GOD'S RIVER

GOD'S RIVER

Exposition of Bible Doctrines,
Taking the Epistle to the Romans as a
Point of Departure

Volume IV

Romans 5:1-11

by
DONALD GREY BARNHOUSE
Editor in Chief, *Eternity* Magazine

Wm. B. Eerdmans Publishing Company
Grand Rapids, Michigan

By the Same Author

Teaching the Word of Truth
God's Methods for Holy Living

Exposition of Bible Doctrines:—

Vol. I   *Man's Ruin*

Vol. II   *God's Wrath*

Vol. III   *God's Remedy*

Contents

Preface

We do not give references to specific editions of the Bible. In all cases I have adopted the translation that I believe nearest to the original. In quotations from the King James Version, I have modernized in some cases such expressions as "thou knowest" to "you know." Other translations used herein are the American Standard, Revised Standard, Catholic Confraternity, and Phillips. When I say "the dictionary says, . . ." I refer to the *Oxford English Dictionary*.

DONALD GREY BARNHOUSE

Τῷ ἀγαπῶντι ἡμᾶς καὶ λύσαντι
ἡμᾶς ἐκ τῶν ἁμαρτιῶν ἡμῶν
ἐν τῷ αἵματι αὐτοῦ.

Rev. 1:5

CHAPTER I

Our Seven-Fold Justification

Therefore being justified by faith, we have peace with God through our Lord Jesus Christ (Rom. 5:1).

ONE of the most triumphant truths in Scripture is that we are justified by God; and one of the most triumphant expressions of this truth is Romans 5:1. The men who divided the Bible into chapters made a correct division here, because chapter four completes one theme, and chapter five introduces a truth that logically follows all that has gone before.

THEREFORE

The first word of the chapter is "Therefore." It has well been said that Paul's "therefores" are there for a purpose. This one opens the door from our past into our glorious present and wonderful future with Christ. It is the stone rolled away from the tomb of Christ, to show us the fruits of His resurrection. "Therefore" refers to all that has been revealed earlier in the epistle.

The first two and a half chapters show us the complete ruin in sin of the human race because of estrangement from the God of all righteousness. The latter half of chapter three and all of chapter four show us that our redemption is the work of God, accomplished by Jesus Christ in His substitutionary death when He shed His blood for us upon Calvary as the sacrifice for our sins. Because of this, God sees us in Christ, completely justified; and, in consequence, has raised Christ from the dead. From now on the epistle is addressed to believers only. The truth of salvation occurs here and there, for a true believer can no more refrain from speaking of salvation in Christ than he can stop breathing. Paul writes to young Timothy, "As for you, always be steady, endure suffering, do the work of an evangelist, fulfil your ministry" (2 Tim. 4:5). Timothy's primary mission was to organize the young churches and supervise their development; but at the same time he was to be an evangelist.

9

In my own ministry, I am not an evangelist in the primary sense. I am not an obstetrician but a pediatrician, although I frequently bring new lives to birth. However, as a Bible teacher, I must include the basic facts of our faith. I must place before men continually the fact that man has been completely ruined in sin and is saved only by the perfect remedy which God has provided in Christ. Thus I do the work of an evangelist. So Paul in Romans speaks of salvation while explaining to believers their position in the risen Lord Jesus Christ.

JUSTIFICATION

Do you know what the Scriptures teach concerning justification? If you are not solidly grounded in the meaning of this heart-word of the Christian faith, you will not be strong in your faith. Many differences between Christians result from failure to comprehend the doctrine of justification. Those who believe that one can be saved and then fall away and be lost, have missed the meaning of justification. Similarly, those who believe that one cannot have full assurance of salvation, and that entrance to Heaven depends upon whether or not one dies in a state of grace, have no true concept of justification.

Many Bible students have noted seven statements in Scripture about justification: (1) We are justified by God (Rom. 8:33); (2) by grace (3:24); (3) by blood (5:9); (4) by the resurrection (4:25); (5) by faith (5:1); (6) by words (Mt. 12:37); and (7) by works (Jas. 2:21). It will be profitable for us to examine them in connection with our present text.

AN EVENT PAST

Now the correct translation of Romans 5:1 is not, as in the King James Version, "being justified"; since it is the aorist participle, it should read, "having been justified by faith." This translation is found in the Confraternity Version published by the Roman Catholic Church, and in the Revised Standard Version. The Confraternity reads, "Having been justified therefore by faith"; the RSV puts it, "Therefore, since we are justified by faith." Between *being* justified and *having been* justified, the difference is very great. "Being justified" indicates a state or condition in which a believer might find himself; "having been justified" points back to an event in history.

BY GOD

The first of these is that it is God who justifies us. "Who shall bring any charge against God's elect?" asks Paul. And the answer comes, "It is God who justifies" (Rom. 8:33). The source of our justification is God. The work is done by Him of whom Solomon said, "I know that, whatsoever God does, it shall be forever: nothing can be put to it, nor anything taken from it" (Eccles. 3:14).

Since the words "justify" and "righteousness" are two forms of the same root word, we could translate this verse, "Having been declared righteous on the principle of faith." Obviously, the only one who can declare a sinner righteous is the Judge before whom all cases involving sin must be tried. Justification is the work of God whereby men who are out of relationship with Him because of sin are brought back into relationship with Him through the work of the Lord Jesus Christ. As a result of sin man became guilty, was condemned, and separated from God. By virtue of the death of Christ, instead of being guilty, we are declared righteous. Instead of being condemned, we are acquitted. Instead of being separated, we are joined to the Lord Jesus Christ and become members of His body. God the Judge does all this. The case has been tried before Him and His is the only verdict. He is the Supreme Judge and can never be overruled.

BY GRACE

The second biblical statement concerning our position as justified ones is that we were justified by grace (Rom. 3:24). God's grace has accomplished the restoration of believers to that oneness with Himself that had been lost in the fall. It was not through anything in any individual, but entirely because of what was in God Himself. Grace is unmerited favor, wholly without a cause in the recipient. Romans 3:24 says that we were justified *freely*. That is, gratis, for nothing, without a cause in us. This is the nature of the heart of God; He is the God of all grace.

BY BLOOD

Third, as to the active communication of justification to the believer, the basis, the ground, the reason, the motive is the blood of Jesus Christ (Rom. 5:9). I am quite aware of the chemical nature of the blood, and am not pushing the word to its literal meaning. The blood of Christ is the biblical phrase for His sacrifice, His death, His atonement. He did not save us by living; He saved us by dying.

BY THE RESURRECTION

In the fourth place, our justification is linked for its proof to the resurrection of Jesus Christ. Our justification did not take place because Christ rose from the dead, but He was raised from the dead because God the Father had declared us righteous, justified freely. The resurrection, then, is proof that our justification is a finished work. If ever I am tempted to doubt my salvation, and eternal position in Christ, guiltless, righteous, forgiven, saved, joined to Him, and maintained by Him, I need only look away from myself, and see Christ at the right hand of God. Then I know that the wonderful things which God declared concerning those upon whom He has wrought this work are indeed true and that they can never be repudiated. For a born-again believer to fall away, history must go into reverse action, like a motion picture film run backwards, until Christ goes back to earth, back into the tomb, never to come out. Then and only then could I finally doubt my salvation.

BY FAITH

Only in fifth place, after four facts which depend on God alone, does the believer's part come into play. We come now to the declaration of our text, "Having been justified by faith, we have peace with God through our Lord Jesus Christ." God is the source, grace the stream; Christ's blood is the ground or cause, His resurrection the proof. And now, the means by which the great and free gift is communicated to the individual. The water of life comes to us by the channel of faith. But we are not to think that we have dug this channel, for even faith is the gift of God (Eph. 2:8). But when God gives faith to a man, He expects him to invest the entire capital with Him. If a Christian seeks to use part of this faith toward God, and squander the rest in small payments to credulity, he will lack assurance, and know little of the power available to him. From the very beginning, faith is the channel by which life and righteousness become ours. Indeed, they are credited to our account long before our faith appropriates them.

In the sixth place, the words of a believer are evidence that he has been justified. Our Lord taught this when the Pharisees founded a council to consider means for His destruction (Mt. 12:14). He tore the mask from their pretensions when He said, "Either make the tree good, and its fruit good; or else make the tree corrupt, and its fruit corrupt: for the tree is known by its fruit. You brood of vipers! how can you, being evil, speak good things? for out of the abundance of the heart the mouth speaks. A good man out of the treasure of the heart brings forth good things: and an evil man out of the evil treasure brings forth evil things. But I say unto you, that every idle word that men shall speak, they shall give account thereof in the day of judgment. For by your words you will be justified, and by your words you will be condemned" (Mt. 12:33-37). What is this justification by words? The explanation is not in the verse itself, and not entirely in the context, but rather in the whole of the Scripture, which teaches that words are the evidence of what has taken place in the life of a man.

One who has turned away from himself and has believed in Christ alone becomes the object of the miracle of regeneration. God plants within that man His own divine life. That man becomes a partaker of the divine nature. He has a new nature. The thoughts of the unregenerate man are vanity, we read in the Word of God, but the renewed man has a new heart, and out of the abundance of that heart his mouth must speak. First of all there will be public confession of trust in Christ. "If you will confess with your mouth that Jesus is Lord, and believe in your heart that God raised him from the dead, you will be saved. For with the heart man believes through to righteousness, and with the mouth he professes his faith unto salvation" (Rom. 10:9-10). From this and other passages it appears that it is impossible for anyone to be a secret believer. If a man has the life of God within him, he must acknowledge it. To withhold public confession of faith in Christ indicates that one does not possess saving, justifying faith, but merely holds an intellectual opinion.

Following the initial confession, there must be continuing witness. A fountain cannot bring forth sweet water and bitter. There
may be denial and cursing, as in Peter's case; but there will be
weeping, and eventually testimony that will feed both lambs and
sheep. The surest evidence of new life is a mouth that is willing
to speak of the Lord Jesus Christ and tell forth His glory.

BY WORKS

The seventh statement about justification is that it is by works.
In James is the famous line so often misquoted and misapplied:
"Was not Abraham our father justified by works, when he had
offered Isaac his son upon the altar? Dost thou see that faith worked
along with his works, and by the works the faith was made perfect?
And the Scripture was fulfilled which says, Abraham believed God,
and it was reckoned to him as righteousness; and he was called
the friend of God. You see that a man is justified by works and
not by faith alone. . . . For as the body without the spirit is dead,
so faith without works is dead" (Jas. 2:21-26).

I have presented here a combination of two translations. The
first two sentences, from the Roman Catholic Confraternity Version,
give the key to the passage in the revealing query, "Dost thou see
that faith worked along with his works, and by the works the faith
was made perfect?" Since the offering of Isaac took place many
years after God reckoned or credited Abraham's faith to him as
righteousness, we see that the works were merely the fruit of that
faith which is the channel of the justification which comes from
God. It comes alone by His grace, on the ground of the blood of
Christ, is proved by the resurrection, and manifests itself in Christian
testimony from the lips and Christian action in the life.

TWO VIEWPOINTS

God looks upon the heart and sees true and saving faith; man
looks upon the outward appearance and sees the outworking of
the new life within the believer. Thus justification is viewed according to the position of the beholder. One who stands beside a great
pyramid sees it only as a vast triangle receding to a point in the
sky. However, from the apex of the pyramid, all its sides are seen
and its true structure is comprehended. Man's view is always biased
and partial. God's vantage point is always perfection; and in these

seven statements He has given us the whole picture of justification.

How great, then, is His justification! How wonderful the work that God has conceived for us, provided for us, and imputed to us! We are justified! This text illustrates how our God calls things that are not as though they were.

One of the commonest errors of popular theological thinking is the confusion of justification with sanctification. How many stumbling babes in Christ fear to enter into the joy of the promise because, aware that sin is still in their hearts, they are afraid to say that they have been justified. But the believer who knows the Word of God and has intelligent faith, knows that he is as sure of reaching Heaven as that Christ is already there. It would be monstrous for a man to say such a thing if there were any thought in his mind of deserving Heaven. But when he acknowledges that all things come from God in His grace and apart from any justifying cause in him, he can claim the promises of God and know that he has eternal life. He has been declared righteous; therefore, he can rest in the quietness of God Himself.

Thus are we justified sevenfold: by God, through grace, on the ground of the blood, evidenced by Christ's resurrection, received by faith, and demonstrated by our testimony in words and works. Thus we praise God.

CHAPTER II

Peace with God

Therefore being justified by faith, we have peace with God through our Lord Jesus Christ (Rom. 5:1).

THE first of numerous results of justification is peace with God. Here is the answer to many problems that arise in the minds of men. We see humanity searching for something; and from the frenzied manner of its search, we know that it lacks something that is vitally important. What are men seeking?

THE MOST SOUGHT AFTER THING

Years ago, when I began to prepare Bible studies, one of my earliest sermons was called, "The most sought after thing in the world." I preached that sermon while still in my late teens; and, in my opening remarks, I asked what was the most sought after thing in the world, and suggested some of the things that men spend their time in seeking. Is it money? A man says he will be happy if he can save up a thousand dollars. He gets his thousand, but he would like to have five thousand dollars. He gets the five thousand, and wants ten. He gets the ten, and wants fifty. He reaches that goal, and starts for the hundred thousand. When he counts his fortune at that figure, he thinks of half a million. As soon as he reaches that figure, he dreams of his million. Let him get his million, and he wants ten million. And the more he gets, the more he wants. After acquiring more money than he or his family can possibly spend, he continues to amass his fortune. His frenzied efforts prove that he is not really seeking money, but something else, an intangible something, which the possession of money has not brought him.

Someone else may think that the most sought after thing in the world is power. Elect a man sheriff, and he will think of the state legislature. Elect him to the legislature, and he will aspire to be congressman. If he reaches Washington, he will want to go back as senator. Let him attain the senate and he will think in terms of the presidency. Elect him president once, and he wants to be president twice. What does this prove? That it is not the mere

place of power that the man is seeking, but something else which
he believes success and power will bring him. Napoleon said,
"What a bore life is! What a cross!"

You may run the gamut of human effort and attainment and it
will always be the same story. The possession of education, fame,
wealth, power, success, does not bring what men really want. This
is proved by the many suicides among the successful, and by the
fact that they keep on striving after they have attained.

PEACE

Robert Burns wrote, in his *Epistle to Davie:*

> If happiness have not her seat
> And center in the breast,
> We may be wise, or rich, or great,
> But never can be blest.

And John Keats described life as

> The weariness, the fever, and the fret,
> Here where men sit, and hear each other groan.

Even the founding fathers did not think of guaranteeing to
us life, liberty, and happiness, but only life, liberty, and the *pursuit*
of happiness.

The explanation is that what they are really seeking can never
be found by man, for it is peace with God. This is the thing most
sought after in the world and our text tells us that such peace is a
gift of God and thus, by implication, teaches us that man cannot
attain peace by his own efforts.

Our God has called Himself the God of peace. When we
understand this characteristic of His nature, we lay the groundwork
for possession of peace in our own hearts. But first, let us ask
ourselves if we know the meaning of the word. There are terms
which we use commonly and which we think we understand, but
when it comes to definition we find that we are far from comprehending all that is involved in them. The dictionary gives fifteen
different definitions of the noun "peace." If we look closely at some
of these, we may have a better idea of what God is talking about
in our text, and perhaps some will learn why their own spirits are
so restless.

DEFINITIONS

The first definition of "peace" is that which describes the relationship between nations and people. Peace is: "Freedom from, or cessation of, war or hostilities; that condition of a nation or community in which it is not at war with another." Another definition concerns the individual: "Freedom from disturbance or perturbation (especially as a condition in which an individual person is); quiet, tranquility, undisturbed state. Emphasized as peace and quiet or peace and quietness." Still another definition concerns the inward man: "Freedom from mental or spiritual disturbance or conflict arising from passion, sense of guilt, etc.; calmness." This meaning we use in such phrases as "peace of mind, of soul, of conscience." Then, significantly, the dictionary states: "In generalized sense including several of the above." Under this heading the dictionary quotes certain passages from the Bible and speaks of the "peace of God" as an illustration.

But I have long since learned that in spiritual matters it is dangerous at times to accept the definitions of the dictionary. It is also very dangerous to accept definitions which have become clichés, especially if hallowed by usage in hymns. There is a great deal of false theology in our minds, accompanied and reinforced by a catchy tune that keeps the error echoing in our thought and gives it a priority in our thinking that is difficult to put aside.

For example, let us consider a famous old hymn by Charles Wesley that is included in practically every hymnbook.

> Love divine, all loves excelling,
>   Joy of Heaven, to earth come down.

In collections which include the second stanza there is an interesting variation in the wording, depending on the theology of the editor of the hymnbook. Wesley wrote this stanza as follows:

> Breathe, O breathe Thy loving Spirit
>   Into every troubled breast;
> Let us all in Thee inherit,
>   Let us find that second rest.
> Take away our bent to sinning
>   Alpha and Omega be;
> End of faith as its beginning,
>   Set our hearts at liberty.

Some theologians were disturbed by the line, "Let us find that second rest." They feared lest people think that there must be a second-blessing experience beyond salvation, some "it" to be sought after instead of Christ and all blessings in Him. There is, of course, that danger. While there are second blessings, thousands of blessings and even millions of blessings *after* one has been saved, there is not, technically speaking, a second experience to be sought by the believer. There is only day-by-day yielding in order to receive all blessings.

TWO KINDS OF PEACE

Some hymnbook editors changed the offending line to read:

Let us find that promised rest.

They probably thought that a "promised" rest was not so liable to misinterpretation, but they missed the point of Wesley's thinking. Undoubtedly he had a great promise of Scripture in mind, and was looking at a verse which sets forth two kinds of peace, two types of rest, and he was seeking to enter into the second.

For instance, in the eleventh chapter of Matthew the Lord Jesus Christ, presenting the first of the gospel invitations, gave us one of the great promises of all Scripture: "Come to me," He calls, "all ye that labor and are heavy laden, and I will give you rest. Take my yoke upon you and learn of me; for I am meek and lowly in heart; and you will find rest unto your souls. For my yoke is easy, and my burden is light" (Mt. 11:28-30). Read it carefully and you will notice that the word "rest" is used twice: "Come to me and I will give you rest . . ." "Take my yoke and you will find rest . . ." There is a rest that is *given*, and a rest that is *found*. Wesley had come into the first of these two rests, and he was praying that he might find the second.

Where the difference between the two kinds of rest is well understood, the Christian can enter into the full joy of Christ, and in knowing the difference between the two, we shall comprehend Romans 5:1. For we are concentrating on a great promise: "Therefore, having been justified by faith, we have peace with God, through our Lord Jesus Christ." God is not telling us here of His own peace with which He fills certain Christian hearts, but of that peace which exists between Him and all Christian hearts. Peace *with* God is far different from the peace *of* God.

In order to understand the peace which God gives to all believers, let us look at the first dictionary definition of "peace," which concerns the relationship between two countries. Peace is: "Freedom from, or cessation of, war or hostilities." Every soul has been at war with God, and therefore every soul must have peace with God through cessation of the hostilities which exist between the individual and the Creator. How is the warfare to be brought to an end?

First, we must realize and acknowledge that the war exists. A man who asserts that there is nothing wrong between him and God is as far from the truth as a Russian ambassador who claims that the attitude and aims of the Soviet are peaceful. There has been, of course, warfare between Russia and the West. Whether hot war or cold war, it is, nevertheless, war. And there is warfare between every soul and God because of the individual's sinful creaturehood. God says that the warfare exists, and that we must admit it. Romans 8:7-8 expresses the situation with finality: "Because the carnal mind is enmity against God: for it is not subject to the law of God, neither indeed can be. So then they that are in the flesh cannot please God!"

Phillips paraphrases these verses thus: "The carnal attitude sees no further than natural things. But the spiritual attitude reaches out after the things of the Spirit. The former attitude means, bluntly, death: the latter means life and inward peace. And this is only to be expected for the carnal attitude is inevitably opposed to the purpose of God, and neither can nor will follow His laws for living. Men who hold this attitude cannot possibly please God."

Because of His holiness and justice, God's wrath must fall on the individual who is hostile toward Him. That is why men are called "by nature the children of wrath" (Eph. 2:3).

How can this state of things come to an end? How does war end between two nations? After World War I a French statesman pointed out that only two types of peace follow a war. First is the peace imposed upon the defeated by the conqueror; second is the peace accepted by the defeated through surrender. There is a vast difference between the peace which one imposes and the peace which one accepts. The peace treaty signed on the deck of the battleship *Missouri* after World War II was imposed by the Allies and accepted by the Japanese. Who can fail to see the difference?

GOD'S TERMS

It should be evident that if there is to be peace between a human being and God, the terms must be imposed by God Himself. The reason men go their way to a Christless eternity is that they will not submit their wills to the Creator. God, being the eternal God, the supreme Being *must* have His way, because He alone is right. Every other way is the way of the creature, the way of earth. Is it mere chance that the two Latin words *humanus* and *humus* are so much alike? *Humus* is a word used by gardeners for the dark brown or black substance resulting from the slow decomposition or oxidization of organic matter on or near the surface of the earth, which, with the products of the decomposition of various rocks, forms the soil in which plants grow. And we all know that, if a human body dies, it soon will go back to the dust of the earth and be the food for plants. Shall, then, the creature that is formed dictate to the Creator who has formed him? Shall a clod of dirt argue with the Maker of the stars?

Yet in spite of the logic that derives from our position and condition, there are those who talk about making their peace with God. The phrase has long been used for settling differences between men. Shakespeare in *Twelfth Night* has one of his characters say, "I will make your peace with him, if I can." So far as we can ascertain, Thomas Fuller, only 300 years ago, first spoke of making one's peace with God. But the phrase is incorrect in such a connection, despite all who have thus used it. For example, it was the custom a century or more ago for obituaries to say, "Having made his peace with God, he departed this life"; but the idea is theologically unsound.

You do not come to God as a victor comes to the vanquished, but as the conquered comes to the conqueror. But when you do come, you find Him all smiles. Only when you insist on having your own way and attempt to dictate terms, must He frown upon you. To the soul who flings himself upon the promises of God, the Creator reveals Himself as the loving Saviour who has made peace, and receives the sinner with grace and tenderness. In Colossians 1:19, 20 we are told, "It pleased the Father that in him should all fullness dwell. And having made peace through the blood of his cross, by him to reconcile all things unto himself." Note the past tense of the verb: "having made peace."

NO OTHER PEACE

This fact is of paramount importance: God has made peace, and no other peace can be made except that which He has already made. To talk about making your peace with God is to reject His peace. What would General MacArthur have said to the Japanese if they had brought their own peace terms? God will have no other peace with man than what He has made at the cross. If a man rejects the peace which God has provided through the Lord Jesus Christ, he remains at enmity with God. He must bear now and throughout eternity the holy wrath of God reserved for those who trample under foot the Son of God, who count the blood of the covenant unholy, and despise the Spirit of grace who pleads with their hearts (Heb. 10:29).

Are you so far from God that the thought of divine wrath shocks you? Do not think that God is not moral because He can be angry. God is perfect morality, perfect justice. If you come in unconditional surrender, you will find Him all peace toward you; then you can go on to find that second rest which is the result of such surrender to Him.

Our text points out that peace with God is an accomplished fact only when we are justified by faith. Everything points to the cross of Jesus Christ. There, traced in characters of blood, are the conditions which God imposes on the soul that approaches Him. We who have come to the cross know that we have peace with God and that He can hold nothing against us who have thus been justified. My experience was typical: I was a sinner, less perfect than God. By conviction of the Holy Spirit I learned that my condition would incur the eternal condemnation of God if I did not submit to His grace. I acknowledged myself a sinner and threw myself on His mercy and grace, recognizing that He had brought salvation to earth through His Son Jesus Christ. After God the Father put God the Son to death on the cross, He could proclaim grace and pardon to all who would submit to Him. I came to the cross, believed His promise about His Son, and God declared me righteous even while I was ungodly and gave me authority to become His child. I ceased to be a child of wrath and became a child of God, justified from all things. Simultaneously, I was declared to be an heir of God, joint-heir with Jesus Christ. I received eternal life, and shall never perish. I was accepted in the Beloved; my body became the temple of the Holy Spirit; I was born of the Spirit into the family of God, baptized by the Holy Spirit into the body of Christ, and sealed by the Holy Spirit unto the day of redemption. I have an inheritance incorruptible and undefiled and that fades not away, reserved in Heaven for me. Although I know myself to be a sinner, I am not concerned about the *penalty* for sin, since the Lord Jesus Christ bore the penalty and declared me righteous. This doctrine, developed in Romans, and throughout the Bible, is lived out in the life of the believer.

The love of Christ becomes the constraining factor in my life, and I seek to glorify Him as Lord. I know Him as my Creator and so have peace of mind. I know Him as Savior and so have peace of conscience. In the measure that I enter into the second rest, I know Him as Lord and find the peace that passes all understanding.

CHAPTER III

Access

By whom also we have access by faith into this grace wherein we stand (Rom. 5:2).

THE fifth chapter of Romans introduces the glorious theme of the life of one who has been justified through faith in Christ. Henceforth we draw a sharp line, lest someone who is not a believer should think that our message is for him.

RESTRICTED TRUTH

One of the most important tasks of a minister is to teach his hearers that from God's point of view there is a vast difference between people. Some truths are applicable only to a certain class of people. If others seek to profit by them, they are before God like criminals before the law, seeking to cash checks in a bank where they have no money.

There is but one truth for the man who has not been born again through faith in the blood of Jesus Christ and that is the offer of salvation. There is the corollary of terrible and eternal judgment if he rejects that offer.

But if you know that your life comes short of the glory of God; if you accept the fact that you are less perfect than God and deserve eternal separation from Him; and if you have come to the cross of Jesus Christ for salvation, then all that follows is for you. One who has been justified is still to live in the midst of an alien world, in earthly circumstances, and certain practical attitudes are necessary if he is to fulfill all that God expects of him.

The late Handley Moule, Anglican Bishop of Durham, has a beautiful paragraph on this Christian life. He writes that it "is to be seen not only as a state whose basis is the reconciliation of the Law, and whose gate and walls are the covenant Promise. It is to appear as a state warmed with eternal love; irradiated with the prospect of glory. In it the man (the truly justified believer), knit up with Christ his head, his Bridegroom, his all, yields himself with

joy to the God who has received him. In the living power of the
Heavenly Spirit, who perpetually delivers him from himself, he
obeys, prays, works and suffers, in a liberty which is only not yet
that of Heaven, and in which he is maintained to the end by Him
who has planned his full personal salvation from eternity to eternity."

We have seen that justification by faith brings peace with God.
The war is over. God no longer holds anything against the believer;
indeed He cannot hold anything against one whom He has justified.
The one who has trusted in Christ is seen by God as perfect as
the Lord Jesus Christ. In God's beloved Son we are accepted even
as He is accepted. This leads us to the next thought; namely, that
by Christ also we have access by faith into this grace wherein
we stand.

MAN'S WAY TO GOD

The doctrine of access is one of the most important in Christian
theology, for it concerns man's way to God. As the preliminary to
understanding this doctrine, we must dispose of false ideas about it.

First, there is the erroneous belief that man has some rights in
approaching God, that anybody, any time, anywhere, may come
to God for help or favors. There is not much difference between
this attitude and that of Aladdin who summoned a genie by rubbing
a lamp. In either case the god is a slave of the one who makes the
request. The verse in the Psalms, addressed to believers, which says
that God "is a very present help in trouble" (Ps. 46:1), has been
twisted to apply to all men, and as though God were a very pleasant
help in trouble.

Scores of Bible verses prove that this is not true. There are
more passages in the Bible where God promises *not* to answer
prayer than where He says that He will. The man who prays, "Oh
God!" but does not acknowledge the truth and holiness of God,
comes under His condemnation. The famous missionary David Livingstone spent a year or two with a certain tribe in South Africa.
Then he went into the interior with his wife and baby, to preach
to another tribe. After a while he returned to the first tribe and
found them in sore straits because a neighboring tribe had attacked
them, killed many men, and captured the chief's son. At the moment
of Livingstone's return, an embassy from the invaders was asking
for friendship and peace. This overture was motivated by fear of

attack by the Zulus. The chief of the injured tribe, who desired
only to live at peace with his neighbors, said to Livingstone, "How
can I be at peace with them while they hold my son prisoner?"

If this attitude is true in the heart of a savage chief, how much
more is it true of God the Father toward those who trample under
foot His Son, who count the blood of the covenant wherewith they
were set apart as an unholy thing, and who continue to despise the
Spirit of grace (Heb. 10:29)? Access to God must be through Jesus
Christ, who set it forth in unequivocal terms, "I am the way, the
truth, and the life: no one comes to the Father but by me"
(John 14:6).

LIP SERVICE

We have sufficiently treated this truth from the viewpoint of
one who denies Christ entirely. But what about those who pay lip
service to God, and even to Christ, but deny the doctrines of access
to God? Take, first, the teaching of those who do not accept Christ as
the way to God, but who speak of Him as the way-shower. A modern
cult sets this forth in *Science and Health* with a "key to the Scriptures" that locks the Scriptures to the mind that tries the key, as
follows: "Jesus' advent in the flesh partook partly of Mary's earthly
condition although he was endowed with the Christ, the divine
spirit, without measure. This accounts for his struggles in Gethsemane and on Calvary, and this revealed him to be the mediator
or way-shower between God and man" (30:10). But most certainly
Jesus Christ the Lord did not claim to be the way-shower. He
claimed to be the way. If you think there is no difference, go to a
sign on the highway that points to the next town. Climb up and
sit on the sign, and see how long it will take you to get to your
destination. You do not need a way-shower to get where you are
going; you need to follow the way. And if someone objects that
he is not sure of the way, the Bible gives unmistakable directions,
and the Holy Spirit will not fail to convict of sin, of righteousness,
and of judgment to come, in order that you may flee from the
wrath to come. Thank God, Jesus Christ is not the way-shower,
He is the way. The doctrine of Christ as the way-shower was
invented by the Devil, the enemy of souls, in order to turn people
from the true way.

OTHER MEDIATORS

Another false idea thrusts other mediators between man and God. These alien beings have been interposed because people have sought peace in ceremonies, vows, religious duties, fastings, prayers, and other observances and have found that these things do not satisfy the heart. In desperation they have turned to those whom they thought to be near God and have asked them to intercede. An analogy may be drawn from the commercial chicanery which was revealed in Washington with reference to government contracts. Businessmen went to the capital in search of contracts and found themselves in the maze of bureaucracy. They became an easy prey for the men who professed to have access and influence, and who, for five percent of any profits, proceeded, with more or less success, to intercede for their clients.

In the spiritual realm there are many such mediators. The difference is that they do not act on their own behalf, but their names have been used by others who have assumed power through such use of their names.

During student days in France, I was the pastor of a little Evangelical Reformed Church in the French Alps. Once a week I went to a neighboring village for an instruction class for its children. En route, I passed the local priest who was on a similar errand in the opposite direction. We became good friends, and often stopped to chat. Once he asked why we do not pray to the saints. I replied by asking why we should pray to the saints. He launched into an explanation that involved an illustration of how one might get an interview with the president of the French Republic. One could go to the ministry of agriculture, or through the departments of war or finance etc., and any one of the cabinet members might succeed in opening the door of the president's office. He smiled with an air of triumph, as though to say that the simplicity and clarity of his argument would preclude any rebuttal. At that time Raymond Poincaré was President of France and lived in the Palace of the Elysée in Paris. I said, "But Monsieur le curé, suppose that I were the son of Monsieur Poincaré? I live in the Elysée with him. I get up from the breakfast table and kiss him goodbye as he goes to his office. Then I go down to the ministry of finance, for example, and ask the fourth secretary of the second assistant if it is possible for me to see the minister of finance. If I do succeed in reaching his office my request is for an interview with papa." My friend appeared thunderstruck, and I went on to say that I am a child of God, heir of God and joint-heir with Christ, that I have been saved through the death of the Savior and thus as a son I have immediate access to the Father.

WITH PEACE COMES ACCESS

Herein lies the importance of the word *also* in our text. "Having been justified by faith we have peace with God through our Lord Jesus Christ, by whom also we have access . . ." The access is in addition to the peace. The peace has been made by Him. The king looks upon us no longer as guilty, rebellious subjects but declares us righteous on the grounds of the death of His only begotten Son. With that justification comes peace, and with peace comes access. Let no one, *no one,* be interposed between me and my God and Savior.

If anyone should ever ask me why I would refuse to pray to the Virgin Mary, I would have a practical as well as a scriptural answer. The practical answer is that I have received all things through Jesus Christ and therefore I need no one to intercede for me.

The Scriptural reason, of course, is that the Bible teaches that the dead are unaware of what is happening upon this earth. Neither the saints, nor the Virgin Mary, nor our loved ones, can glimpse what goes on in our lives. Death ends all awareness of things on earth.

NO APPROACH THROUGH MARY

With regard to the mother of our Lord, Jesus Himself blocked off approach through her. I do not appeal primarily to the miracle of turning water into wine. On that occasion (John 2), our Lord's mother informed Him that the wine had run out. He replied, "Woman, what have I to do with thee? Mine hour is not yet come." This was His preliminary announcement that she was not to presume upon their relationship. As to all the disciples, He would also have had to say to her, "You are from beneath, I am from above" (John 8:23).

On another occasion this truth was brought out even more

sharply. There came that day when the Lord was forced to break with the leaders of His people. They had revealed their antagonism to spiritual principles and had formed a council against Him that they might destroy Him. (Mt. 12:14). The Lord changed the whole fashion of His message: in chapter eleven He pronounced woe upon the cities and said that they would be brought down to Hell; He announced that He would now turn to the Gentiles; then He snatched the mask from the hypocritical Pharisees and called them whited sepulchres, sons of snakes, dirty cups. There must have been something of divine wrath in His words and attitude that caused them to draw back from Him. He turned and began to speak to the crowd. Meanwhile Mary and her other children, Jesus' half-brothers, were summoned by someone. Finally, when they arrived outside, a messenger came to tell Jesus. There seems to be a timidity in the approach of the messenger who, remembering His fury of a moment before, is trying to get Him to go away quietly. "Behold . . . your . . . mother and . . . your brethren are outside, desiring to speak with you . . ." (Mt. 12:47). The Lord Jesus turned upon the man and said, "Who is my mother? and who are my brethren?"

Here He set forth definitely and clearly that He could not be approached on the basis of any earthly tie. The grace of God is grace, pure, unmerited grace, and is not to be doled out like patronage in politics. And His mother and brethren remained outside so far as any answer to their plea was concerned. They had no influence with Him then; and, since they are now with Him awaiting the consummation of the age when they too shall become like Him, they are not in a position either to hear requests made to them by deluded earthlings, or to be channels of access for such prayers.

Then, after the Lord Jesus had refused the intercession of His mother, He turned to His disciples and said, "Behold, my mother and my brethren. For whosoever shall do the will of my father in heaven, the same is my brother, sister and mother" (Mt. 12:49, 50). That is why I would crave the prayers of any living soul who trusts in Christ as His Savior. I would a million times prefer that some poor laborer, forced to leave school early but who has been to the cross of Calvary for the atonement provided in the shed blood of the Savior, pray for me than to have all the prayers that all the population of earth might address to saints or the Virgin Mary. Jesus said, "Whosoever does the will of my Father . . ." Such a one has power to prevail with God in prayer. And the first step in doing the will of the Father is to believe on His Son. Christ's words are the foundation for that which was written later by James: "The effectual, fervent prayer of a righteous [a justified man] avails much" (Jas. 5:16). But prayer ministry is ended, so far as intercession for human needs is concerned, when life, ceasing to exist upon earth, is transferred to Heaven where it is lived on a plane which does not include knowledge of affairs on earth.

DIRECT ACCESS

Finally, the positive truth set forth in this Scripture is that the believer who is justified by the atoning work of the Savior has direct access to the grace of God. It should be realized that access to this grace is much more than the possession of grace.

There are some beautiful passages by Alexander Maclaren about our access into the grace of God. "I said that the Apostle was using a metaphor here regarding the grace as being an ample space into which a man was admitted, or we may say that he is thinking of it as a great treasure house. We have the right of entrance there where, on every side as it were, lie ingots of uncoined gold, and masses of treasure, and we may have just as much or as little as we choose. It is entirely in our own determination how much of the wealth of God we shall possess. We have access to the treasure house; and this permit is put into our hands, 'Be it unto thee even as thou wilt.' The size of the sack that the man brought in the old story determined the amount of wealth that he carried away. Some of you bring very tiny baskets and expect little and desire little; you get no more than you desired and expected.

"That wealth, the fullness of God, takes the shape of, as well as is determined in its measure by, the magnitude of the vessel into which it is put. It is multiform, and we get whatever we desire, and whatever either our characters or our circumstances require. The one gift assumes all forms, just as water poured into a vase takes the shape of the vase into which it is poured. The same gift unfolds itself in an infinite variety of manners, according to the needs of the man to whom it is given; just as the writer's pen, the carpenter's hammer, the farmer's ploughshare, are all made out of the same metal. So God's grace comes to you in a different shape from that in which it comes to me, according to our different callings and needs, as fixed by our circumstances, our duties, our sorrows, our temptations.

"So, brethren, how shameful it is that, having the possibility of so much, we should have the actuality of so little. . . . There are a great many Christian people who ought to be ashamed of their moderation. They have gone into the treasure house; stacks of jewels, jars of gold on all sides of them—and they have been content to come away with some poor little coin, when they might have been 'rich beyond the dreams of avarice.' Brethren, you have access to the fullness of God. Whose fault is it if you are empty?"

CHAPTER IV

Christ the Way

By whom also we have access by faith into this grace wherein we stand (Rom. 5:2).

THE doctrine of access to God is one of the most important in Christian theology. It is not merely a matter for academic discussion; it also affects our daily life as believers, since it concerns our way to God, the means of receiving answers to prayer, and the way to power for living, moment by moment. The subject takes on all the more importance for Protestants since the time of the papal definition of the doctrine of the Assumption of the Virgin. It is only right and proper, truly American, and in line with the basic antecedent freedoms of our religious worship, that we present the truth which so many of us hold dearer than life. If anyone protests that such a presentation is controversial and impugns the religious faith of a segment of our population, we reply that we did not start the discussion, and that the doctrines of the assumption of the Virgin and access to Christ through her impugn the entire basis of biblical faith. These doctrines negate the Scriptures, much of the teaching of church fathers, the statements of earlier Popes, and the entire Reformation. Many would be willing to die, and many have died, a martyr's death rather than submit to these false teachings.

ALL MEN PRAY

How to reach God has been the preoccupation of the minds of men through countless generations. Turn to such great works on anthropology as J. G. Frazer's *Golden Bough* and read how every tribe of men, no matter how degraded, has sought to establish contact with the supernatural. Primitive men pray to the winds, the storms, the sun, stars, roots of trees, shadows in the forest; or to animals, reptiles, and insects; nevertheless, they pray. In Asia, men pray to literally a million gods and seek to approach these gods in a variety of ways. Within Christendom are those who limit prayer to God the Father alone, and also those who add to the Trinity a host of saints and the Virgin Mary.

In this chapter we are occupied with one thing—what the Bible teaches about access to God. Every man has the right to pray as he desires, but the Bible teaches that there is but one way to God. Christ did not say, "I am one of many equally good ways, I am a phase of truth, I am an aspect of life." The very heart of the Christian faith is in the words of the Lord Jesus Christ: "I am the way, the truth, and the life; no man comes to the Father but by me" (John 14:6). Again, "He that climbs up by some other way, the same is a thief and a robber" (John 10:1). And finally, "There is one God, and one mediator between God and men, the man Christ Jesus" (1 Tim. 2:5). Even the proponents of prayer through the saints or the Virgin admit that there is not a line in the Bible on which to base their teaching, but that it is founded solely on tradition that postdates the Bible by several centuries.

WHAT THE BIBLE TEACHES

Our chief concern is, What does the Bible teach? We are not considering the ideas of those who do not accept the Bible as the supreme court from which there is no appeal. Differences of opinion will be settled at the judgment bar of God. We are in the position of a lawyer who knows that a majority of the judges before whom he argues may be adverse to his just cause. He is doing everything possible to marshal his evidence, to cite his authorities, and so to present his case that all will be accepted for the record—a record to be submitted to the Supreme Court. There he knows, from the Constitution, the Supreme Judge will overrule his adversaries and decide according to truth.

Our text reads, "Therefore, having been justified through faith, we have peace with God through our Lord Jesus Christ through whom we have had our access by faith into this grace wherein we stand" (5:1, 2), and the Supreme Judge will one day reveal that He was reached only through His Son our Savior.

In one sense it might be said that the whole progression of thought in the Bible is the development of this doctrine of access. In the first chapter of Genesis, we find that man is created by God and has friendly fellowship with Him. Almost at once man determines to rebel against God, to seek his own way instead of God's way. By that sin man loses his fellowship with God and finds himself naked of righteousness and alone in a world that has become hostile to him. It should be noted that man did not seek God. God sought man. The Bible everywhere teaches that man never seeks the true God by himself. Every idea of religion that has ever sprung from the human heart has been an attempt to find a substitute that could give surcease from the gnawing of conscience. Thus a thousand religious ideas have developed throughout the world of humanity. This is why, as Karl Marx said, religion is the opiate of the people. We heartily agree. Religion is the opiate of the people, but Christianity is the salvation of the people.

THE BLOOD OF THE LAMB

In the story of the fall we learn that God sought man. In the cool of the day He came down into the garden and said, "Where are you?" (Gen. 3:9). This was the first establishment of relations between a holy God and a man estranged from Him by sin. The altar was set up and God Himself, by providing a covering of skins for the man and woman who first believed His word about the coming Messiah, shed the first blood ever poured out. From then on, throughout the Bible, the story is told in increasing detail. Man is to come to God through shedding of blood of a sacrifice provided by God. Cain hated this idea so desperately that he murdered Abel who adhered to it and practiced it. The lamb Abel presented is a faint picture of what was later provided by God through Christ. With Abel there is one lamb for one man (Gen. 4). By the time of the passover, a lamb is killed for one household (Exod. 12). Its blood is applied to the doorposts of the believer's house, and the angel of judgment passes over the homes where there is this public manifestation of faith in the lamb of God. Then, as God's revelation unfolds, the people of Israel are set apart and on the great Day of Atonement—Yom Kippur—one sacrifice is made for the whole nation. This portrays the fact that God intends to save Israel and govern the world through this ancient people whom He chose for that purpose (Lev. 16). And, when John the Baptist identifies the Lord Jesus as the Savior, it is to show God's ultimate purpose for the whole creation: "Behold the Lamb of God, who takes away the sin of the world!" (John 1:29). A lamb for one man, a lamb for a family, a lamb for a nation, and a lamb for the world!

The fact that Jesus Christ was to be the Lamb, and thus the means of access for the soul of every man, was also progressively set forth in the Bible. Abel's lamb was a type of Christ. Did Abel understand all that was involved in his sacrifice? That God told him to do it is certain, for in Heb. 11:4 we are told that "by faith Abel offered a more excellent sacrifice than Cain"; and if by faith, there must have been the command to obey. When Abraham offered his only son Isaac on the mountain of sacrifice the Lord intervened to provide a substitute to die in his stead. There the Almighty revealed a new name for Himself, *Jehovah-jireh*, and Abraham told Isaac, "God will provide himself a lamb" (Gen. 22:8, 14). At the passover, when the lamb was slain and the blood applied (Exod. 12), there was a further development as God revealed that His death angel would pass over those who applied the blood, and would slay those who were not thus protected. Centuries later, He revealed to Isaiah a startling truth now common to us—the Lamb would be a man (Isa. 53).

When John the Baptist came, his role was to point to one man in the midst of the crowd and set Him forth as God's Lamb (John 1:29). Is it any wonder that the theme of the believers in Heaven is to magnify (Rev. 5) and to glorify God's Lamb (Rev. 22)? Typified, prophesied, applied, personified, identified, magnified, and glorified—there is the development of the doctrine of the Lamb, the doctrine of access—Jesus Christ who is man's one and only access to the triune Godhead.

ACCESS UNDER LAW

When God began to prepare Israel for His service, He revealed to them that He was holy and could be approached only in the way which He set forth. Read the books of Moses and see how carefully access to God was hedged about. When God came down on Mt. Sinai, He warned Moses that the people must be barred from the mountain: "And you shall set bounds for the people round about, saying, 'Take heed that you do not go up to the mountain or touch the border of it; whoever touches the mountain shall be put to death; no hand shall touch him, but he shall be stoned or shot; whether beast or man, he shall not live'" (Exod. 19:12, 13). When it is properly comprehended, the Levitical code given to Moses and set in order by Aaron was a pageant showing how to approach God.

If a group of men and women had come over the brow of a hill and observed below them the camp of the Israelites, several things would have been noted. First of all their attention would have been attracted to the mark of the glory of God that hung over the center of the camp, far more wonderful than the mushroom atomic cloud that blossoms out of the death of nuclear fission. Above the holy of holies a pillar of cloud by day and a pillar of fire by night spread over the whole vast camp, for a glory and a covering for God's people. But how would one approach that marvelous manifestation of God? Let us join that group and walk down the hill. We make our way past the tents of the camp of Israel. Some of the dwellers look at us curiously, but they are silent for they see that our group includes not only several Gentiles, but also Jewish men and women, including several priests and Levites, and, leading the group, the high priest, successor to Aaron.

Our group wanders at will among the tents of Israel, but as we near the center there is a sharp division. A wall stands before us, and at this point it is explained to all the Gentiles that they are not permitted beyond that barrier—no Gentiles had access to the presence of God. But as the Jews draw nearer to their Tabernacle, there are further divisions. All the women must stop at the court of the women, for there is no access for them beyond that point. The diminishing company continues on, and soon reaches the gateway of the sacred area; there, all men except those of the tribe of Levi stop. The Levites pass this barrier and take stations for their various duties. Since no religious service is going on, some of the Levites, depending on their descent from one or another branch of the family of Levi, immediately go about the janitor service of the Tabernacle. But, at time for a service, they retire. Another branch of the family furnishes singers and conducts worship. But, when it is time for closer access to God, they too must retire.

A PRIESTHOOD ORDAINED

Of the Levites, only the descendants of Aaron could touch the sacrifices. These were the priests who shared with their cousins who supplied music and menial service the food given by the people through the tithe exacted from all. At the hour of sacrifice, the priests slew the lamb brought by the sinner, while the sinner leaned over the gate, his hand on the animal's head, and confessed his sins before God. This scene is pictured in one of our great hymns:

> Not all the blood of beasts
> On Jewish altars slain
> Could give the guilty conscience peace
> Or wash away our stain.
>
> But Christ the Heavenly Lamb,
> Takes all our sins away;
> A sacrifice of nobler name,
> And richer blood, than they.
>
> My faith would lay her hand
> On that meek head of Thine,
> While as a penitent I stand,
> And there confess my sin.
>
> Believing, we rejoice
> To feel the curse remove;
> We bless the Lamb with cheerful voice,
> And trust His bleeding love.
>   —Isaac Watts, original version.

After confessing his sins, the sinner watched the priest offer the sacrifice for him. First, the priest went to the altar, offered the sacrifice, and then walked a few steps to the laver where he washed his feet. Returning to the altar, he took the blood of the animal in a bowl and placed it on the north side of the altar, toward the Tabernacle itself. Taking the censer with sweet-smelling incense, he walked into the Tabernacle but only into the first room, the Holy Place, and there offered the incense at its special altar.

A PAGEANT OF THE CROSS

This altar stood just in front of a great veil—the one torn in two when Christ died on the cross. Everything here was of the highest spiritual significance. God was teaching us a great object lesson, the hidden meanings of the sacrifice of Christ for our sins. At this point the priests could proceed no further. Aaron's own sons were struck dead on their ordination day for lighting their censers with fire other than that kindled by God Himself to consume the body of the lamb—a picture of the fact that God wishes us to light the fires of worship at the cross of Jesus Christ. He will not tolerate any approach other than what He has Himself designated. Some believe that they may approach God through Mohammed. It is their privilege so to believe, and it is God's privilege to tell us through Christ that such worship is not acceptable unto Him. Even within the bounds of Christendom there are those who believe that they may find access to God through other intercessors. It is their privilege to pray to the saints and Mary if they wish, but it is God's privilege to reject such worship, since those prayers are actually offered to demons (John 14:6 with 1 Cor. 8:4-6 and 1 Cor. 10:19-21).

Finally, once a year one man could go beyond the veil of the Temple. On the great Day of Atonement, the high priest of Israel offered two sacrifices. First, he sacrificed an animal for his own sins and, after purifying ceremonies, prayers, and offering of incense, he returned to the altar and killed a second animal for the sins of the people. Then he went to the laver, washed his feet once more, entered the first room of the sanctuary, burned the incense before the altar, and—solemn moment—drew back the veil and entered into the holiest of all, filling the little room with incense. He then placed the blood of the second sacrificial victim between the overshadowing cherubim whose statues were on top of the ark of the covenant. Here was the climax of access. All this pageant taught that man cannot come to God in his own way; he must come to God in His revealed, divine way. It is the height of insolence and arrogance to attempt to worship in a way which does not conform in every detail to that which is set forth, in type and in fulfilment, in the Word of God. God will not, He *cannot* accept man's way; for man's way always leaves out the blood of Jesus Christ.

THE VEIL RENT

God Himself, of course, has the right to modify the worship. He did so when Christ died on the cross. In that sublime and awesome moment, we read, there was an earthquake, and the veil of the temple was torn in two from top to bottom (Mt. 27:51). It was the sign that God was through with priests, altars, and blood sacrifices. No longer was there to be incense and ritual but simple worship from the human heart, in Spirit and in truth (John 4:24).

When the Protestant Restoration took place under Luther and Calvin (for the Reformation was a restoration), these truths began to be perceived afresh through the overlay of tradition and the encrustations of ceremony that had all but obscured the original meaning of the sacrifice of the cross. Calvin, especially, understood this fact and ordered the altars removed from the churches. There was to be a pulpit, high and lifted up where all could see, with a Bible on the desk before the minister. This was not to be at one side of the room but in the very center, where every line of architecture could carry the eyes toward the sacred Book which God had given for the government of His church during this age, under the teaching of the Holy Spirit who is the true vicar of Christ for all who have been born again.

THE WAY IS OPEN

The veil has been torn away, the way is open. We need not approach God as cringing creatures, afraid of the shadow of our sin. We do not have to hang back like rebels before an offended monarch. We do not hesitate in fear because of the pollution of our Adamic natures. The veil has been torn in two. We come with holy boldness. We need no intercessor other than Christ.

There is in a simple story about Abraham Lincoln an illustration of what we have a right to expect. A Southern soldier, who had been freed from prison camp because he was wounded too sorely to return to active duty, was seeking access to the President in order to intercede for his brother, the sole support of their mother, who was then in a prison camp. The soldiers on guard at the White House would not let him in. One day as little Tad Lincoln, the President's son, was walking near the White House, he observed the crippled veteran seated on a bench, crying. The boy asked what the matter was. The man explained that he wanted to see Mr. Lincoln to tell about his brother but the soldiers would not let him in. Tad took the man by the hand and led him past the guards into the presence of his father. When I was desolate and alone, wounded by sin and mourning my lost state, the Son of God came from Heaven, died to pay the debt of my sin, and was raised from the dead in order that He might take me by the hand and lead me to His throne, past angel guards that might have barred the way, and in spite of the forces of the enemy of souls who would love to keep me from the place of comfort and blessing. The Son of God is my access into the grace where I now stand, and I need no other. I need not His mother; I need not any of the others for whom He died. I need only Jesus, and praise God, I have Jesus—the Lord Jesus Christ—my Jesus.

CHAPTER V

Standing in Grace

By whom also we have access by faith into this grace wherein we stand, and rejoice in hope of the glory of God (Rom. 5:2).

ONE autumn a great hurricane ripped across the middle Atlantic states and left a swath of toppled trees. I was much concerned, not only because I love trees and have planted several thousand of them, but also because a great pine tree, almost a hundred feet tall, fell across the roof of my kitchen, ripped a hole four by five feet, and brought a stream of water into the house. When the storm had subsided, I went out and examined the root structure of the pine and was amazed to see how shallow it was. Though it had spread out in large circumference, seeking its food, it had no taproot to anchor it, and the storm had bent it with ease. As I drove through the countryside and studied the effects of the wind, I saw hundreds of such trees, similarly uprooted. I decided to replace the fallen monarch, not with another pine, but with a tree that would develop a strong taproot; and while I would not live to see it, the years would bring strength and beauty to the spot in a tree that would stand and withstand the gales of the future.

STANDING

People are like trees. Some are brittle and snap with easy pressure; some bow before the winds of adversity; and some stand the severest tempests and live into the ages, as the cedars of Lebanon and oaks of Mamre. The Christian should be able, thus, to stand. If there is no dry rot of sin infecting the heart, the Christian should be able to withstand whatever pressures life may bring.

Our text states that we have access into this grace wherein we stand. We have discussed in some detail the question of our access; not by works but by grace; not by earthly mediators such as saints or Mary, but by the Lord Jesus Christ; not by an earthly priesthood but by the merits of the Savior. Now we look at the grace wherein we stand.

40

First, God says that the natural state of the true Christian is one of standing. Second, we are not propped into our standing position by external, human influences. Third, our standing, like our salvation, is entirely by grace.

Everywhere the Bible teaches that the Christian is to stand firm in this life. It is necessary to define the nature of the Christian because some have false ideas of what constitutes a Christian. Jews, for example, are inclined to make "Christian" synonymous with "Gentile." But there are multitudes of Gentiles, even in so-called Christian countries, who are not Christians; and there are many Christians who were not originally Gentiles. Others apply the name "Christian" to those who live in civilizations predominantly perfumed by Christian ideas. Many years ago, in a train, I asked a man if he were a Christian. He replied, "Do you think I was born in Africa?" Still others define Christians as church members. Billy Sunday exposed that fallacy by saying: "You can baptize a bicycle, but that doesn't make it an automobile." Finally, some think that a Christian is one who pays lip service to the so-called ethics of Jesus Christ and seeks to pattern his life after His supposed ideals. The Lord Himself blasted such a view by announcing that in the day of judgment He would banish to eternal separation from Himself many who claimed that they had wrought mighty works in His name.

There is not one line outside the Bible that defines a Christian. If we turn to that source book of all knowledge concerning the origins of the Christian faith, we must accept its teaching that a Christian is a member of the human race who ought to go to the lake of fire like any other sinner. However, he is going to Heaven because God Almighty has declared him righteous even though he is unrighteous. This declaration is based not on his character or deeds but solely on the ground of the atonement which Jesus Christ furnished by dying on the cross of Calvary to satisfy the demands of divine righteousness.

What are the characteristics of the man who has been thus declared righteous, justified in the sight of God by the redemptive work of the Savior? Since "man looks on the outward appearance, but the Lord looks on the heart" (1 Sam. 16:7), God tells us in the epistle of James, that the proof of our salvation, manward, will be good works. But in Romans, the proof of our salvation, Godward, is that God sees what He did within us when He declared us righteous in Christ. The whole process of becoming a Christian is like the erection of a beautiful building. The first two and a half chapters of Romans—like a bulldozer clearing away the ground—destroy all hope of man's participation in salvation through his own efforts. The next chapter and a half, by showing that God provided Christ as the means of our salvation, place a foundation that goes down to the very rock.

Now, the walls of the building begin to rise. We see effects of the new life within us. To change the figure of speech, the Christian learns, like a woman with child, that there is life within. As the expectant mother feels the first little taps which rapidly increase to strong movements, so the Christian realizes the presence of Christ in his life, and nourishes himself so that Christ may be fully formed within. In the eighth chapter of Romans the child is born, and stands as a personality. In the last five chapters of the epistle, the child is walking and leaping, ready to enter into the responsibility of being an adult, to which the end of life brings the true Christian as he steps into Heaven, fitted to exercise the function of government with God forever. For that he has been chosen, called, saved and matured.

GROWTH

The true function of the Christian is to stand in the midst of this world that crucified Christ, to grow spiritually and to witness to the Lord who has become his life. This is the natural state of the true Christian, but "natural" here means supernatural. It is "natural" in the physical state for an individual to sleep approximately one third of the time, to breathe at a certain rate per minute, and to have his blood circulating at a certain arterial tension. This is a description of things as they should be. In the spiritual life, the life of Christ dominates the old Adamic life with which we were born. As Christians we should allow the life of the Lord Jesus Christ to dominate every phase of our life. But such a condition is not natural to the Adamic nature; it comes from Jesus Christ in a supernaturalness that is evident at every moment.

Failure to understand that Christ must furnish the life which we live moment by moment leads to misunderstanding of the concept of the Christian life. Half a century ago Charles Sheldon's *In His Steps*, which was sold by the millions of copies, set forth that men should follow in the footsteps of Christ and try to do what they thought He would do in similar circumstances. Later, Glenn Clark wrote *What Would Jesus Do?* This idea is alien to the Christian life as set forth in the New Testament. Under this method, the old, Adamic nature would paint a facade to hide man's natural sinfulness. The Christian life is not an attempt to do what Jesus Christ might do if He were head of an advertising agency or running a department store. It is almost blasphemous to think thus, for Jesus Christ came the first time not as a citizen but as a Savior; He will return, not as a citizen but as a Ruler.

Meanwhile, we who have been born again are not to visualize a Unitarian Jesus, an ordinary member of the human race, doing ordinary things. Rather, we must see ourselves as empty gloves through which His hand performs tasks impossible to our Adamic being.

So we are to stand in our circumstances as redeemed men and women, placed there to show forth the life of Christ and witness against the world which is alien to the person and work of Christ, and always will be.

GIFTS AND GRACES

If we seek outward props by which to stand, we shall be but scarecrows—only a part of the scenery. The crows will fly down and lodge on our shoulders the better to survey the field and find out where the grain is thickest or the corn most tender. They will use us as their vantage ground for pillaging.

It is possible for unregenerate men to compete with and even surpass true Christians in the development of courage, charity, kindness, politeness, thoughtfulness, tolerance, gentleness, patience, and a thousand other virtues. But these are not the marks of true Christianity. In non-Christians they are works and attributes; in a Christian they are gifts and graces, from an entirely different source. A gold nugget no larger than a pea is valuable because it is pure gold. A gawdy trinket, though much larger and more glittering, will not stand the acid test because it is base metal, coated over with a thin wash borrowed from reality. The gifts and graces in the life of the believer come from Christ Himself in the measure that the individual surrenders his life to the dominance of the Savior. To put it in another way, the Christian life will become manifest as the individual who has accepted Christ as Savior truly acknowledges Him to be Lord.

In the first chapter of Romans we read, "The just shall live by faith"; or, as another translator puts it, "The righteous, on the principle of faith, shall live." The chapters before us tell of living by this principle of faith. As Bishop Anders Nygren of Sweden says, "Through Christ the believer has been delivered from the age of death and received into the age of life. What does it mean to live, in this pregnant sense? That is the question Paul is about to discuss. Each of the next four chapters has its contribution to make to the answer. Chapter five says it means to be free from wrath, chapter six says it is to be free from sin, chapter seven says free from the law, and chapter eight says free from death."

THROUGH CHRIST

The standing of the believer is in grace, as all of salvation is by grace. It should be noted that the King James Version states that our access is by faith into this grace wherein we stand. When all the great revisions are consulted, we discover that they agree with the Greek original in omitting the words "by faith," and in stating simply that "By Christ we have access into this grace wherein we stand." God has taken the believer out of Adam and placed him in Christ. This is entirely by grace, and we have nothing to do with it, either in the conception of the idea, the execution of the method which makes it possible, or the transaction which brings salvation and standing to us, or, more properly, which brings us into salvation and standing. "Through Christ we have confidently entered into this new relationship of grace, and here we take our stand."

We can easily comprehend what it would mean to have access to the gold stores at Fort Knox, where the major portion of the world's precious metal is stored. The man who could take from those stores at will would never want for anything material. This prospect is now set before us in the spiritual realm. We have access into the grace wherein we stand. It should be realized that every other promise in the Bible is based upon this spiritual fact: we have

access into the grace of God. When we read that God shall supply
all our need according to His riches in glory by Christ Jesus (Phil.
4:19), it is because grace has been opened up to us in Christ. When
we are told that we have comfort in time of sorrow, strength in time
of weakness, consolation in time of bereavement, a Father's chastening when we stumble, pardon when we sin, it is all because we
stand in grace. When we are told that we have been admitted to the
fellowship of the Father and the Son, and that, when broken by our
sin, fellowship may be restored and maintained, it is because
we have already been placed in the relationship of grace which can
never be broken.

RELATIONSHIP

Someone may wonder why all Christians do not live in these
glories that are so readily accessible. The answer is in the words
relationship and *fellowship*. Relationship has been conferred upon
the believer without any strings attached. We are taken from our
relationship to fallen Adam and placed in the new relationship to
Christ, and there we remain forever.

The blessings are all there for us in that relationship: we have
access into the grace wherein we stand. If Christians do not
appropriate the spiritual resources available in Christ, it is not God's
fault. Indeed, after an individual has been justified, his whole life
is subjected to the whittling and sandpapering process that God
must use to bring His children into blessings which He wishes them
to have.

We have all read the story of some old woman who went from
garbage can to garbage can, taking crusts of bread that had been
left from someone's dinner. After her death police discover bank
books among her effects, showing deposits totalling $100,000. A man,
who picked up old newspapers in the subway and sold them as
junk, dies, leaving deeds to ten properties, and safe deposit boxes
filled with gilt-edged bonds. Why do some people go through life
in misery while actually possessing tremendous resources? Why do
multitudes of Christians, who believe truly in Christ as Savior,
possess eternal life, have access into the grace wherein they stand,
and are accepted by God in His beloved Son, live as starvelings?

LOVE FOR THE UNSAVED

The Lord Jesus turned, almost pathetically, to the unbelievers of His day, saying, "O Jerusalem, Jerusalem, killing the prophets and stoning those who are sent to you! How often would I have gathered your children together as a hen gathers her brood under her wings, and you would not! Behold, your house is forsaken and desolate!" (Mt. 23:37, 38). And that cry is repeated to those who have believed in Him but who do not rest in His love and live by His grace. One appeal from the heart of God to His ancient people can be addressed to all who are His own in every age. "My well-beloved had a vineyard in a very fruitful hill: and he fenced it and gathered out the stones thereof, and planted it with the choicest vine, and built a tower in the midst of it, and also made a winepress therein: and he looked that it should bring forth grapes, and it brought forth wild grapes. . . . What could have been done more to my vineyard, that I have not done in it? Wherefore, when I looked that it should bring forth grapes, brought it forth wild grapes?" (Isa. 5:1, 2, 4).

The sweep of the promises of God for those who are in Christ is from eternity to eternity. There is nothing that God would withhold from the one who is chosen in Christ and who has put his trust in the Savior. "He that spared not his own Son, but delivered him up for us all," the Holy Spirit cries out, "how shall he not with him also freely give us all things?" (Rom. 8:32). And after having chided them for the carnality of their daily lives, the Apostle tells the Corinthian believers, "All things are yours; whether Paul, or Apollos, or Cephas, or the world, or life, or death, or things present, or things to come; all are yours; and you are Christ's; and Christ is God's" (1 Cor. 3:21-23).

Let us possess our possessions. God takes us to Calvary, shows us the bright prospects of eternity, and places the Bible in our hands as a chart of all that He promises to give us. Go in and possess your possessions, He cries out to us. Every promise that you appropriate will bring forth its fruit in your life, for I have called you in love, and through Christ I have given you access into this grace wherein you stand.

CHAPTER VI

Hope of Glory

By whom also we have access by faith into this grace wherein we stand, and rejoice in hope of the glory of God (Rom. 5:2).

THE true believer in Christ has been accepted in the Savior and placed in a position of all grace. Because we have been given eternal life we look forward even now to its glories. Our text says, "We rejoice in hope of the glory of God" (Rom. 5:2). It is significant that the hope of the glory of God is the first to be set before the believer in considering the blessings that flow from grace.

Several years ago I traveled extensively in China. One of the trips was by railroad from Peking, northwest through Mongolia, and into the province of Shansi. During part of the journey, the train went for several hours along a shelf of hills overlooking plains stretching southwest as far as the eye could reach. These plains were filled with farm lands and dotted with villages. The missionary accompanying me asked how I would go about evangelizing those villages where there had never been a missionary. Even though in full possession of the language, how would I go about preaching the gospel of Christ to people who had never even heard His name?

FIRST THINGS

We discussed this problem at some length and he then asked me if some villagers should trust Christ as Savior, what doctrines would I teach them first? They had already received the irreducible minimum of Christianity: they believe that they are sinners before the one true God, and that God sent His only Son to die in order to remove their sins; and now they stand before God, accepted in Christ. Should I teach the doctrines of prayer, the virgin birth of our Lord, of justification, sanctification, redemption, the new birth, inspiration, revelation, of the Holy Spirit, or something quite different? We discussed this question for perhaps two hours.

Two or three weeks later, back in Peking with the same missionary, while reading my Bible, I found a verse that made me

47

exclaim, "Oh I was wrong when I outlined the succession of doctrines to be taught to young Christians! Here is a verse which gives quite another idea of the matter." Paul was confronted with this problem when dealing with the Ephesian church. When the gospel was first preached in that city, there was a riot fostered by the silversmiths whose occupation was threatened by the coming of the gospel; for a biblical Christian could have no statues or images in connection with his worship. The Ephesian pagans understood this implication of the gospel; and, for two hours, thousands of milling people cried out, "Great is Diana of the Ephesians!" This Diana, one of the forerunners of the modern cult of the counterfeit Virgin Mary, the people believed was able to hear and answer their prayers. Paul left soon after the uproar; and after the experiences that led to his arrest and imprisonment, he reached Rome to be judged by Caesar.

THE HOPE OF GOD'S CALLING

While there he wrote to the Ephesians and recounted the effect that their behavior had produced on him. He said that after he heard of their faith in the Lord Jesus, and their love unto all the saints (living people, of course, not dead saints) he ceased not to give thanks for them, making mention of them in his prayers. And what did he pray for this infant church? The answer is given in some detail and shows that he prayed that they might come to know certain doctrines. And of all the doctrines in the catalogue of the Christian faith, which did he esteem so important that they should be known first by the young believers? To these former Devil-worshippers the Holy Spirit moved Paul to write that he ceased not to pray "that the God of our Lord Jesus Christ, the Father of glory, may give unto you the spirit of wisdom and revelation in the knowledge of [Himself]; that the eyes of your understanding being enlightened you may know" three things: (1) "what is the hope of his calling"; (2) "what are the riches of the glory of his inheritance in the saints"; and (3) "what is the exceeding greatness of his power toward us who believe" (Eph. 1:15-19).

Notice that first he prayed that they might know the hope of God's calling. And here in Romans we see that the first blessing that flows from our access into divine grace is our rejoicing in hope of the glory of God.

The hope of the Christian is threefold. There is the far distant, future hope of our life with God in Heaven forever; there is the intermediate hope of our position in Christ immediately after death until the Lord ushers in the permanent, eternal state; and there is our present hope concerning all that may befall us in this life while we wait for death or the coming of the Lord Jesus Christ.

HEAVEN A PLACE

The far hope of the believer in Christ is that we shall dwell with Him in Heaven forever. This is not wishful thinking, but is founded on the Word of God and guaranteed to us by the honor and integrity of our God.

First, let us face the objection that is brought against the doctrine of Heaven by those who have a smattering of science, who are aware of the distance which light travels in a second and in a light year, who know the various theories in modern cosmology, and who have read the early findings that have come to us from Mount Palomar's 200 inch telescope. They say that they cannot find Heaven in space. They say that the areas of space now becoming known by the arrival of pinpoints of light are so far removed from earth that it would take light a trillion years to reach our speck of dust. They insinuate that only a medieval obscurantism could think that our earth is the center of the universe. They say that if Christ, ascending into Heaven, had traveled with the speed of light, He would not yet have reached the farthest star.

I am willing to admit the importance of the argument, for if there is no material, spatial Heaven, the Lord Jesus Christ did not ascend into Heaven in His body. If we admit this, we must abandon the doctrine of the physical resurrection of the Savior, unless we hold that the body is lurking around earth somewhere. If we abandon the resurrection, we must abandon the redemptive meaning of the crucifixion. These doctrines are so infrangibly welded to each other that, if one be destroyed, the others fall with it.

THE SPEED OF THOUGHT

A student once asked me the trick question about Christ ascending at the speed of light and being still within the inner universe. I replied, "Why do you wish to slow the Creator to the speed of light? He who created the universe is able to move with the speed of thought, and it is possible to think from here to the remotest point of the universe as quickly as it is to think down to the corner drugstore." I wonder at the great patience of God Almighty with the little minds which seek to reduce Him to the level of man!

As to the question of earth being the center of the universe and Heaven existing for the after life of earth creatures, it is well to remain within the bounds of the Bible and not go beyond what is written. It is true that men have conceived of the earth as being the physical center of the universe but this is nowhere stated in the Bible. Indeed, amid hypotheses that held that the earth was supported on the back of Atlas, or on the back of an elephant standing on the back of a turtle, the Bible shines clearly with its vivid testimonies of truth. He "hangs the earth upon nothing" said Job, hundreds of years before Christ; while to Isaiah was revealed the phrase, "the circle of the earth" (Isa. 40:22). Our Lord Jesus spoke of His return as occurring in an instant of time and then described life on a turning globe at that instant: two in bed, night; two grinding at the mill, morning; and two working in the field, midday.

But let us ask the skeptics: What constitutes the center of a room? Someone might answer by drawing lines to opposite corners, and calling the point of intersection the center of the room. A mason would erect a perpendicular from a point to the ceiling and find the center halfway up that line. An actor would know without a question that the center of a theater is the stage. And a Christian should know that the center of a church is the pulpit on which the Bible rests, behind which the minister stands to feed the people. Thank God the center of our churches is not a chancel, not an altar, for Christ has died once for all, but the pulpit with a Bible, the Word of God containing all the answers that we need for our pilgrim journey.

GOLDEN STREETS

There are certain false concepts about Heaven which must be brushed aside if we are to know the hope of the glory which lies before us. One idea is that Heaven is a hard, glittering place with streets of gold and gates of pearl, where the believers will wear golden crowns and fly about playing harps. C. S. Lewis of Cambridge has demolished this concept in one of his books. He points out that the Bible contains many symbols, and that it was written for grownups who could understand these symbols. When the Bible speaks of streets of gold, it is presenting us with an idea of something rare, precious, that does not rust away. A crown symbolizes royalty and government, and sets forth the fact that we shall be associated with God in the government of the universe forever. The harp is the symbol of music, the nearest thing to ecstasy on earth. Combining these symbols, we see that God is teaching that our eternal destiny is to dwell with Him in closest fellowship, companions of His heart, partners of His plans, willing agents of His desire, in a place of unchanging wonder and beauty, and in ecstasy beyond anything we can imagine.

Such a picture is far removed from that set forth in an old hymn that described Heaven as a place

> Where congregations ne'er break up
> And Sabbaths have no end.

It is difficult to comprehend how anyone could think that Heaven will be eleven o'clock Sunday morning, all timepieces eternally frozen at that moment when the doxology is intoned.

HEIRS OF SALVATION

The danger of visualizing the symbols of Heaven in terms of earthly objects can be seen from an incident that occurred when I was holding meetings in Miami, Florida. One of the ladies of the church came to the morning meeting each day and brought her cook with her. While teaching the first chapter of Hebrews, I pointed out that Christians were not angels and that we never would be angels. I was invited to luncheon in the lady's home and was told that the cook was depressed since hearing me speak. I went to the kitchen to find out what the matter was. The woman had lived with the expectation that some day she would be an angel. Probably she visualized the moment when wings would be attached to her human frame and she would fly around in a golden Heaven, her crown properly adjusted, her harp in full melody. "Sally," I asked, "do you want to sweep floors and dust chairs in Heaven forever?" She looked at me, wide-eyed, and answered that she did not. "Well," I told her, "the Bible definitely says that the angels are domestic servants of Heaven, and that they are the servants of God and of us whom they guard." I turned to the first chapter of Hebrews and asked her to read aloud, "Are they not all ministering spirits, sent forth to minister for them who shall be heirs of salvation?" (Heb. 1:14). Then I asked her if she knew who were the heirs of salvation. Since she hesitated, I urged her to sing, "Blessed Assurance."

> Blessed assurance, Jesus is mine
>   O what a foretaste of glory divine,
> Heir of salvation . . .

I stopped her and asked who were these heirs of salvation. She answered that we, believers in Christ, are the heirs of salvation. Then I showed her that she was not going to be an angel, doing the domestic work of the universe, but she would be joined to Christ, made like Him, associated with Him forever, the fullness of Him who fills all in all. I then asked her, "Do you really want to be an angel?" She replied, "Not if it's like that." I pressed the matter one step more: "The Bible says that it is like that, doesn't it?" She nodded her head, and I asked her, "Don't you think it would be much better to be the bride than to be the one who ties the shoes for the bride?" By now she was smiling, and resumed preparation of an excellent luncheon.

FACE TO FACE

Our hope of glory is a wonderful thing. Most wonderful is the fact that we shall behold the Lord Jesus Christ face to face, and express to Him in fitting language praise and thanksgiving for the love He showed to us in leaving Heaven to come to earth and die for needy sinners. This inspired Fanny Crosby to write:

> Some day the silver cord will break,
>   And I no more, as now shall sing;
> But, O, the joy, when I shall wake
>   Within the palace of the King.
>
> And I shall see Him, face to face,
>   And tell the story: Saved by grace!
>
> Some day my earthly house will fall,
>   I cannot tell how soon 'twill be;
> But this I know: My All-in-all
>   Has now a place in Heav'n for me.

> And I shall see Him face to face,
>   And tell the story: Saved by grace!
> Yes I shall see Him, face to face,
>   And tell the story: Saved by grace.

This hope is one of the greatest themes of our hymnody, and it is not hard to understand why so many have been moved to song at the thought of seeing Him who loves us and has loosed us from our sins through His own blood (Rev. 1:5).

FREEDOM FROM SIN

To me, however, there is another thought of Heaven that runs a very close second to the prospect of seeing the Lord Jesus Christ, and that is that we shall be free from sin. This desire has always been in my heart with earnestness and intensity. I recall that while in my teens I read a Sunday School lesson on King Solomon. He was allowed to ask for any gift from God, and he chose wisdom. The committee which made up the lessons had given this one the title "Solomon's Wise Choice." I pondered it for some time, and decided that it was not wise; that if I had been in his place I would not have asked God for wisdom, but rather to be like Him in holiness. Through the years, my soul longs intensely for that day when there will be no more sin. The heart, like a garden, produces weeds when left to itself, and brings forth flowers only when cultivated with intense care. How wonderful that day when only flowers will grow, and we shall be like our Lord forever!

And with sin will go all the ugly army that has marched in its train. There will be no more evenings when we must review the day with contrition because of self. There will be no more need to confess sin and seek forgiveness. Our blood will no longer run hot in our veins in anger or in lust. We shall be like our Lord Jesus Christ. There will be no more sickness, pain, sadness, crying, loneliness, separation, sorrow, or death. No wonder believers throughout the ages, like John Bunyan's Pilgrim, have gazed upon this city from afar and counted the toil of the journey as nothing!

Though some smile superciliously when they hear God's people sing it, there is great comfort for the believer in these words:

> There's a land that is fairer than day,
>   And by faith we can see it afar;
> For the Father waits over the way
>   To prepare us a dwelling place there.
> In the sweet bye and bye,
>   We shall meet on that beautiful shore.

Do not waste your time in telling me that such a hymn is poetically gauche, and that it lacks the finish of a Shakespearian stanza. We know that well; these lines have welled up from childlike hearts of God's common people. In the simple words and simpler melody we find a stream coming forth from the rock in an arid desert. The pilgrims are no longer thinking of the toil that has brought them weariness, of the labor that has calloused their hands, of the age that has wrinkled their faces, of the sorrow that has saddened their countenances. Forgotten are the pains of life and the deceptions of earthly promises. Like the traveler who quickens his step at first sight of the distant city to which he journeys, these raise the melody of hope, and I gladly join them in singing the praise of Him who has given us access into grace where we rejoice in the hope of the glory of God.

CHAPTER VII

Hope in Death

We . . . rejoice in hope of the glory of God (Rom. 5:2).

CHRIST our Lord has not only redeemed us from our sin, so that
we are justified before God, but also with that redemption has
opened the door to the storehouse of God's grace, that we might
have all spiritual blessings in Him. This justifying redemption has
brought us to the place of peace with God, and access into the grace
wherein we stand; and the first blessing that flows from this grace
is that we rejoice in hope of the glory of God. In the preceding
chapter we looked at the far hope of Heaven; here we consider hope
that has to do with death and life immediately after death, until
our eternal status is perfected at the coming of the Lord Jesus Christ.

DEATH IN THE PAGAN WORLD

The entrance of Christianity into the pagan world of Greece
and Rome must have been like a fresh breeze which enters a cavern
when the wall is broken.

When the angels rolled the stone from the door of the cave-
tomb in which the Lord Jesus Christ had been buried, they changed
life upon the earth. The pagan world was filled with the noxious
fumes of false philosophy. Satan had brought sin to man, and with
sin came death; with death came the errors of mortal mind, and
with these errors came the end of hope. Men lived in abject fear
of death. Here and there Stoics confronted the unknown with brave
resolution, but the religions of the ancients show that there was no
hope in any of them. Except for the revelation which God gave His
people Israel, the world was shrouded in darkness, even as it is
today wherever the light of Bible truth concerning the future has
not penetrated. The underworld of the ancients was a dark, fear-
some abode; the dead were ferried across the river Styx by Charon,
boatman of despair. Even today when archaeologists open an ancient
grave where all has turned to dust, the head may be distinguished
from the feet by the coin which the friends of the deceased placed

in the mouth of the corpse to pay the boatman. Literature is filled with allusions to fear which gripped the hearts of multitudes as they faced the terrors of death.

STEPHEN'S MARTYRDOM

Such fears were banished for those who had been redeemed by the Lord Jesus Christ. As soon as the persecution of Christians began, it was evident that here was a new source of power that brought joy even in the midst of death. The first martyr, Stephen, preached truth that flayed his hearers and filled their hearts with rage. We read that "they gnashed on him with their teeth. But he, being full of the Holy Spirit, looked up steadfastly into heaven, and saw the glory of God, and Jesus standing on the right hand of God. And said, Behold, I see the heavens opened, and the Son of man standing on the right hand of God. Then they cried out with a loud voice, and stopped their ears, and ran upon him with one accord, and cast him out of the city and stoned him. . . . And they stoned Stephen, calling upon God, and saying, Lord Jesus, receive my spirit. And he kneeled down, and cried with a loud voice, Lord, lay not this sin to their charge. And when he had said this, he fell asleep" (Acts 7:54-60). This was not soul sleep, but merely a figure for the death of the body.

AN OPEN DOOR TO GLORY

Here was something new in the world. Henceforth men and women would die without fear, since they knew that the end of this life would be entrance into the eternal life of all joy. An ancient legend illustrates this truth. A pagan monarch wished to destroy Christianity in his realm. One of the Christian leaders incurred the hatred of the king, who told his servants to put him to death. They informed the ruler that this would greatly please the Christian because it would take him at once into Heaven. The king answered that the Christian should be tortured, but short of death. The servants replied that the man would thank God that he was privileged to suffer for the name of Christ. The king cried out, "Is there nothing that will displease these people?" His servants replied that the only way to offend the true Christian would be to force him to commit sin. Suffering and death held no terrors for the Christian.

The hope of the glory of God filled the eyes of Stephen and

all who followed him. How can we fear that which brings us to the end of evil? How can there be hesitation or doubt when death for the believer is an open door to glory?

DREAD OF DEATH

It is not so for those who do not have the hope that is ours in the gospel of Christ. Fear grips the pagan world at the thought of death, but such fear is not the exclusive possession of the dark lands of heathenism. Right around us are evidences of the fear that holds highly intelligent men in bondage.

To know what fear exists in the dark lands without Christ, we have only to study their horrible religions. The hideous masks of the witch doctors, the incantations of the voodoo workers, the warfare against evil spirits waged by wounded hearts throughout the Christless world are witnesses to the terror of death. I close my eyes at times and hear the drums for the dead in India and the hired mourners shrieking in the night. Or I visualize the frenzied dance of the Chinese round and round the coffin as the funeral train proceeds toward the resting place of the corpse. These dancers drop myriads of pieces of paper, each with a hole in it, thinking that the evil spirits must pause to pass through each hole before reaching the deceased.

But we need not go to Africa, India, or China to find the dread of death in the heart of one who does not know Christ. We turn to the volume of published correspondence of Lord Pollock and Oliver Wendell Holmes. Chief Justice Holmes was one of the most brilliant minds in our history; his keen analysis of problems did much to shape the interpretation of law under which this republic now lives. The relationship between the two friends is clearly revealed in the correspondence, and they wrote without camouflage or artifice. In one of the most somber of passages Mr. Holmes expresses abject terror of death; underneath the light exterior of his life was the stark reality of growing old with fear and trembling, and facing death with the hopelessness of one who does not know the redemption from sin and fear that comes through faith in the Lord Jesus Christ.

As a minister, I have been in many a sick room and have conducted many a funeral. In those moments when the veil is lifted and death enters the household, one sees the difference between faith and non-faith. Still ringing in my ears is the shriek of a godless daughter whose life of sin brought her mother to an early grave. And I can see the trusting smile on the face of the bereaved Christian who watched the passing of a saved loved one with all the confidence and assurance that is his right in Christ.

The Devil hates the Christian doctrine of hope in death. Satan wages war to keep souls from believing in Christ; and when any are translated out of the kingdom of Satan into the kingdom of God's beloved Son (Col. 1:13), he seeks to destroy their confidence and dim their hope. He has often heard believers sing:

> The soul that on Jesus hath leaned for repose,
> I will not, I will not desert to his foes.
> That soul, though all Hell should endeavor to shake,
> I'll never, no never, no never forsake.

Satan knows that God will never desert the soul that has trusted in Jesus Christ. But Satan will do the next thing to recapturing the soul—he will attempt to destroy the peace of that soul. Some Christians find the road to Heaven a miserable one because they fail to take the Word of God at face value.

But the enemy of souls discovers that among God's children are many who lay hold upon promises with full assurance of faith, and go forward steadfast unto the end. We are just as sure that we are going to be in Heaven as we are sure that God the Father, the Lord Jesus Christ, and the Holy Spirit are there. Our assurance is based not on anything in ourselves, but upon the fact that, though we deserve Hell, the Lord Jesus Christ has borne our Hell, and therefore God Himself can give us nothing less than His Heaven.

CHRIST THE DOOR

As a child I heard frequent jokes concerning two Irishmen who died and went to Heaven, and how at the door they met St. Peter who said to them one thing or another that ended in a laugh. But I have learned from the Word of God that Peter is not at the door of Heaven, and has nothing to do with our entry. Jesus Christ said, "I am the door; by me, if any man enter in, he shall be saved, and shall go in and out, and find pasture" (John 10:9). Here is the joy of the believer: Christ is the door, the door is open wide; we have already entered into Christ, and we are therefore assured of Heaven. No keys are needed for an open door.

Another idea from which we have been freed is that death is a long sleep. As Longfellow wrote,

> Dust thou art, to dust returnest,
> Was not spoken of the soul.

When the Bible speaks of the sleep of death it is speaking of the body, not of the soul. I saw one of my children so still in her cradle that I feared she was dead; but when I touched her she was vibrant with life. And I know of a woman who thought her husband was asleep but he had been dead for several hours. I mistook sleep for death, and the woman mistook death for sleep. The proof that sleep does not affect the soul lies in all that the Bible teaches concerning what occurs after death.

JESUS PAID IT ALL

We have also been released from the fear of undergoing suffering for our sins after we die. Of all false doctrines, most obnoxious is the idea that Jesus Christ did not pay enough to redeem our souls, and that we must pay after we die. We sing:

> Jesus paid it all;
> All to Him I owe:
> Sin had left a crimson stain;
> He washed it white as snow.

How wonderful is that truth! I will never sing

> Jesus paid it ninety per cent;
> Only ten per cent I owe.
> Sin had left a crimson stain,
> He washed it light pink.

Thank God, such an idea is not even remotely true. The Bible tells us that the blood of Jesus Christ, God's Son, cleanses us from *all* sin (I John 1:7). Since God says that He has cleansed us from *all* sin, no one can tell me that He cleansed me from only a part and that I must pay for the rest. There is no purgatory.

Two magnificent passages set forth this great hope of the believer that at the instant of death the soul of the Christian is immediately and forever in Heaven. The first is in 2 Corinthians 5. I quote it from the Roman Catholic Confraternity Version. "And indeed, in this present state we groan, yearning to be clothed over with that dwelling of ours which is from Heaven . . . Always full of courage, then, and knowing that while we are in body we are exiled from the Lord—for we walk by faith and not by sight—we even have the courage to prefer to be exiled from the body and to be at home with the Lord" (2 Cor. 5:1, 2, 6-8). Is it any wonder that the early Christians met death with the shout of triumph and the hope of glory? And is it any wonder that Satan has sought to rob God's people of this hope? What a travesty to teach purgatory in the light of this truth!

TO DIE IS TO GAIN

The second passage I take also from the Roman Catholic Confraternity translation. Paul was writing to the Philippian church that his trial was about to come up before Nero, and that he did not yet know whether he would be freed or sentenced to death. But, he says, "with complete assurance now as at all times Christ will be glorified in my body, whether through life or through death" (Phil. 1:20). Having shown that he has perfect confidence and trust in Christ the apostle continues, "For to me to live is Christ, and to die is gain." Note that he does not say that to die is soul-sleeping or unconsciousness or purgatory; to die is gain. He does not say that to die is separation from Christ and suffering penance for sins; to die is gain. He continues, "But if to live in the flesh is my lot, this means for me fruitful labor, and I do not know which to choose. Indeed I am hard pressed from both sides—desiring to depart and to be with Christ, a lot by far the better" (Phil. 1:21-23). Isn't that wonderful! Paul declares that a Christian is much better off dead than alive, because death means instantaneous departure to be with Christ in Heaven: absent from the body, present with the Lord.

In spite of these unequivocal statements of Scripture, many Christians hold to life on earth, even though they have but a few breaths left. Here is a man who has scraped and slaved for forty years to save several thousand dollars. He knows he is going to die, but he is willing to spend it all to be kept in his body for a few more days. I once remarked to an audience, "Do not act as though life on earth were more wonderful than life in Heaven. Give your money to one of the Bible societies and go to Heaven three weeks sooner!" The audience laughed, but it is indeed strange to see Christians who are unwilling to rejoice in hope of the glory of God.

REJOICE IN HOPE

Because of this hope that death will take every believer, fully cleansed by the blood of Jesus Christ, immediately and directly to Heaven, it is strange that any believer should fear death. An analogy will show how silly such fears really are. Suppose a young soldier from your town has been fighting against the Communists in the hard Korean winter. He is sent up to a certain ridge in the night and digs his foxhole, completing it just as dawn breaks. An enemy shoots at him and he is forced to lie low throughout the day. He eats K rations, and knows how a horse feels who has hay and oats on one day and oats and hay the next. He knows he must hold his ground and lies there throughout the day and night, and the next day and the next night. Along about the third night he hears a voice behind him: "Hey! Are you Private John Smith of Hometown, Anystate?" "What's it to you?" replies the soldier. "Are you serial number 768-99-74?" "Yes, I am; but what of it?" The relieving soldier answers, "I have orders to replace you. You are to go out on the next Red Cross flight to the States. You will get a hot bath and clean clothes. You are going home and eat Southern fried chicken with mashed potatoes and gravy, and apple pie with ice cream." Now suppose the G.I. should answer, "You don't mean that I have to leave this nice foxhole and give up my K rations?" We smile at the absurdity of the idea, and yet some believers, perhaps you who read these lines, are unwilling to leave your earthly foxhole for the Heavenly home and sit down at the banquet table of our God and to fellowship with Him in Heaven among all your loved ones who have gone before.

I could appreciate the desire to remain here if there were the prospect of lapsing into unconsciousness, even if only to the day of the Lord's return; for loving consciousness with Christ here is better than unconscious sleep. I could imagine wanting to stay here even though afflicted with incurable disease, if dying meant departure to purgatory to remain there in torment while purging oneself from sin. But for the soul who has leaned upon Jesus Christ and knows Him as Savior, for the soul whose sins have been cleansed, removed as far as the east is from the west (Ps. 103:12), cast behind God's back (Isa. 38:17), cast into the depths of the sea (Mic. 7:19), blotted out as a thick cloud (Isa. 44:22), remembered against him no more forever (Heb. 8:12), it is indeed a strange aberration to wish to remain here, even though it be in the halls of royalty or in the mansion of a Midas. The best that earth can produce is but a foxhole compared with Heaven. Paul says, "I reckon that the sufferings of this present time are not worthy to be compared with the glory that shall be revealed in us" (Rom. 8:18).

CHAPTER VIII

The Present Hope

By whom also we . . . rejoice in hope of the glory of God *(Rom. 5:2).*

THE thousand-year-old proverb—"If it were not for hope, the heart would break"—is a fitting commentary on Romans 5:2. We have seen the far distant hope of Heaven, and the nearer hope of all that is ours at the instant of death. Let us now look at our present hope in the midst of this world of sadness and fear. Paul wrote to the Corinthian believers, "If in this life only we have hope in Christ, we are of all men most miserable" (I Cor. 15:19). Our present text augments this thought: knowing the future is sure, we rejoice in the present.

Satan is always seeking to emasculate the power of words and deprive them of meaning. Some words have been so misused that the spiritual power which God meant to convey through them has drained away. One of the values of expository Bible study is that the preacher goes deep into the meaning of words and makes them live again with power to stir the soul. Thus he can bring comfort to the sorrowing and strength to the weak. For example, "awful" has almost lost the original meaning, "that which is worthy of, or which commands, profound respect or reverential fear"; it has degenerated to "frightful," "monstrous," or merely "distasteful."

"HOPE"

The word "hope" is so wonderful that it is not surprising that Satan has endeavored to rob it of its power and insinuate despair into its meaning. To many thoughtless people, hope is little more than a desire, fulfilment of which is in doubt. This meaning has an interesting philological background. The great *Oxford English Dictionary* was issued in fascicles over a period of forty-five years. When the volume containing the word "hope" came out half a century ago, the editors stated that intransitive use of the verb "to

hope" was obsolete except as a biblical archaism, and that the
transitive usage was chiefly poetic. Then they added what they
called colloquial usage: "often in a weakened sense, expressing no
more than a desire that the event may happen, or that the fact may
turn out to be as stated." But in the ensuing half-century, the trends
then noted have become predominant and the word "hope," except
as used by writers on biblical themes, has become little more than
a term of politeness: "I hope I don't disturb you," or of mere desire:
"I hope it doesn't rain." Various proverbs reflect this kind of hope
such as: "Hope for the best, but prepare for the worst"; "Hope is
a good breakfast, but a bad supper"; "He who lives on hope will
die fasting"; "Hope is cheap as despair"; and Friedrich Nietzsche's
"Hope is the worst of evils for it prolongs the torment of man."

    These are the vilest counterfeits. François Voltaire wrote of
another hope which is also a counterfeit more dangerous than the
others because it has a grain of truth. In his *Philosophical Dictionary*
he defines hope as "a Christian virtue which consists in our despising
all poor things here below in the expectation of enjoying, in an
unknown country, unknown joys which our priests promise us for
the worth of our money."

    Now it is evident that strong hope, true hope, biblical hope,
is not akin to any of these. Voltaire was but the precursor of those
who in our own generation have taunted Christians by saying that
faith promises nothing more than "pie in the sky bye and bye."

    We accept with gratitude and praise to God His great prom-
ises for the future; but we rejoice also that there are hopes for today.
The *Oxford English Dictionary* defines the strong hope, the true
hope, as: "Expectation of something desired; desire combined with
expectation." The Bible uses words of confidence and trust, of assurance and certainty. Thayer's lexicon of the Greek New Testament
defines *elpis* as "expectation of good, hope; joyful and confident
expectation of salvation." And since salvation is always presented
as a present possession, our hope is also a present possession.

BY-PRODUCTS

    The Christian can look into the Bible, back over history, and
out over the world and rejoice in the fact that the hope that is his
in Christ has transformed society. The ideal state is certainly not
the communist state, the socialist state, or the welfare state, but

the Christian state. This has never existed upon earth, and we know from Scripture that it will not exist until our Lord returns to rule in power and to establish His sovereignty by force over the world that crucified Him. But that does not mean that we may not expect tangible, social blessings from our faith. In fact, all social gains are by-products of the Christian faith.

We go back into history and discover that there were no hospitals for the sick, no asylums for the aged or fatherless, no dignity of human personality, before the advent of God's revelation in the two Testaments. This may be seen in our present civilization by the following test: On several outline maps shade with black those parts of the world where the sick are least cared for; where the aged are neglected and where the insane are treated as beasts; where unwanted children are exposed to destruction by animals; and where women have no rights. Then shade with dark gray, places where progress has been made in those fields. Color light gray places where there is considerable progress. Leave white those places where there is the highest degree of care, the greatest value placed upon the rights of the individual. Take another map and repeat the same process with reference to the knowledge of Christian truth: black where the Bible is unknown, dark gray where the sun is rising, light gray where there is lip service to Christianity, and white where there is general acceptance of evangelical truth. Now examine the maps, and you will discover that they are all alike. Where the Word of God has not come, bringing the life of Christ to certain hearts, gross darkness manifests itself in every sphere of life.

Madam Chiang Kai-shek pointed out that the religion of China was ancestor worship, but Confucianism has never built a home for the aged. In Africa a wife can be purchased in exchange for a few goats. And if a woman desires to leave a brutal husband, and runs away from the harem after delivery of the goats, the law demands that she be arrested as a common criminal and restored to her husband. He has a right to beat her for she is his property. The colonial powers of Africa, Portugal, Belgium, France, and Britain all support the husband in these barbarous practices.

But follow the missionaries as they penetrate these countries and watch the transformation. Homes are established for the or-

phaned, aged, and insane; leprosaria are built for untouchable
lepers; women take a place of dignity in society as companions of
their husbands.

Some who live in our civilization and enjoy its benefits sneer
at Christianity which has conferred these benefits upon them. There
are Negroes who reject Christ, not realizing that they would still
be slaves if William Wilberforce had not cried to God for the freedom of the bondmen of the world and launched the abolitionist
movement. And those women in western countries who treat Christ
with flippancy owe their freedom and all the rights that they enjoy
to reforms effected because of Him.

MERE SOCIAL WORK

Some will dispute my thesis and point to social efforts which
have been made during the past century by non-Christian groups.
I have read the *Communist Manifesto* and other works of Karl
Marx, Friedrich Engels, and their followers, and I maintain that
their writings are not original, but perversions of Christian truth.
Great movements of reform are always started under the guidance
of the Holy Spirit in transformed lives of believers. When they come
to the notice of the world, Satan's forces seize them and twist them
to social ends without regard for the souls of men, and claim credit
for their origination. Movements for youth, for laborers, for the
unfortunates of life, have all been launched by believers in Christ.
When their benefits are manifest, unbelievers seize the work and
attempt to perpetuate the material benefits without the spiritual
benefits that come from the regenerating work of the Holy Spirit.
Thus the Y.M.C.A., fundamental in its beginnings, has changed
considerably from its original concept. The Salvation Army, founded
by William Booth for the salvation of souls, has slipped into mere
social work—so much that during World War II it insisted that a
woman worker be able to dance with the soldiers rather than that
she have any spiritual gifts. And there are travesties of social Christianity in both Romanism and in Protestantism which have no
biblical basis. We hold no brief for the terrible things that have
been done by Christendom, as distinguished from biblical Christianity, no matter in what form of organization such spiritual per-
verts work. In the days of our Lord Jesus Christ men made long

prayers in public, and secretly devoured widows' houses. Our Lord tore the mask from their hypocrisy and set the standard whereby pharisaism may be exposed in any setting.

THE ENTRANCE OF LIGHT

Some years ago I stood on the porch of a summer hotel talking with some men who were deriding evangelical Christianity, saying that believers in Christian truth were not sufficiently socially minded. I saw the fallacies in their arguments, but it is difficult to dissipate fixed prejudice. The task was undertaken for me by a young man who joined the group and monopolized the talk for some time. He said that he and his immediate family were the complete refutation of the attack. He described his background. The dingy street in which they lived was lined by houses joined each to each without a square inch of lawn to break the monotony. Husbands and fathers squandered their wages on gambling and liquor. The street was dirty, the people were slovenly and in despair. Then the gospel came into his home; mother and father became Christians and endeavored to bring up the children in the nurture and admonition of the Lord. The children were better fed and educated. The house was painted and furnishings were renewed. This young man, oldest of the children, entered the university and succeeded brilliantly in his studies. His brothers and sisters followed in his steps; and today the entire family stands in careers of service and honor, respected and emulated. As he described the transformation, the critics listened in silence. He concluded somewhat as follows:

"In that dingy street there was no difference in mental background or in economic ability. All the families came from approximately the same stock; the men were employed in work that brought comparatively the same wages. The other homes remained in squalor. One home stood out above the others. The difference was the Lord Jesus Christ. The explanation of the lack of ideals, ambition, and incentive was simple: the others were living without Christ. Into one family came the gospel of Jesus Christ, the power of God unto salvation, and the dynamic change that resulted was proof that social betterment, as a by-product of Christianity, has permanent results."

STRANGERS HERE

Finally, the present hope of the believer is what it is because of the nature of our citizenship. As soon as a man is born again, he is taught by the Holy Spirit that he was not made for this life alone. The life planted within the believer at his conversion bears the characteristics of eternity. We live the life of Heaven even in earthly surroundings. Our awareness of eternal things changes our perspective and helps us to see things of time and sense in their true measurements. We look not at the things which are seen, but at the things which are not seen, and the things which are not seen are eternal. (2 Cor. 4:18).

An American who has lived abroad knows what it is to be a stranger in a strange land. His outward circumstances may be the same as those of the people among whom he lives, but he never forgets that he is an alien. He knows that he belongs in another land, and that some day he is going back to it. The present discomforts can be accepted with equanimity. The knowledge of his true citizenship is a pure joy. Now, America is not Heaven, although it unquestionably leads the world in material comforts. Without pushing my illustration too far, the thought is this: We Christians are citizens of Heaven. We eat food that is not of this world; we breathe an atmosphere that is not of earth's deadly miasma. Our interests are centered in Christ; and so we do not have to create an escapism of daydreams, for our minds are fixed on Christ who is our life.

This awareness of Christ and consciousness of Heaven make the difference between believer and unbeliever. In the first chapter of Colossians Paul writes of the riches of the glory of this secret truth, hidden from the unsaved and revealed to believers. This secret was unknown to men of past ages, but is now clearly known by believers. It is not merely for the future, but for the present— "Christ in you, the hope of glory" (Col. 1:27). This transforms the individual, furnishes incentive to the poor and ignorant to change their lot and rise with Christ into newness of life. It banishes doubts and gives clear knowledge of truth. Christ in the believer loves the unlovely, touches the leper, comforts the lonely, ministers to the

If you are unsaved, observe the life, not of a professing Chris-
prisoner, and offers strength to the needy.

tian, but of a possessing Christian—one in whom the Word of the Lord has been fulfilled that "He that believeth . . . out of his innermost being shall flow rivers of living water" (John 7:38). How many people have been brought to Christ by recognizing that a friend had something which they lacked—Christ, our present hope of future glory! This is why Paul could say, "Be ye followers of me, even as I also am of Christ" (1 Cor. 11:1); and this is why we tell you to put your trust in our Savior that you may have the present certainty that flows into future glory. We are the children of hope.

CHAPTER IX

Glory in Tribulation

. . . we glory in tribulations also: knowing that tribulation worketh patience (Rom. 5:3).

WE HAVE presented the three aspects of our hope in reverse order, beginning with the future and working back to today, because the present passage in Romans shows that the power of God enters into every phase of the believer's life during his earthly pilgrimage.

This question of difference between the future and the present is most interesting. Eternity is beyond us, entirely outside of time. We who are creatures of time must understand that we are dealing with our Lord who is the Creator and dwells in eternity. God Himself speaks to Isaiah in a way that shows that He is in a sphere totally different from ours and yet within our ken, for He comes down to us and dwells with us. Theologically stated, He is both transcendent and immanent. "For thus says the high and lofty One who inhabits eternity, whose name is Holy; I dwell in the high and holy place, and also with him who is of a contrite and humble spirit, to revive the spirit of the humble, and to revive the heart of the contrite" (Isa. 57:15). God tells us that He dwells both in Heaven and with us. In His essential nature He is high and lofty, remote, untouchable—but He is also near at hand and can be touched with the feeling of our infirmities. Perhaps the most important study for a Christian is how to realize this presence of the eternal with him in time, and know the infinite in his finite life.

AN EVER-ROLLING STREAM

The unsaved man cannot know what the believer knows: that eternity rushes into time, and the infinite rushes into our lives. Isaac Watts wrote:

> The busy tribes of flesh and blood,
>   With all their lives and cares,
> Are carried downward by Thy flood,
>   And lost in following years.
>
> Time, like an ever-rolling stream,
>   Bears all its sons away;
> They fly forgotten, as a dream
>   Dies at the opening day.

There is a sense in which that is terribly true; the stream of time sweeps from us into the past, and bears men and events into a lost valley of which we have little knowledge. Much of our own life swirls into what Shakespeare called "dark forgetfulness and deep oblivion." And we may thank God that our imperfect past is gone forever and that He, the omniscient God, has forgotten our dark deeds and thoughts, and will remember them against us no more forever (Heb. 8:12, 10:17).

But in another sense we may consider the stream of time as coming toward us. We look upstream, not down. All the glorious future comes to us, flood upon flood, and fills the reservoir of our souls. As we allow God to enlarge our capacity, He fills us with Himself until we expand to contain more and more of Him. This process will continue forever. The very essence of eternal life is that we might know God the Father and God the Son (John 17:3). Let us be careful, then, in every moment of meditation to turn our hearts toward Him so that His grace may pour into our beings. Then we shall begin to comprehend the exceeding greatness of His power to us who believe. Then we shall crave more and more of God, with an appetite that will ever be insatiable.

All this is part of our rejoicing in hope of the glory of God. It is not an attitude of otherworldliness, of being uninterested in the present life in that alien sense of which enemies of truth accuse us. We are otherworldly only in the sense in which the electric lamp which now floods my room with light may be called other-roomly! When there is no flow into it from the distant power plant, that bulb is dark and useless. But when connected to the current, it glows with brilliance and illumines all that is around it. Thus must the Christian live empowered by Heaven in order to shine upon earth. Thus men will see life that is not our own and will glorify our Father who is in Heaven. (Mt. 5:16).

BORN TO TROUBLE

The first visible aspect of our rejoicing in hope is that we glory in tribulations (Rom. 5:3). Tribulations are the common lot of humanity, and only the Christian, as captive to the will of God, can triumph over them in utter glory. One of Job's comforters expressed a truth that has become proverbial: "Affliction comes not forth of the dust, neither does trouble spring out of the ground; yet man is born to trouble, as the sparks fly upward" (Job 5:6, 7). Trial and suffering are the common lot of man, and no one will escape this heritage. The Hebrew of this passage in Job is very beautiful, for the comparison between the trouble of mankind and the flying sparks is couched in most poetic language. The two Hebrew words translated by our one word "sparks" are literally "the sons of flame." The fire on the hearth produces an offspring of sparks. Life is a similar fire, and each generation is placed upon the burning embers of the past. Coming from fallen Adam as we all do, there is nothing for us but the trials and sorrows, adversities and afflictions common to all men. When we sing

> Take the name of Jesus with you,
> Child of sorrow and of woe . . .

we properly name our ancestry. We are by nature of the lineage of trouble.

Very interesting theories have been advanced by some of the school of depth psychologists to account for man's attitudes toward pain. We all know the old proverb that a burnt child dreads the fire. These psychologists hold that every member of the human race is fearful of pain because of the very first experience of conscious life. Before birth the child rests easily in the mother's womb, warm, comfortable, fed, and with no cares for any bodily functions. Suddenly, great pressure is placed upon the body of the child. The child is pulled and pushed, the bones of its cranium are dislocated, and, finally, the supply of oxygen which it has been receiving from the mother's blood is cut off. In an experience akin to strangulation, its body cries out for oxygen, and its introduction to a world of air is a scream that is the reaction of its gasping struggle for life. Several of the depth psychologists believe that many of the later experiences of life are forceful reminders of this early trauma.

After the birth of the child the mother cares for all of its needs, but each social advance knocks away a prop and forces the child to depend upon his own strength and resources. Little by little, he learns to feed and clothe himself, to take care of his bodily functions; he goes to school, and ultimately earns his own livelihood. Sooner or later death will enter his circle. He will make plans that fail and will see his most cherished desires frustrated. He will pass through the refinement of physical suffering, and the mental anguish of seeing loved ones suffer. Finally, he will come to his own deathbed and face life beyond this world. Man is born to these troubles; he is a child of the flame.

TRIBULATION

The believer who has entered into the redemption that is in Christ and has been introduced to the endless supply of grace provided among the spiritual blessings which are ours in Christ Jesus (Eph. 1:3) rejoices in hope of the glory of God and glories in tribulations. That this is a supernatural experience is evident from the meaning of the words that describe the suffering which purchases for us rejoicing and glory. "Tribulation" has been taken over from the Latin. The verb is *tribulare,* which means, "to press, to oppress, to afflict." The Latins had a *tribulum,* a threshing sledge which separated grain from chaff. It consisted of a wooden platform studded underneath with sharp flints or iron teeth. As this instrument passed over the pile of grain the wheat was separated from the straw. We can well understand how a man undergoing afflictions would compare his sufferings with those which would be inflicted if such an instrument passed over him. Now, how could a believer rejoice in such grinding pressure?

The Greek word brings us the same terrible thought, couched under slightly different imagery. The word is *thlipsis,* and originally conveyed the idea of "pressing together, pressure." It is interesting to note from the lexicons and dictionaries of the ancient language that the application of this word to human suffering was first employed in the New Testament. The Christians were the first to think of themselves as being in the vat like grapes or olives, and being pressed to the point where their joy ran out like wine or oil. How can we press joy from sorrow as one presses wine from grapes or oil from olives?

OIL AND WINE

Oil and wine are biblical symbols of joy. For instance, oil was used as a cosmetic to make the face shine (Ps. 104:15). Thus it became a symbol of joy and gladness. "The Lord bless thee, and keep thee: the Lord make his face shine upon thee, and be gracious unto thee" (Num. 6:24, 25). The Lord of the shining face was the Lord of joy and peace for His children. Of Christ it was prophesied, "God, thy God, hath anointed thee with the oil of gladness above thy fellows" (Ps. 45:7). Another symbol of joy in the Bible was wine. References may be multiplied to parallel the declaration of praise to God because He brings forth "wine that maketh glad the heart of man" (Ps. 104:15).

The Lord has told us that He wants our joy to be full. In spite of this, many of His children come short of the great grace that He has for us in this life. They are fundamental and know the doctrines; they are instructed and know the vocabulary; they are saved and have the potentialities, but do they have fullness of joy? They have olives but no oil, grapes but no wine.

Olives and grapes are fruits which produce oil and wine but they are not oil and wine themselves. In Palestine we find olives and grapes that have never fulfilled their true destiny. The olive shrinks and is wrinkled. A hungry man will eat such olives, and the poor people put them into their food; but the richness has evaporated. Grapes that remain on the vine harden, and after a time are pulpy and dry. They will keep for months, dry all the time, and will still be nourishing, but the wine is gone, and the raisins excite a thirst for the juice that is not there. Such olives and grapes are better than nothing, but they are not substitutes for oil and wine.

Are you satisfied with olives and grapes? Be sure that they will dry up in your storehouse and will never furnish the shining face or the merry heart. Oil and wine bring joy, not olives and grapes. And surely you can see that it is not possible to have oil and wine unless olives are pressed and grapes crushed. Even the finest fruit will not yield its essence without this process. Indeed, the finer the fruit the firmer the skin, and the heavier the pressure that must be put upon it to burst its surface that the juices may spurt. If you are to be splashed with joy, you must be crushed.

OLIVES AND GRAPES

I would suggest to you, then, three steps to joy. First, to have oil and wine you must have olives and grapes. The unsaved man can have no true joy because he has no fruit from which joy can be produced. Be sure, therefore, that you are rooted and grounded in Christ so that the Holy Spirit may bring forth His fruit. If you are unsaved, you can have no joy because you have nothing but thorns and thistles. Crush them and you get thorn juice and thistle milk which never make the face shine or the heart rejoice. The unsaved can have the wildness of revelry and the froth of mirth, but never the shining of gladness and the depths of joy. These come only from God's oil and wine; and these, in turn, are pressed only from God's olives and grapes.

You answer me that you are certain on this score. You know that you are saved and even take some pride in the olives and grapes in the garden of your life. You have digged the earth and pruned the trees and vines; you have watered them with care and have even gathered fruit. I recognize the truth of what you say. You are, in comparison with the wild trees and weedy fields of your unsaved neighbors, a fruitful bough and a fertile garden.

You are correct in believing that neither oil nor wine can be produced without the fruit which you have grown; but you seem unaware that no small skill is demanded to make oil and wine, and that such skill must be accompanied by patient labor and wise attention to details. Stop pointing to your work for the Lord, as though the presence of fruit could give you the oil of the shining face or the wine of the gladdened heart. The second step to possession of oil and wine is to become dissatisfied with mere production of olives and grapes. If you are satisfied with grapes, you will never know the wine of joy.

The third and final step to fullness of joy is for olives and grapes to be crushed. For this the Lord has many different processes. In all vintage countries proprietors of great vineyards have their own secrets for making wines. Connoisseurs tell the difference between the products of one vineyard and another by their tastes. Soil, sun, method of preparation, all enter into the final product.

So the Lord works in all of us to bring forth a particular brand of joy that He and we may share. Each of us will have a new name,

which no man knows saving him that receives it (Rev. 2:17). To
that end our Lord now works, first growing choice olives and grapes
within us, and then pressing them out so that there may be oil
and wine and our lives may be shining and glad for Him.

In the measure that we welcome infirmities and tribulations,
we shall glory in them and realize afresh the power of Christ to
transmute the suffering into glory and distill joy from pain. Shall
we not be willing to glory in tribulation if it produces joy, and
opens up the fountain of blessing to others?

SONS OF OIL

A verse in Zechariah can be put with the one in Job to show us
further the blessed results of tribulation. Man is born to trouble as
the sparks, the sons of fire, fly upward, says Job. Zechariah tells of
two men called olive trees. The older versions translate the passage,
"These are the two anointed ones, that stand by the Lord of the
whole earth" (4:14); but the Hebrew is very plain: "These are the
two sons of oil, that stand by the Lord of the whole earth." For
this the Lord works in our lives, and we are confident of this very
thing, that He who has begun a good work in us will keep on perfecting it until the day of Jesus Christ (Phil. 1:6). He will grow
His fruit—olives and grapes—and He will press out His oil and
His wine. He will give us the shining face and a heart so filled with
His joy that nothing else in the world—no, not even the work of
the Lord—can charm us like the knowledge that we are the sons
of His oil, sons of His joy, and that we shall be occupied with Him
and His joy forever.

It is evident that this type of living is miraculous, for it is not
natural for us to undergo suffering and endure it patiently. It is
natural to whine and sigh and cry in adversity. The worldling often
lives such a life of failure, and, alas, too many Christians settle
down to the same low level. Nevertheless, provision has been made
for us to glory even in tribulation, if we will appropriate the resources that are ours for moment-by-moment living in Christ.

The Christian does not go out of his way to seek trouble, for
he is not the victim of a martyr complex or a delusion of persecution
symptomatic of paranoia. But when the crushing load of life comes
down upon him, the true believer faces it with calmness and equanimity, knowing that God means it for good and that out of it will
come rejoicing and the possibility of glorying afresh in God.

CHAPTER X

God's Purpose in Human Suffering

. . . we glory in tribulations also: knowing that tribulation worketh patience (Rom. 5:3).

EVERY human being, at some time, must experience suffering, sickness, and finally death. Only true believers who are alive when the Lord Jesus returns will be transformed in a moment and go to Him without dying. With this exception, it is the lot of all men to suffer and die.

The Bible teaches that in the life of an unbeliever the causes and results of suffering are quite different from those in the life of a believer, although they may not appear different. If a lion, for example, could think, and in his lion mind could see two men suffering from blindness, he might conclude that causes and results were the same. But an angel, seeing the suffering of these two men, would comprehend the spiritual factors; he would understand that in the one case the Devil was doing as he pleased with a member of his kingdom; in the other, an all-wise Heavenly Father was permitting one of His children to suffer, for a purpose. The Bible tells us what should be our attitude toward the world of unbelievers: "In meekness instructing those who oppose themselves; God may perhaps grant that they will repent and come to know the truth, and they may escape from the snare of the devil, after being captured by him to do his will" (2 Tim. 2:25, 26).

But although Satan can do as he pleases with those who have never been born again, we know from Job's experience that Satan cannot lift a finger against a child of God, without the direct and definite permission of God, and can do no more than God permits.

DIVINE PURPOSE

When suffering overtakes the regenerate man, he may immediately perceive divine purpose. This prevents him from becoming a fatalist. The follower of Islam may shrug his shoulders and say that

kismet, fate, has overtaken him; and in that belief he will settle
down in the darkness of credulity. But when ill comes upon a Christian, he can look up with confidence into the face of his Heavenly
Father who has never made a mistake and who does all things well,
and expect the event to work out for his good, no matter how terrible
the grief or anguish of the moment. Thus the Christian can say,
"We know that all things work together for good to them that love
God, to them who are the called according to his purpose" (Rom.
8:28). Such a truth brings a calm in the midst of suffering which
far surpasses the grim resignation of the stoic. Thus God Himself
said to His chosen people in the midst of their suffering, "For I
know the thoughts that I think toward you, saith the Lord, thoughts
of peace and not of evil, to give you a planned future and hope"
(Jer. 29:11, Heb.). God has planned a future for us.

There are at least three purposes of suffering set forth in the
Bible. Because as believers we can know these varied purposes of
tribulations, it is possible for us to glory in them. What a history is
ours! We have been justified! And so, we have peace with God! In
addition, we have access into the grace of God where we live and
move and have our being. Because of this ready access to the grace
of God, we rejoice in hope of the glory of God. And not only do we
have this rejoicing in our hope, but we glory in tribulations also.
Why not? Did not our Father plan it all? Is He not working out a
determined purpose? Then shall we not receive whatever He meas-
ures out to us, knowing that it will have its effect upon us, even in
eternity?

God has arranged the varied sufferings of man so that no out-
sider can know His purposes, but the suffering soul can know. The
sufferings that come to a believer may be classified as corrective,
constructive, and exemplary, but we can glory in our tribulations,
no matter what their purpose may be.

Before proceeding to specific verses, we should understand that
all suffering is caused by sin. By one man sin entered and death by
sin, so that death passed upon all the race. The wages of sin is
death. All members of the human race are bound in the bundle of
life with fallen Adam and must partake of the changes and ills that
confront human life. Nevertheless, we see wide variations in the
sufferings of different individuals.

CORRECTIVE SUFFERINGS

First, there are sufferings that are corrective. Just as a child who has done wrong receives a spanking (or does if he has a proper father and mother), so some sufferings come to a believer because he has stepped out of the will of God. Ignorant people have imagined that all suffering was the result of individual acts of sin and that any tribulation could be set down as a payment by the sufferer for some wrong he had committed. We shall see that this is false when we consider instances of suffering which God permits to come upon the innocent. And certainly no man's suffering ever pays for his sin. Only Jesus paid the price of our atonement.

The outstanding paragraph on corrective suffering is in the twelfth chapter of Hebrews. Speaking of the difficulties that come to true believers the Holy Spirit says, "You have forgotten the exhortation which speaks unto you as unto children" (Heb. 12:5ff.). Phillips has paraphrased it as follows: "You have perhaps lost sight of that piece of advice which reminds you of your sonship in God: 'My son, regard not lightly the chastening of the Lord, nor faint when thou art reproved of Him; for whom the Lord loveth He chasteneth, and scourgeth every son whom He receiveth.' Bear what you have to bear as 'chastening'—as God's dealings with you as with sons. No true son ever grows up uncorrected by his father. For if you had no experience of the correction which all sons have to bear you might well doubt the legitimacy of your sonship. After all, when we were children we had fathers who corrected us, and we respected them for it. Can we not much more readily submit to a Heavenly Father's discipline, and learn how to live? For our fathers used to correct us according to their own ideas during the brief days of childhood. But God corrects us all our days for our own benefit, to teach us His holiness. Now obviously no 'chastening' seems pleasant at the time: it is in fact most unpleasant. Yet when it is all over we can see that it has quietly produced the fruit of real goodness in the characters of those who have accepted it in the right spirit. So take a fresh grip on life and brace your trembling limbs. Don't wander away from the path but forge steadily onward. On the right path the limping foot recovers strength and does not collapse."

THORNS AND WALLS

This comparison between the right path and the meandering way of the one who steps off into uncharted territory reminds us of a beautiful story in the Minor Prophets. Hosea likens Israel to a wayward wife who has left her husband for other men. When we wander from God, we commit spiritual adultery. God must correct us to bring us back into the way in which we should go. God says, "Therefore, behold, I will hedge up your way with thorns and I will build a wall against you, so that you cannot find your paths" (Hos. 2:6). Notice that the thorns are not in the path of God but in the willful path of departure; there is no wall across the path of God, but one is placed across the path of self-will.

When a Christian finds himself in a thorn patch, he should at once recognize that he has stepped out of the will of God. Instead of thrashing about to get past the thorns, he should try to be still. One of the important verses for the conduct of the Christian life is, "Be still, and know that I am God" (Ps. 46:10). If you thrash around in the thorn patch, you will only get more scratches. If you stand quiet and allow the Lord to speak to you, you will find Him only too glad to extricate you. The Lord is slow to anger and of great compassion, plenteous in mercy. He takes no delight in chastising His own, but He does delight in the upright walk of the corrected one. It may not be pleasant to go back, but the route to the main highway from the thorn patch is usually back to where you left the road. In God's dealings with His children, this is the purpose of the thorns.

The other part of the illustration is that of the wall across the path. The Lord has no pleasure in blocking our road, and He never does so if we are in the path that He knows is best for us. But sometimes He must block our path because He has become our Father and because He sees ahead and knows the end from the beginning. At almost every point in life there are two ways before us. The one seems beautiful, and slopes gently downhill, making the journey simple and easy. The other path leads upward, and seemingly is ill-paved and tortuous. But the easy path soon leads to a bend in the road where it narrows and finally diminishes in a wilderness beyond our sight. If we follow the road that is seemingly harder, we soon discover that beyond the bend it becomes easy, and our Lord waits to be our companion. There are no walls across the path of His will, but we may thank God that He places walls across our own paths. Jeremiah lamented, "He has walled me about so that I cannot escape; he has put heavy chains on me; though I call and cry for help, he shuts out my prayer; he has blocked my ways with hewn stones, he has made my paths crooked" (Lam. 3:7-9).

When we find ourselves confronted by a stone wall, it is best to sit down and survey the situation. In front of a wall is a great place to pray. If we seek the Lord with our whole heart, if we come to Him in our difficulties, He will be found by us. All that He requires is a heart that says in advance that it is willing to go right or left, to turn around and go back, or to confront the wall.

FACING A WALL

When I find a wall in my path, from long experience I have learned to move rapidly. I first say, "Lord, I would be absolutely surrendered to your will. I have no knowledge that could help me, and I dare not trust in human sense. I trust you with all my heart and lean away from my own understanding. I acknowledge you and ask for direction of my paths" (Prov. 3:5, 6). At times this is sufficient; the Lord leads me to the main highway, and with little ado I am back on the road I should have traveled. Then there are other times when, after I have said all this sincerely, as the Lord sees and knows the heart, there is no denying that the wall is still there. Then I confront the wall, because the Devil, who is an imitator, frequently builds imitation walls, like the papier maché prop of a stage set. I then say, "Lord, you do love me. You don't want me to be hurt. But I see no other path than that which lies beyond this wall. Perhaps I have missed a turn. I want to be on the right road and am willing to go in any direction. But, Lord, perhaps the Devil built that wall. I am going to take a run and heave myself against it. If it is truly your wall, keep me from getting too much bruised, for I want to be in your full will. But if it is Satan's imitation wall, then open the way before me, and give the enemy a mouthful of dust for attempting to block the way of your child." Then I take a run and jump at the wall. If it is Satan's imitation, there is a rip and a tear, and I am on the other side, well on the Lord's path. I know that I have served Him well in the invisible war, and that the enemy has been discomfited by one who was willing to draw all strength from Him who is mighty. But if the rock is unyielding and I fall at its base, and if I find that the wall grows higher as I try to climb it, and if it widens as I attempt to go around it, then I must wait for God to reveal His path to me. At times He does not want movement, but He wants me to sit still, perhaps for a considerable period, and there learn, in silence, lessons that can never be grasped in the heated course of the pilgrimage. Then the wall disappears, and His path is opened once more. Happy the believer who is sensitive to the slightest indication of thorns or wall and seeks to be on the path traced for him by the Lord God, Saviour, Redeemer, and Lord of all paths. Thus the believer can glory in tribulations that are for his correction.

Second, the believer endures sufferings which are constructive. The Lord desires to form Himself in us. We now change the figure from paths with thorns and walls to that of the sculptor's marble block. The great artist Benvenuto Cellini tells us in his autobiography how he felt as he stood before a block of marble that had been brought to Florence for him to form into a great statue. Several chapters are devoted to the design and creation of the work of art which still stands in his native city as his greatest monument. Between the rough-hewn block of marble and the finished statue were all the love and care of the artist, and the infinite patience of releasing from stone the vision of beauty which he saw before he began to work. Thus the Heavenly Father is at work in the life of everyone whom He has foreknown as believing in the Savior. There is a difference between ourselves and a block of marble, however, in that we have feelings and can shrink back from the strokes with which the divine Sculptor would cut away the marble so that the likeness of Christ may emerge in our lives.

In the great Psalm on the theme of revelation, David tells us that before he was afflicted he went astray, but after affliction he observed the Word of God (Ps. 119:67). Affliction was a factor in his growth, and so it is in the lives of many of God's children. We may face tribulations with joy, therefore, since we know that when we have gone through the trouble we shall be more like our Savior.

A POLISHED SHAFT

Similar to the image of the sculptor, Isaiah says, "The Lord called me from the womb. . . . He made my mouth like a sharp sword; in the shadow of his hand he hid me; he made me a polished arrow, in his quiver he hid me away" (Isa. 49:1, 2). In the British Museum I saw a finely polished arrow-shaft, displayed beneath a magnifying glass. When observed from the side, its surface appeared as smooth as a billiard ball; but when seen through the glass, it revealed a thousand facets, cut so finely that the shaft appeared to be burnished.

When Isaiah tells us that God turned him into such a shaft, he is saying that he underwent the cutting of the chisel. It was a process filled with pain, but when it was completed, Isaiah tells us, he was a polished shaft. What is more, the Lord made him a useful instrument, hidden under His hand, and, when such an instrument was needed, he was available. Here is the Christian's highest joy in this world, for the Lord never uses one of His children without communicating Himself to him both in suffering that makes him usable, and in the ordering of the service.

This constructive suffering the Lord will continue to send into our hearts and lives until He has us ready to take home to Himself. Through Malachi He spoke of Himself as a refiner of silver, sitting through the process of cleansing His people (Mal. 3:3). In oriental bazaars the silversmiths sit with molten metal before them while the flame does its purifying work. From time to time the workman removes dross which rises to the surface and continues this process until he can see his own image, as in a mirror, reflected in the cleansed metal. Thus our Lord works upon those whom He has redeemed. We are worth far more than gold to His heart, and He is eager to see Himself in us. Thus, He who has begun a good work in us will keep on perfecting it until the day of Jesus Christ (Phil. 1:6).

In Peter's first epistle we find the summary of the teaching on constructive suffering. He speaks of the glory of our future salvation when all the work of the Lord in our behalf will be terminated, and we shall be forever in the land of joy with our Savior and our God. He speaks of our rejoicing in that hope, and continues, "Though now for a little while you may have to suffer various trials, so that the genuineness of your faith, more precious than gold which though perishable is tested by fire, may redound to praise and glory and honor at the revelation of Jesus Christ" (1 Pet. 1:6, 7). It is not pleasant to be put into the fire, but the result is the burning away of dross and the refining of the metal.

Thus we may sing:

> Let sorrow do its work,
> Send grief and pain:
> Sweet are Thy messengers,
> Sweet their refrain,
> When they can sing with me,
> More love, O Christ, to thee
> More love to thee!

Thy messengers? Cancer? Polio? Blindness? Yes, Thy messengers.

It is certainly possible for the Christian to glory in tribulation that turns him from wandering into by-paths and brings him back into the way of God. It is also possible for the believer to glory in the tribulation that chips away the unimportant things of life, the secondary things, the dirty things, the alien things, and reveals the life of the Lord Jesus Christ within.

The third phase of suffering is the exemplary suffering which God sends in order to prove to the invisible world that He can win and hold the allegiance of His children, even though surrounded by Satan's host and wooed by all the seductions of the flesh, the world, and the Devil. That phase of suffering is so important that we shall devote the next chapter to it.

CHAPTER XI

Exemplary Suffering

And not only so, but we glory in tribulations also: knowing that tribulation worketh patience (Rom. 5:3).

HAVING considered suffering that is corrective, and suffering that is refining and purifying, we now consider those sufferings which are exemplary. God chooses some of His children to suffer for reasons of His own, entirely apart from sin in their lives, even with no apparent constructive purpose, although those who pass through such sufferings do indeed grow in grace and in the knowledge of God.

SIN AND SUFFERING

Through the centuries the false idea developed that there was a definite relationship between sin and suffering. Many people believed that any suffering was evidence of sin, open or secret, and that all sin was punishable in this life. Such ideas, alien to the Word of God, produce great errors. For example, if a man does not suffer great sorrow or affliction, he may get the idea that God is not displeased with him, and that what he is doing is not sin. This is false, for the Bible tells us that in many cases evil men are allowed to sin with impunity, and that the wicked often flourish like the green bay tree (Ps. 37:35). At the same time, we shall see that God subjects some of His finest children to the most terrible suffering so that He can manifest His glory in them.

Another error that arose from this false idea that sin was always punished by suffering was that God must protect virtue and punish sin immediately. This gave rise to the practice in the Middle Ages known as the Ordeal. If there was controversy about the innocence or guilt of a person, and it was impossible to obtain proof, the victim was subjected to an ordeal such as fire or water to prove his innocence or guilt. For example, a person under trial might be bound hand and foot and thrown into deep water. If he sank and drowned, he was guilty. If God worked a miracle in his behalf, he was innocent. Needless to say, the victim always drowned and was thereby judged guilty. If legend says that some were saved miraculously, we know such stories are false for this is not the day of miracles. This is the day of the Bible.

Though centuries have passed since the practice of trial by ordeal, many people still believe that there is a necessary connection between sin and suffering. There are passages in the Bible, however, which refute this notion. Let us turn to some of these and see the glory of sufferings which God allows to come into the lives of His children, and which, as marks of His deepest affection, He even plans for them. Indeed, some sufferings come to people as degrees of honor conferred upon them by their God. The world may give a brave man a medal of honor, or confer upon him an honorary doctorate, but God decorates some of His people with anguish and honors them with a doctorate of tribulation. And when they have passed through the fires which His love has planned for them, He brings them to the place of triumph and rewards them with eternal glory because they have won honors for Him.

THE MAN BORN BLIND

In the ninth chapter of John's gospel, our Lord and His disciples passed by a man who had been blind from birth. The disciples asked, "Master, who did sin, this man or his parents, that he was born blind?" They too were afflicted with the common delusion that suffering is the necessary result of sin. The Lord Jesus Christ dissipated their error by answering, "Neither has this man sinned, nor his parents, but that the works of God should be made manifest in him." Then the Lord said, "I must work the works of him that sent me, while it is day; the night comes, when no man can work. As long as I am in the world I am the light of the world." Having thus spoken, He performed a miracle and gave sight to the man who had been blind from birth.

Would God Almighty allow a man to be afflicted with total blindness so that he might be the object of a miracle by the Lord Jesus Christ? We answer that such is indeed possible. If anyone asks how a loving God could do such a thing, we answer that God is perfect and does all things well. He has infinite purposes, which all that our God is doing, we most certainly are not qualified to criticize Him, for we are born in sin and live in sin. He, the Creator, the God of holiness and righteousness, has never made a mistake. From this story we must learn never to draw the conclusion that a person is suffering because of his own sin or the sin of his parents. It may be that God is working out an eternal purpose in the invisible realm, beyond the discernment of man.

CHOSEN BY GOD

I believe the Bible reveals that God chooses some people to suffer intensely, and the choice of these heroes of pain is made in two ways but with one object. God's object is to demonstrate to the invisible world, and especially to Satan, that He can hold the allegiance of those who have become His children through faith in Christ Jesus, and that nothing can swerve them from confidence and trust in Him, even though the enemy brings his heaviest artillery to bear. The choice is made sometimes at the nomination of God, sometimes at the nomination of Satan. This conclusion is based on the biblical teaching that God is not the Father of all men. I am convinced that among the most devilish of all theological errors are the doctrines of the universal fatherhood of God and the universal brotherhood of man. The Bible teaches that all men are children of wrath and disobedience, and that only a few become children of God through faith in Christ Jesus. These are translated from the kingdom of Satan into the kingdom of the Son of God's love. This present world system is organized by Satan, and every part of our civilization is Satanic. Here and there a few fields have been faintly perfumed by the presence of Christians, but we must accept the verdict of God's Word that "the whole world lieth in the lap of the wicked one" (I John 5:19 Greek). In every civilization and stratum of society, God has His own who live in opposition to the principles which govern the surrounding fallen world.

SATAN'S ATTACK ON JOB

The outstanding example of suffering on earth inflicted for its effect in Heaven is the story of Job. It is easy to understand why the Devil hates that book and why he has raised up many theologians to deny its validity. But we know from the witness of the Holy Spirit that the book is indeed from God. Briefly, the outline of the conflict is as follows: When Satan came into the courts of

God to report, as he must do at intervals, God pointed out to him
a man whose walk and ways were in righteousness and holiness
and whose trust was in God alone. Though in the midst of Satan's
world, Job was giving no allegiance to him. This was a mouthful
of dust for the Devil, who cried out: "Hast thou not made an hedge
about him, and about his house, and about all that he hath on
every side?" (Job 1:10).

Incidentally, that is one of my favorite Bible verses, because
Satan admits that the power of God which surrounds all of us who
trust Him is so effective that no event can touch us unless God
lowers the hedge and permits it. The believing mother who sees
her boy go off to war knows that nothing will happen to him
without God's permission. Our God, who guides the fish through
the sea, can order incidents of history and details of circumstance
to fit the pattern of life which He had designed for His redeemed
children. A shell can explode in the midst of a dozen men. Some
will be killed, some will be wounded. One will have only a scratch
on his ear. All will happen exactly according to the plan of God.
The Lord of shell fragments has numbered the very hairs of the
heads of His children.

To the charge that Job was faithful because God protected him
and blessed him with great possessions, the divine reply was given
that the hedge would be lowered to permit Satan to touch the
family and property of Job, but he must not touch Job himself.
Immediately the Devil goes into action. Storms rage, an army
marches, bandits move from their lair, lightning falls from the sky.
The houses and barns of Job are destroyed, his property ravaged,
his children are killed. Only three servants escape to bring the news
to Job. It should be noted that these events were caused by the
Devil, even though permitted by God. One day an insurance agent
asked me if I were insured against acts of God. I replied that I
was but asked him if he could write a policy that would insure my
property against acts of the Devil. He was astonished until I opened
the Bible to the book of Job and showed him that the Devil is the
author of war, banditry, tempest, and lightning. We read in the
second epistle to Timothy that Satan can do as he pleases to all who
have not been born again (2 Tim. 2:26), and he uses the forces of
nature for his ends. Let those who are not Christians realize that
the enemy of souls is the cause of their misery. The Christian knows

that when life strikes a blow the enemy means it for evil but God intends it for good.

JOB'S ATTITUDE

Job received the news of his losses with quiet trust in God. He arose, tore his mantle and shaved his head—marks of mourning in those days—and then fell down on the ground and worshipped God. That must have been a bitter moment for Satan. Job cried out, "Naked I came from my mother's womb, and naked shall I return; the Lord gave, and the Lord has taken away; blessed be the name of the Lord." (Job 1:20, 21). His words have been dust in Satan's mouth for thousands of years, for multitudes of God's children have repeated Job's words when similar ills have befallen them. What an illustration of our text in Romans, "We glory in tribulations also!" How wonderful that when we are blinded by tears, we can nevertheless see our God. In fact, our tears become crystal lenses through which He is magnified; and in the midst of suffering we realize the greatness of His power and the tenderness of His love.

Following this event in the life of Job there came another day when Satan presented himself before God and was called to account concerning Job. He could not argue that Job loved God because of his prosperity, so he fell back on a lie, and made a charge against humanity that shows his own lying, cowardly nature. He alleged that Job was groveling before God so that nothing worse might happen to him: "Skin for skin! All that a man has will he give for his life" (Job 2:4). A thousand examples disprove this calumny. We constantly read of men who give their lives for noble causes and, alas, for frivolous ones. We read of men who die as show-offs before a crowd of empty-headed witnesses looking for a thrill. We read of men who gamble their lives for the smile of a worthless girl. All of these deaths prove Satan a liar even where his own citizens are concerned. And when it comes to those who have become subjects of the Lord God Almighty through faith in Christ, he is even more wrong, and the lie reveals his frustration. God now permitted the hedge to be lowered further, to permit Satan to afflict Job with anything short of death. Satan immediately launched an attack on the body of Job. Boils covered the poor man from head to foot.

ETERNAL PURPOSE

Once more Job triumphed and praised God in the midst of pain. He was confident that there was an eternal purpose behind his suffering, and knew that the events of time were unimportant in the light of eternal issues. This illustrates a principle of modern warfare. A commander in chief has a grand strategy and wishes to take a certain objective. He knows that he must pay for it with the lives and suffering of men. He will pay so many casualties to achieve a certain end, and he will pay so many more to attain each further object. The famous phrase, "They were expendable," is very expressive of war and its costs. We must not forget that an invisible war —a rebellion of Satan against God—is being fought in the lives of men. God in His Word and by His actions in the lives of His people tells us that we are expendable in this invisible war. But, where an expendable man dies in an earthly war, a suffering saint lives eternally, shining as the brightness of the firmament and as the stars forever and ever.

PETER SIFTED

Not only did God vindicate Job, and do battle with Satan in the life of that Old Testament saint, He sometimes also accepts battle with Satan in the life of a Christian. There is a true story in the New Testament, not in the lines of type but in the white space between two verses. We do not find it written in Scripture, but I can prove from Scripture that it happened. One day Satan came to the Lord Jesus Christ and said something like the following: "Do you really think that that boasting, bragging Simon Peter is worth anything? He is nothing but a bag of wind, and if I had a chance to blow on him, he would disappear like a puff of smoke." The Lord answered in effect: "You think that he would be carried away by your blowing? I will give you permission to blow on him. Begin tomorrow night at 11:15, and not before." Someone asks, "How do you know that such a conversation took place?" The Lord Jesus told Peter about it. "Simon Simon, behold, Satan demanded to have you, that he might sift you like wheat" (Luke 22:31).

In Palestine wheat was sifted by tossing the grain into the air and allowing a gentle breeze to carry away the chaff, while the grain fell in a pile on the threshing floor. The Lord Jesus told Peter that Satan would blow on him, but when the blowing was over, the chaff would be gone and the pure grain would remain. He told Peter that He had already prayed for him, and thus victory was announced before the test. The Devil brought all his power to bear against the braggart fisherman; when the test was done, the chaff was blown away, and Peter was commissioned to feed the Lord's lambs. Again, the Devil got a mouthful of dust.

However when suffering comes to us, we should not immediately think that we are suffering for God in His war with the enemy. First, we should ask whether we have wandered from His path. Second, we should ask Him to use our tribulation to form His image in us, in order that we may become like Christ. Then we may ask Him to use our suffering for His honor and glory. For, if God can be thus glorified, and if Satan can be made to eat dust, we are delighted that God does with us whatever He pleases.

CHAPTER XII

Steadfast Endurance

And not only so, but we glory in tribulations also: knowing that tribulation worketh patience; and patience, experience; and experience, hope (Rom. 5:3, 4).

As A child I heard my father recite this bit of doggerel:

> Patience is a virtue,
> Possess it if you can;
> Seldom found in woman
> And never found in man.

I will not vouch for its theology or veracity, but it illustrates the fact that patience is among the rarer virtues. Romans 5:3 teaches a great lesson about patience.

Students and commentators have rendered this simple phrase in a variety of translations. Bishop Handley Moule of the Church of England translates it: "Tribulation works out, develops, patient persistency." Calvin renders it: "Tribulation produces patience." The Catholic Confraternity translation reads: "Tribulation works out endurance," which is a duplication of the Plymouth Brethren translation by William Kelly. The excellent American Standard Version translates it: "Tribulation worketh steadfastness." W. R. Newell emphasizes the present action of the verb by using the present participle and putting it: "Tribulation is working out endurance"; and the RSV renders it: "Suffering produces endurance."

FRUIT IN THE BELIEVER

Everything that the believer has up to this point is sovereign grace, grace unmerited, a gift from God. Faith is counted as righteousness to the man who works not but believes on God who justifies the ungodly (4:5). But now we see that the believer is to produce good works. They are not the works which are cursed if offered as payment for salvation, but are the works which flow out of salvation we see in fragments. If we cannot comprehend with our puny minds

(Eph. 2:8-10); they are the fruit that grows out of the root that is Christ. The old edifice of character and works having been demolished, and the solid foundation of justification having been established, the superstructure of the building of God in our lives begins to appear.

I once heard of a man who had a very hasty temper. He constantly exploded in violent outbursts of wrath. When he was chided for such behavior, he said earnestly, "You know, other people have told me this, and I have studied my life to see if it is true. But I have found that it is not true, for I am never cross as long as I have things the way I want them, and I never lose my temper when things go the way I have planned." In other words, "I am patient when there is nothing to make me impatient." To endure patiently means to be calm in circumstances which normally cause impatience. But there is much more in the truth set forth in our text than merely holding one's tongue and temper.

The first virtue produced in the life of the Christian is (variously translated) patience, persistence, endurance, steadfastness. The reason for the variation in translation is that the Greek word has several shades of meaning, all imply something that continues; in some cases this continuance is passive and in some it is active. Several verses use this word for the patience we must exercise while waiting for the return of the Lord Jesus Christ, even though He tarry until the eye becomes dim with looking for Him. This quality comes most often to mind in the modern use of the word "patience." The idea of bearing the trials of life without complaint is in the English word. But there is something far more in the Greek than calmness and content. Thayer's lexicon translates the word as "steadfastness, constancy, and endurance"; in the New Testament it is "the characteristic of a man who is unswerved from his deliberate purpose and his loyalty to faith and piety by even the greatest trials and sufferings."

PROGRESS

There is an idea of dogged plodding in the word, but with definite progress. It may not be progress on the run; rather it may be progress step by step, but it is progress none the less. The progress of mountain climbers will illustrate this meaning. Men undertake to climb a difficult mountain which involves a great deal of skill and courage. While scaling the face of the cliff, they measure their progress, at times, in inches. Suddenly, however, a point is reached from which they gaze back and see that hundreds of feet have been gained. This is progress in tribulation. While in it, we are conscious of nothing but the inching toil of the climb. But suddenly we look back and see that we are solidly on higher ground.

THE POWER OF HOPE

Someone may point out that unregenerate people go through trials and sufferings and do not steadfastly endure. The reason is that they have nothing to look forward to except more suffering and desolation. The Christian's afflictions lead to perseverance because they are connected with his hope. If some Christians fail to grasp triumph in the midst of trial, it is because they have lost the connection between the fire and the future; they have failed to grasp hope, the cord that binds the pain to the prize. If our eyes are on the stars, we cannot see our sorrow. If we keep in our hearts the glory that is to follow, then the gloom of the present will have no significance. Bishop Anders Nygren of Sweden has written: "Life in Christ reaches forward toward consummation and glory. But that does not mean flight from the world. Even this present life is made new through the Christian hope. To him who lives his life only in the *present* age and in *this* world, the sufferings which come to him can only be something negative. But for the Christian, suffering is precisely the point where the power of hope most clearly proves itself. He knows that the sufferings of this present time are not worthy to be compared with the glory which shall be revealed in us (Rom. 8:18).

"Suffering receives a new meaning. It becomes a means in God's hand to carry us on toward consummation. When God lets the weight of suffering rest on us, He does so to exercise us in patience and endurance. Suffering has the very effect of making the Christian hope the more eagerly for the 'glory' which God has promised him. Suffering is thus not something of which we must be ashamed. Hope makes it something positive, in which we can actually rejoice. If there were no suffering, hope would never have the opportunity to attain its full strength. It is by suffering that hope is tested and strengthened. The role of suffering in the Christian life is to develop endurance 'and endurance produces character and character produces hope.'"

It should be noticed that the virtue produced in the Christian by the ploughing of tribulation is not mere tolerance. There is no thought of, "I can stand it." The pagan, in dull hopelessness, bows to the inevitable. The Christian accepts the suffering, knowing that God is bringing him through to glory; and from the hope of the past to the hope of the future, he sees the connection running through his suffering like a thread that binds all together. His life is like the turbulent rapids of a river, but he knows that the river comes from a still spring and is flowing to a calm ocean. In this knowledge, the Christian has settled peace.

Bishop Moule paraphrases this passage as follows: "Not only so, but we exult too in our tribulations, with a better fortitude than the Stoic's artificial serenity, knowing that the tribulation works out, develops, patient persistency, as it occasions proof after proof of the power of God in our weakness, and thus generates the habit of reliance; and then the patient persistency develops proof, bringing out in experience, as a proved fact that through Christ we are not what we were; and then the proof develops hope, solid and definite expectation of continuing grace and final glory."

EXPERIENCE

The tribulation which has wrought in us the habit of reliance on God, the patient persistence of endurance, develops in us still further virtues. The King James Version says that our patience develops experience. This is a very unsatisfactory translation, for the word "experience," in our day, refers to "the actual living through an event," and hence, "the effect upon the judgment or feelings produced by personal and direct impressions"; and thus "the knowledge, skill, or technique resulting from practice." The Revised Version translates it to show that steadfastness develops approvedness. Kelly says, "Endurance develops proof." The Catholic Confraternity translation states: "Endurance develops tried virtue." Certainly the Greek word does not mean "experience" in the modern sense of that English word. Thayer's lexicon says of *dokima:* "(1) in an active sense, a proving, trial . . . (2) approvedness, tried character . . . (3) proof, a specimen of tried proof." The whole sense of the passage is better brought forth in Phillips' para-phrase: "This doesn't mean, of course, that we have only a hope of future joys—we can be full of joy here and now even in our trials and troubles. Taken in the right spirit these very things will give us patient endurance; this in turn will develop a mature character, and a character of this sort produces a steady hope, a hope that will never disappoint us."

In Paul's own life and experience, everything that came to him only heightened his joy and deepened the certainty of his faith and calling in God. He knew and taught that they that "live godly in Christ Jesus shall suffer persecution" (2 Tim. 3:12). In the story of his missionary journeys we read that he went from city to city "confirming the souls of the disciples, and exhorting them to con-tinue in the faith, and that we must through much tribulation enter into the kingdom of God" (Acts 14:22). When persecutions broke out he wrote his very first epistle, that to the Thessalonian church, comforting them concerning their faith and saying, "No man should be moved by these afflictions: for yourselves know that we are appointed thereunto" (1 Thess. 3:3).

PERSECUTIONS

And what Paul told the early Christians to expect, he did not shirk in his own life. He spoke of the glory that was given to every believer in Christ, and continued, "But we have this treasure in earthen vessels, that the exceeding greatness of the power may be of God, and not from ourselves; we are pressed on every side, yet not straitened; perplexed, yet not in despair; pursued, yet not forsaken; smitten down yet not destroyed; always bearing about in the body the dying of Jesus" (2 Cor. 4:7-10). He wrote in the same epistle that he was in everything commending himself as a minister of God, "In much patience, in afflictions, in necessities, in distresses, in stripes, in imprisonments, in tumults, in labors, in watchings, in fastings . . . by evil report and good report: as deceivers, and yet true; as unknown, and yet well known; as dying, and, behold, we live; as chastened, and not killed; as sorrowful, yet alway rejoicing; as poor, yet making many rich; as having nothing, and yet possess-ing all things." (2 Cor. 6:4, 5, 8-10). And yet again, in the same epistle, he contrasts himself to those who criticized him so sorely. The comparison was forced upon him by the inspiration of the

Holy Spirit, and it was all in Paul's favor. "Are they ministers of Christ? (I speak as one beside himself) I more; in labors more abundantly, in prisons more abundantly, in stripes above measure, in deaths oft. Of the Jews five times received I forty stripes save one. Thrice was I beaten with rods, once was I stoned, thrice I suffered shipwreck, a night and a day I have been in the deep; in journeyings often, in perils of rivers, in perils of robbers, in perils from my countrymen, in perils from the Gentiles, in perils in the city, in perils in the wilderness, in perils in the sea, in perils among false brethren; in labor and travail, in watchings often, in hunger and thirst, in fastings often, in cold and nakedness. Beside those things that are without, there is that which presseth upon me daily, anxiety for all the churches. Who is weak, and I am not weak? Who is caused to stumble, and I burn not?" (2 Cor. 11:23-29).

What did all these afflictions do for Paul himself? Exactly what they will do for every child of God who takes hold of them by the right end and accepts them as the Father sends them for our chastening, edification, and glory. We shall know that the tribulations of life will work a steadfast endurance. We will keep on in the Christian life and when maintaining progress seems hardest, we shall call upon God for His spiritual reserves of determination; and we will keep on.

APPROVED BY GOD

It appears to me that it is necessary to say a word to those who are not Pauls and who are not to be martyrs burned at the stake. Multitudes of Christians live out their lives in the simplest of circumstances. Not only will they never set the world on fire, but also they will never be noticed by the world. Millions of the Lord's children are like the flowers in Gray's "Elegy":

> Full many a flower is born to blush unseen
> And waste its sweetness on the desert air.

But we may be sure that devotion to the Lord, though unnoticed by the world, is observed by Him and will not go unrewarded. These multitudes know the joy and power of steadfast endurance and resultant maturity of virtue and character. They have the sense of being approved by God, even though they have not done anything that would call for special citation. Some of the greatest battles and victories are fought and won in the dark recesses of secret lives, well away from man's historical writing. What secular historian would mention Job? There was nothing in his life to evoke notice from the world. But we can be sure that all Heaven was regarding, with intense interest, the conflict raging in the life of that ancient cattle raiser, and that the glory of God was manifest in all that he did.

Let all humble souls take comfort in this. It may take more of the grace of God for a man to go to his office each morning and sit at the same desk that he has occupied for the last forty years than for a martyr to be burned at the stake. It may take a greater supply of the grace of God for a housewife to resume the daily round of household chores than for a missionary to be shot by the Reds in China.

Our text is a New Testament expression of the Old Testament truth that they that wait upon the Lord shall renew their strength (Isa. 40:31). Not only shall they mount up with wings as eagles, but also they shall run and not be weary (which is not so spectacular but seems to cover more distance in less time); and what is more, they shall walk and not faint, which is the miracle of God's provision for the humdrum of everyday life.

THE JOY OF THE LORD

Let us see in Job's life this chain reaction of God's dealings with His people in the midst of pain. Job knew the terrible pressure of suffering. This caused him to examine his position before God; he realized that he was nothing in himself, that he had no rights so far as God was concerned. This conclusion led him to look to God and to accept absolutely anything from His hand. When God allowed the severest blows to strike him, Job perceived the corresponding grace and love of God toward himself. This taught him steadfast and persistent endurance. As his sorrows increased, Job sensed that he was being proved by God and approved, so he looked to God with even greater confidence, and with the expectation that the Lord would reveal Himself to him in a fresh way. Since his hope was from God, his heart was filled with the joy of the Lord. This is what our text sets forth. God is working within us. "Whom the Lord loveth he chasteneth, and scourgeth every son whom he receiveth" (Heb. 12:6).

If we are to experience all this, we must not apply these verses apart from the first verse in this fifth chapter of Romans. To do so is to think of the river without thinking about its source. Tribulation leads to steadfast endurance; steadfast endurance produces maturity of character and a sense of being approved by God, which increases our further hope. But all this results from the truth that we have been justified by the grace of God in Christ.

VICTORY

Our victory over daily tribulation comes from the fact that Christ took our place upon the cross, and died in order to bring us back to God and to bring God back to us. Our lives have ten thousand facets, and God wants the light of His being to reflect from every one of them. He wants to show the world the great sufficiency of His grace. Do we have a problem? God is able to meet that problem. Do we have a need? God is able to supply that need. Do our hearts have a cavity of loneliness? God is able to fill it with Himself and to be all things to us through Christ. Do we stumble? God is able to strengthen us and make us stand. Do we waver between two choices? God is able to direct us. Are we feeble in our wills? God is able to give us the power to choose for Him.

Thus God's work in us leads us from Himself and to Himself. Thus we learn to glorify God and enjoy Him forever.

CHAPTER XIII

The Sources of Hope

By whom we have access by faith into this grace wherein we stand, and rejoice in hope of the glory of God. And not only so, but we glory in tribulations also: knowing that tribulation worketh patience; and patience, experience; and experience, hope (Rom. 5:2-4).

ONE of the disadvantages of detailed Bible study is that we pay such close attention to words, phrases, and doctrines that we are apt to lose sight of the forest while studying the individual trees. So let us survey the ground covered to this point. For the purpose of this survey, I am basing the content of this chapter on the excellent study by Alexander Maclaren entitled *The Sources of Hope*, full of rich thoughts on Romans 5:2-4.

THE GLORY OF GOD

In Romans 5:1-2 the apostle is sketching the grand outline of the ideal Christian life. Rooted in "being justified by faith," it flowers into "peace with God" and "access into grace." In verses 2 to 4 he proceeds to complete the outline by delineating the true Christian attitude toward the future. I have ventured to take so pregnant and large a text, because the very striking and close connection throughout the verses is lost unless we consider them together. Note, then, "we rejoice in hope," "we glory in tribulation." Now, one and the same word in the original is here rendered "rejoice" and "glory." The latter rendering is better than the former, because the original word denotes not only the emotion of joy, but also the expression of it in speech. So it is frequently rendered in the New Testament by the word "boast," which, of course, has an unpleasant connotation. So, you see, Paul regards it as possible, and more than possibly characteristic, that in a Christian the same emotion can be excited by that great, bright future hope and also by the blackness of present sorrow. Hope can make us rejoice, and tribulations can make us rejoice. That is strong meat! So he goes on to explain how it can and must be so, and points out that trouble, if rightly borne, illuminates more brightly the hope that has grasped the glory of God. We have here not only a wonderful designation of the object around which Christian hope twines its tendrils— namely, the glory of God—but also of the double source from which that hope may come, and of the one emotion with which Christian people should face the darkness of the present and the brightness of the future. Ah! how different our lives would be if that ideal of a steadfast hope and an untroubled joy were realized by each of us! It may be! It should be! So I ask you to look at these three points.

First, consider that wonderful designation of the one object of the Christian hope which should fill with unflickering light all that dark future.

"We rejoice in hope of the glory of God." Now, I suppose I need not remind you that "the glory of God" is used in the Old Testament for the light that dwelt between the cherubim above the mercy-seat, the symbol of the divine perfections, and the token of the divine presence. The reality of which this light was a symbol is the total splendor, so to speak, of that divine nature as it shines out into all the universe. And, says Paul, the true hope of the Christian is nothing less than that he shall actually possess that glory of God, in an eternally growing degree. This tremendous claim leads us into deep places. We shall be like the Lord and shall manifest His glory. It is the closest possible union with God and His glory.

WE SHALL BE CHANGED

Our personality will survive and our individual consciousness will be intensified; nevertheless, we shall be drawn into the glory of God as only those could be drawn who have become sons through the redemption that is in Christ. The hope of the Christian is that our humanity will be clothed with as much of that glory of God as can be imparted to redeemed sons. That means perfect knowledge, perfect purity, perfect love. That means the acquisition of new powers, the dropping away of all weaknesses. It will end the schism between what I will do and what I ought to do and the other schism between what I will do and what I can do. It means what Paul says elsewhere, "whom He justified, them He also glorified," and again, "we all, beholding as in a glass"—or rather, perhaps, mirroring as a glass does—"the glory, are changed into the same image."

The very heart of Christianity is that the divine light, of which that shekinah glory in the temple was but a poor and transitory symbol, has "tabernacled" among men in the Lord Jesus Christ, and has from Him been communicated, and is being communicated, in such measure as earthly limitations and conditions permit. Our present reception of these glories points out that they are but a down payment on what shall come to us hereafter when "we shall be like Him, for we shall see Him as He is." The three men in Daniel's day could walk in the fiery furnace because there was One with them, "like unto the Son of God." How can we walk in the divine light and fire of the holiness of God? How can we dwell in the fire of that divine perfection? Only because the Lord Jesus Christ has walked with us in that fire. He brought us first into the light of His grace, and He will bring us one day into the fire of His glory.

It is of great importance that when we think of the future life we should think of it in the highest terms. It is well to speak of rest from toil; it is well to speak of all the sorrowful things which will disappear and be unknown in that future life. Perhaps it is when we realize some of the things that will not be in Heaven that we are the most deeply stirred. Our very deepest feelings are aroused when we know that "there shall be no night there," "there shall be no more death, neither sorrow, nor crying"; there shall be no toil there. But we must rise above all that, for our Heaven is to live in God and to possess His glory. Do not let us dwell upon the symbols lest we lose sight of the realities. Do not let us think of Heaven in terms of its differences, oppositions, and contradictions to earth. Let us rather rise high above negations to the positive truth. Let us not be content with saying, We shall be full of knowledge. Let us rather think of that which embraces them all— we shall be full of God.

DOUBLE SOURCE

So much, then, for the one object of Christian hope. We have here, in the second place, the double source of that hope.

Observe that the first clause of our text comes as the last term in a sequence. It began with "having been justified by faith." The second rung of the ladder was, "we have peace with God." The third, "we have access into this grace." The fourth, "we stand." And then comes, "we rejoice in hope of the glory of God." That is to say, the facts of a Christian life—justification, peace, access, and so on—are the best brighteners of the hope that lies ahead of us. Of course, that is so. "Justified by faith," "peace with God," "access into grace"—what, in the name of common sense, can death do with these things? How can the blunted sword of death cut the bond that unites a soul with the source of all grace when that soul has known and experienced such fruits of life as these? Nothing can be more grotesque, nothing more incongruous, than to think that death, subordinate and accidental—that death whose region is the physical, and which touches nothing but our bodies—has anything whatsoever to do with the higher region of our consciousness.

And further than that, to a man who has known and experienced these gifts of justification, peace, and access, it is unthinkable that these gifts should ever cease to be. In fact as we realize that these emotions and blessings are our very own possession, here and now, we rise to the belief that they are not for an age but for all time, and not just for time but for eternity. This belief becomes a settled feeling in those who have known these joys, and that feeling, though not a proof, is a very strong presumption (if you believe in God) that a man, who thus feels that he was not made to die because he has grasped the Eternal God in salvation and blessing, is right in so feeling.

WHAT WE SHALL BE

Also, if we look at the experiences themselves they all have the stamp of incompleteness and suggest completeness by their own incompleteness. We look up at the new moon and see that its crescent prophesies the completed silver round of the full moon. In the same way, the experiences of the Christian life, here and now, in their greatness and in their smallness, are but the first quarter of glory and declare that there will come a time and an order of things in which thwarted tendency will be accomplished result. The tender green spikelet, pushing up through the brown clods, does not more surely prophesy the waving yellow ear than the seeds of Christ's life within us attest the full flowering that is to come. When a man enters a broad highway in the lonely country, he knows that there is a town at the end of it; and when we come across the path of the grace of God, we know that the glory of God lies at the end of it.

> Then we shall be where we would be,
> Then we shall be what we should be,
> Things that are not now, nor could be,
> Then shall be our own.

And so, if you wish to brighten that great light that fills the future, see to it that your present Christianity is fuller of "peace with God," "access into grace," and the firm, erect standing which results from these. When the springs in the mountains dry up, the river in the valley shrinks; and, when they are full, the river glides along level with the top of its banks. So when our Christian life in the present is richest, our Christian hope of the future is brightest. Look into yourselves. Is there anything that witnesses to that great future? anything that is obviously budding, and destined to greater growth? Some tropical plants manage to grow, weakly, at 40 degrees north latitude. Their leaves are dwarfed and their flowers scanty; their fruits are shriveled and sourish; their whole existence is a cold dream of their warm native land. Thus the virtues and the graces which the Spirit grows in us in the arctic land of earth are but the promise of what they will be when transplanted to Heaven, their native land. God has destined you for Heaven. The great 200-inch telescope on Mt. Palomar reflects the heavens in a mirror, and the astronomers must look down to see what is above them. Look down into your heart today and see whether on the polished plate of your Christian life there are any images of the stars that move around the throne of God. Are you beginning to be like Him?

THE REFINER'S FIRE

Let us turn to the second source to which the apostle traces the Christian hope; Paul says that trouble works patience; that is to say, not only passive endurance but also brave persistence in a course in spite of antagonisms. That is what trouble does to a man when it is rightly borne. Of course the apostle is speaking of the ideal operation and not of the reality which, alas! often is seen when our tribulations lash us into impatience or paralyze our efforts. "Tribulation worketh patience, and patience experience."

That last word is difficult to put into English. Underlying it is the frequent thought, familiar in Scripture, of trouble of all kinds testing a man, be it the refiner's fire or the winnower's fan. It tests a man, and if he bears the trouble with patient persistence, he passes the test and is approved. Patient perseverance thus works approval, or proof of the man's Christianity, and, still more, proof of the reality and power of the Christ whom his Christianity grasps. And so, out of that approval or proof which comes through perseverance in tribulation, there rises in that heart that has stood the test a calm hope that the future will be as the past. Having fought through six troubles, by God's help the seventh will be vanquished also, till at last troubles will end and Heaven be gained.

There is the true point of view from which to look not only at tribulations but also at all the trials that lie in duty and in enjoyment and in earthly things. They are meant to convince us of the reality of our grasp of God and of the reality of the power of the God whom we grasp. If we took that point of view with regard to all the changes of this changeful life, we should not so often be bewildered and upset by our darkest sorrows. The shining lancets and cruel cutting instruments that the surgeon lays out before he begins the operation are very dreadful. But they are there to remove from a man what does him harm to keep and, if not taken away, will kill him. So life with its troubles, great and small, is all meant for this: to make us surer of, and bring us closer to, our God, and to brace and strengthen us in our own personal character. Then blessed be everything that produces these results and leads us to glory in the troubles by which shines out a brighter hope.

So there are the two sources, you see: the one is the blessedness of the Christian life, the other the sorrows of the outward life, and both may converge upon the brightening of our Christian hope. Our rainbow is the child of the marriage of sun and rain. The Christian hope comes from having been "justified by faith, having peace with God . . . and access into grace," and it comes from tribulation, which "worketh patience," and patience which "worketh approval." The hope that comes from our knowledge of salvation and its fruits is like a fire kindled through a glass directly from the sun. The hope that comes from our tribulations is like a fire that is struck with hard flint and cold steel; both are fire, whether they come from the glorious sun or the flint and steel.

STEADFAST JOY

In the third place we have here the one emotion with which the Christian should face all the facts, inward and outward, of his earthly life.

"We glory in the hope," "we glory in tribulation." I need not dwell upon the lesson that is taught us by the inclusion, in this series of Christian characteristics, of steadfast and all-embracing joy. I do not believe that we Christian people realize how imperative a duty, as well as how great a privilege, it is to be glad always. You have no right to be anxious and fretful. You are wrong to be a hypochondriac and depressed, weary, and melancholy. True, many events in life bring sadness. True, Christian joy looks very gloomy to a worldy eye. But there are far more occasions which, if we were right, would make joy instinctive, and which, whether we are right or not, make it obligatory. If that hope were brighter than it commonly is with us and if it were more constantly present to our minds and hearts, we would sing with gladness:

> Come, we that love the Lord,
> And let our joys be known;
> Join in a song with sweet accord,
> And thus surround the throne.
>
> Let those refuse to sing
> Who never knew our God;
> But children of the Heavenly King
> May speak their joys abroad.
>
> There we shall see His face,
> And never, never sin;
> There, from the rivers of His grace,
> Drink endless pleasures in.
>
> Yea, and before we rise
> To that immortal state,
> The thoughts of such amazing bliss
> Should constant joys create.

By a great and wonderful paradox, sorrow and joy coexist. The sorrows are on the surface; beneath there may be rest. All the winds of Heaven may rave across the breast of ocean and fret it into clouds of spume under a storm-swept sky. Deep down there is stillness but not stagnation, because there is life and freshness.

Though there will be wind-vexed surfaces on our too-often agitated spirits, there ought to be, deeper than these, the calm setting of the whole ocean of our nature toward God Himself. It is possible, as the apostle says, to be "sorrowful, yet alway rejoicing." It is possible as his brother apostle puts it, to "rejoice greatly, though now for a season ye are in sorrow through manifold temptations." Consider your life from the point of view that your tribulation is an instrument to produce hope, and you will thank God for all the ways by which He has led you.

Now, the plain lesson of all this is that we have in these texts a chain, one end of which is wrapped around our sinful hearts and the other fastened to the throne of God. You cannot drop any of the links, and you must begin at the beginning if you are to be carried to the end. If we are to have joy immovable, we must have a "steadfast hope." If we are to have a "steadfast hope," we must have a present grace. If we are to have a present grace, and access to the fullness of God, we must have "peace with God." If we are to have "peace with God," our condemnation and guilt must be taken away, and Jesus Christ must take them. If Jesus Christ is to take them away, we must have faith in Him. Then you can begin at your own end of the chain and say, "If I have faith in Jesus Christ, then every link, in due succession, will pass through my hand, and I shall have justification, peace, access, grace, erectness, hope, and exultation, and at last He will lead me by the hand into the glory for which I dare to hope, the glory which the Father gave to Him before the foundation of the world, and which He will give to me when the world has passed away in fervent heat."

CHAPTER XIV

The Breath of God

And hope maketh not ashamed; because the love of God is shed abroad in our hearts by the Holy Spirit which is given unto us (Rom. 5:5).

THIS text is like a fruit tree which may be studied in different ways. A botanist might begin with the root structure, then proceed to study the tree above ground, and come at last to the fruit. Most other people would begin with the fruit; then, if they looked at the tree at all, would perhaps examine the root structure. Our text has three parts and reads: "And hope maketh not ashamed, because the love of God is shed abroad in our hearts by the Holy Spirit who was given unto us" (Rom. 5:5). The hope that makes not ashamed is the fruit. The love of God which is shed abroad in our hearts is the tree itself. The Holy Spirit who brings the love of God to us is the root. Let us begin with the root and work backwards to the fruit, so that we may see why our hope is in us like a beacon light or a waving banner. We shall discover the solid structure of our faith which blossoms in a hope so confident and glorious that we shall never be able to doubt again that we are on the rock, that our goings are established; and we shall burst forth in singing the new song which He has put in our mouths.

Our text, though simple, is one of the most important in the Bible: "the Holy Spirit has been given unto us" (using the past tense as the Greek and revised versions have it). I must state, however, that I do not expect any unbeliever to understand what follows, for "the natural man [the soulish man as the Greek has it] receiveth not the things of the Spirit, for they are foolishness unto him, neither can he know them, for they are spiritually discerned" (1 Cor. 2:14). But all who are believers in the Lord Jesus Christ will be able to comprehend, because "the Holy Spirit has been given unto us."

"SPIRIT" VS. "GHOST"

First, we must define "spirit." This has been slightly compli-
cated by the fact that older versions use the term "the Holy Ghost."
Here is one of the innumerable instances which illustrate what happened to the English language after William the Conqueror and
his French-speaking Normans brought their language into Anglo-
Saxon England. Little by little the two languages amalgamated to
form our mother tongue, but in the process the child adopted
thousands of words from both parents and brought them into the
new language sometimes using two words interchangeably, sometimes splitting a meaning into two parts and giving words from
the parent languages to the new parts. For example, if a Frenchman and a German were talking, each would understand the other
if they used *ochsen* or *boeuf*. Either word describes both the ox
in the field and its meat on the table. This same process has been
followed with "Holy" and "Spirit." A German would say "Holy
Ghost" and a Frenchman would say "Saint Spirit." If you picked
up a German Bible, you would see on the title page the words
Heilige Schriften, "Holy Writings." Inside you would read Holy
Matthew, Holy Mark, Holy Luke, and Holy John. In a French Bible
you would find Saint Matthew, Saint Mark, Saint Luke, and Saint
John, and on the title page, *Sainte Bible.* In English we have taken
the two words and used the one most often for inanimate things—
holy communion, Holy Scriptures, holy week, holy days (and holi-
days!). The other word is more often used for animate beings—
Saint Paul and the other saints (in biblical usage, all believers;
hence, "communion of the saints").

The same fusion and division of words has taken place with
"ghost" and "spirit." A German and a Frenchman would each translate the other's word by his own. But if either talked to an English-
man, clear distinctions must be made. Today we use the word
"ghost" for the spirit of a dead human being, supposedly returning
to haunt persons or places. The French have an entirely different
word for that—*revenant,* "a returning one." This idea was formerly
expressed in English by either "ghost" or "spirit." Thus Horatio tells
Hamlet that he has seen his father's ghost. But the Lord Jesus
Christ, speaking of His own physical body after His resurrection,
said, "Handle me and see; for a spirit hath not flesh and bones, as

ye see me have" (Luke 24:39). Because of this tendency to identify the word "ghost" with the spirits of the dead, I have abandoned the word and always use "Holy Spirit," except in the Doxology or in the Apostles' Creed.

THE HOLY BREATH

What, then, is the Spirit? The word itself has some beautiful and instructive ramifications. The English "spirit" comes from the Latin *spiritus*, which means "breath." We have it in such words as aspire, conspire, inspire, perspire, expire. You lift your head and draw in a deep breath when you aspire. You put your head together with the heads of others and inhale and exhale together when you conspire. When God breathes into a man, he is inspired. You breathe through your pores when you perspire, and your breath goes out when you expire. It can readily be seen from these illustrations that the idea of breath is deeply rooted in the word "spirit."

In the Greek the word is *pneuma;* you meet it in some English words. Rubber tires were first called pneumatic tires because they contained breath or air. A drill run by compressed air is a pneumatic drill. When our lungs are attacked by a disease, we take the Greek word for lungs, the breath-box, add a suffix to it, and call the sickness pneumonia. *Pneuma* is used scores of times in the New Testament for the Holy Spirit. He is the Holy Breath.

The Breath of God came on the day of Pentecost as a rushing mighty wind (Acts 2:2). Many hymn writers speak of the Holy Spirit as the breath of God, or the wind of God. John Keble wrote:

> So, when the Spirit of our God
> Came down His flock to find,
> A voice from Heaven was heard abroad,
> A rushing, mighty wind.
>
> It fills the Church of God; it fills
> The sinful world around;
> Only in stubborn hearts and wills
> No place for it is found.

Alfred Henry Vine wrote:

> O breath of God, breathe on us now,
> And move within us while we pray;
> The spring of our new life art Thou,
> The very light of our new day.

William Henry Parker wrote:

> Holy Spirit, hear us;
> Help us while we sing;
> Breathe into the music
> Of the praise we bring.

Andrew Reed wrote:

> Come as the wind, with rushing sound
> And pentecostal grace,
> That all of woman born may see
> The glory of Thy face.

James Montgomery wrote:

> Like a mighty rushing wind
> Upon the waves beneath,
> Move with one impulse every mind,
> One soul, one feeling breathe.

And Edwin Hatch wrote:

> Breathe on me, Breath of God;
> Fill me with life anew,
> That I may love what Thou dost love,
> And do what Thou wouldst do.

And, above all, we have that great Keswick hymn by B. P. Head:

> O Breath of Life, come sweeping through us,
> Revive Thy Church with life and power;
> O Breath of Life, come, cleanse, renew us,
> And fit Thy Church to meet this hour.
>
> O Wind of God, come bend us, break us,
> Till humbly we confess our need;
> Then in Thy tenderness remake us,
> Revive, restore, for this we plead.
>
> O Breath of Love, come breathe within us,
> Renewing thought and will and heart;
> Come, Love of Christ, afresh to win us,
> Revive Thy Church in ev'ry part.
>
> O Heart of Christ, once broken for us,
> 'Tis there we find our strength and rest;
> Our broken, contrite hearts now solace,
> And let thy waiting Church be blest.

Now, just as the English, Latin, and Greek words for "spirit" all refer to "breath," so does the Hebrew word. Indeed, when we look at the word translated "spirit," from its first usage throughout the Old Testament, we find that the word itself is a breath. In the first paragraph of Genesis we read, *Braisheeth bara Elohim* . . . as almost every Jewish boy learns by heart: "In the beginning God created the heavens and the earth; and the earth became a wreck and a ruin, and darkness covered the face of the deep. And the Spirit of God moved upon the face of the waters." The Hebrew word is beautiful. It belongs to the class of words that are onomatopoeic, that is, formed in imitation of natural sounds, like the buzz of bees, the quack of ducks, the crackle of fire, the hiss of a serpent. The Hebrew word for breath is the sound of exhaling, *ruach*.

REVELATION BY THE SPIRIT

How may the word "spirit" be said to reveal the being of God? Speaking to the woman at the well, the Lord Jesus Christ said that worship should not be limited to form, ceremony, and location, such as a shrine, an altar, or a building, because "God is Spirit; and they that worship him must worship him in Spirit and in truth" (John 4:24).

It is evident that if we could understand God fully, we would ourselves be God, but we can go to the Word and learn much about Him. He has said, "My thoughts are not your thoughts, neither are your ways my ways. . . . For as the heavens are higher than the earth, so are my ways higher than your ways, and my thoughts than your thoughts" (Isa. 55:8, 9). Surely one difference between His ways and ours is that He is eternal and we are creatures of time: He is Spirit, not tied down by flesh and blood, but we are in bodies, limited by physical laws.

Only as God communicates His thoughts to us can we understand Him. A simple illustration will reveal the dilemma and show how it may be partly solved. We live in a world of length, breadth, and height, but imagine a world that is totally flat. We might even call it Flatland. It would be peopled by creatures who measured distance horizontally, who could understand a circle but not a globe, who could comprehend a square but not a cube. They would know plane geometry but not solid geometry. They would understand long and short, but would have no words for down and up, or high and low. We might talk to them about the third dimension but they would not comprehend it. But if we were able, by a supernatural birth, to give some of them a nature capable of understanding up and down, high and low, then they would know what we were talking about, even though the other citizens of Flatland might think them slightly crazy. But those who had this new knowledge would understand each other.

THE SPIRITUAL DIMENSION

Thus it is with our three-dimensional world. There is another dimension outside the bounds of human thinking: the spiritual dimension. The Lord God knows that we live in the little world of length, breadth, and height, and that by nature we cannot understand the fourth or spiritual dimension. But He came to this earth to die for us and to impart to us a new nature which enables us to comprehend that the spiritual is much more important than the physical, that the eternal is much more important than the temporal, that our little affairs are not worthy to be compared with what will be revealed to us and in us. Thus Paul could say, "I reckon that the sufferings of this present time are not worthy to be compared with the glory which shall be revealed in us" (Rom. 8:18).

A being, a personality, from the spiritual point of view, has knowledge, feelings, and will. We know that we possess these three characteristics independent of the body. Those who have lost eyes, arms, or legs say there is no diminishing of what they knew, felt, and determined before being deprived of those parts. All of us feel that we exist apart from our physical being. We awaken from a dream feeling that we have been away from ourselves, and awaking brings us back to the prison of our bodies. And believers know what it is to live above and beyond the things of time and sense.

Now it is difficult to express this in the infinite, but such expression is the beginning of the knowledge of God. He is not limited by time and space. Even the Heaven of Heavens cannot contain Him, as Solomon said when he dedicated his temple (1 Kings 8:27). God is the source and end of all knowledge. He is infinite omnipotence. (We risk redundancy here, for we are seeking to push our thought beyond the limit of the human mind.) God is the infinite of feeling. His love is beyond us. God is the infinite of determining will. Nothing can be outside His control or beyond

His dominion. This is why we think of foreknowledge not simply as advance knowledge, but also as knowledge that has decreed and determined all things and is working out all things for a purpose, after the counsel of the eternal, divine will (Eph. 1:11).

A NOSEFUL OF BREATH

An illustration which has helped me to understand God a little better is one hidden in the Hebrew of Isaiah 2:22. This verse contains the word *ruach*, translated in our King James Version as "breath." "Cease ye from man, whose breath is in his nostrils: for wherein is he to be accounted of?" (Isa. 2:22). It might be translated, "Cease ye from man who has only one-noseful capacity of breath: what is he worth, anyway?" Americans should be able to comprehend that verse with ease, for we are accustomed to the supremacy of a sixteen-cylinder car over an eight or a four; and our minds can grasp jet propulsion, rocket projectiles, and supersonic speeds. Now, if instead of cylinders we think in terms of nosefuls, God is saying here, "When will you human beings realize that you are only one-noseful creatures, and that I am infinite, eternal Breath? You dive under water and, even though you are the world's champion swimmer, you can stay under only for the brief moment of the one deep breath you have inhaled."

We turn to the Book of Genesis and read that God said, God spoke, God moved, and the result was creation. He exhaled; and from His Spirit came all things. We read that man was formed out of the dust of the ground and God breathed into his nostrils the breath of life and man became a living soul (Gen. 2:7). But there is no thought of God's having to inhale. He is forever breathing out; He will never have to draw a breath. He is the eternal Spirit, the eternal Breath. Man draws himself up to his full height and fills his lungs until his eyes almost pop out and then says, "Watch me blow! I can blow so hard that I can blow Hiroshima down with one breath! And man sucks in a little of God's power and blows out an atomic bomb that destroys a city, is as proud as the Devil of what he has done, and becomes frightened because he cannot control what he has blown out. Shortly after Hiroshima, God blew the small breath of an earthquake in a corner of Japan which was a thousand times more destructive than man, but all the time He knew what He was doing. And a little later in New Guinea the top

of a mountain blew off in a volcanic eruption, and the cloud was
so vast that it made the atomic cloud look like a smoke ring from
a man's mouth.

All that is happening today is calculated by the eternal God
of the eternal Breath, the source of all life. He is trying to teach us
by history and experience that there is no good in man, no power
in man; that we must turn away from all things human and trust
the living God. But man will not learn this lesson. There are a
few to whom God has given His eternal Spirit. We redeemed ones
know a little of what He is doing, since He has been pleased to lift
the veil and give us a glimpse of the scene.

Our text says that God has given us the Holy Breath; He has
given us of Himself. We shall have to look at this more closely, but
here we have seen enough to know that salvation came to us in
that moment when we turned away from ourselves and accepted
His verdict that we were nothing and could do nothing to satisfy
Him, and accepted our position as objects of His love and mercy
and participants in His grace. Thus, we have eternal life and no
longer carry on with the noseful-at-a-time of earth's atmosphere,
but are learning that we are to inhale forever and draw all things
from Him.

CHAPTER XV

Born into God's Family

The love of God is shed abroad in our hearts by the Holy Spirit who is given unto us (Rom. 5:5).

HAVING seen the Spirit as the eternal Breath of God, we now see that the Holy Spirit is not a power from God, but is God Himself. Perhaps here we find the weakness of the Church in the midst of the world. For too long the Church has looked upon itself as having some strength, and has thought of the Holy Spirit as a power which the Church must take hold of and use. But the Bible teaches that the Holy Spirit is a Person—the third Person of the Godhead. He wishes to move in His eternal sphere. In His eternal wisdom and according to His eternal purpose, He takes hold of us and uses us to His honor and glory as He pleases. The Christian who attempts to use God is bound to be fruitless and frustrated. The Christian who yields to the control of the Holy Spirit will be filled and fruitful, and forever satisfied.

THE SPIRIT A PERSON

Because the Holy Spirit is a Person, I have changed the pronoun in our text from *which* to *who*. The nature of language demands the change. Languages differ, and the thought of one language cannot always be expressed in another by an exact, word-for-word translation. Therefore, it is not only necessary to enter into the genius of the language, but also to grasp the thought of the work. It is not enough to understand the Greek of the New Testament; we must know the Author, the living God, who breathed the truth of His revelation through the minds and hearts of the writers. The Bible everywhere teaches that the Holy Spirit is the third Person of the Godhead; that He has the three marks of personality—knowledge, feelings, and will. He has knowledge, for He is the Spirit of wisdom (Eph. 1:17); He has feelings, for it is possible to grieve Him (Eph. 4:30); and He has will, for He is the active executive of the plan and purposes of God (1 Cor. 12:11). Understanding this, we shall nevermore speak of Him as "it," and

116

shall not consider ourselves masters of a power given to us to use, but servants of a Person who wishes to possess and use us.

Thus God has not given us something small and limited; He has given us Himself; and, having given us Himself, He has given us all things.

THE FIRST SCHISM

How and when did He give Himself to us? The Church has been split into many denominations over these questions. When the first great schism divided the Christian world into Eastern and Western churches, Greek and Roman, it was ostensibly over a difference concerning the coming of the Holy Spirit to the Church. But, as a matter of history, Rome and Constantinople actually split over supremacy in power and government. Rome claimed that all authority was vested in her bishops; those of the East, under the domination of Constantinople, wanted equal power in the government. But when men separate in church matters, they do not say, "I am going my way because I want to run things; since you won't let me run things, I'll start a new group." Instead, they seek a theological difference, and then salve their pride and instill devotion into their followers by claiming that they are "warring for the truth."

Thus, in the fourth century, the battle between the Eastern and Western churches was like that between Hollywood and Broadway for control of the entertainment world, or between the New York and Chicago Stock Exchanges for control of market commissions. In the worlds of entertainment and finance, the warfare is open, but in the world of theology it is hidden, since Christians are supposed to love one another and not seek personal gain. Alas, reality has often been far from the principle set forth in the divine revelation. The church council, in process of writing a creed, was discussing the doctrine of the Holy Spirit. The Roman Church wanted to write that the Holy Spirit proceeded from the Father and the Son, for so the Bible teaches. But in the battle for political control this was seized upon by the men of the Eastern Church who demanded that the Latin word *filioque,* "and the Son," be stricken from the creed. There was heated argument, and finally the Eastern delegates walked out. The breach has not been healed to this day.

THE COMING OF THE SPIRIT

Other differences have arisen concerning the time and manner
of the coming of the Holy Spirit. The Church of England differs
from the Roman Church on this point; and in the midst of Protestantism many of the new branches, which are growing very rapidly,
have made this doctrine the point of separation. The Pentecostal
group, for instance, have adopted a position quite different from
that of the major denominations.

Concerning the dilemma that faces the expositor of Scripture,
Alexander Maclaren writes: "The first question is, when was that
Spirit given to these Roman Christians? The Christian Church
has been split in two by its answers to that question. One influen-
tial part says 'in baptism,' and the other says 'at the moment of
faith.' . . . I am not going to be tempted into controversial paths
now, for my purpose is a very different one, but I cannot help just
a word about the form of these two answers. 'Given in baptism,'
say our friends, and I venture to think that they thereby degrade
Christianity into a system of magic, bringing together two entirely
disparate things, an external physical act and a spiritual change.
I do not say anything about the disastrous effects that have followed
from such conception of the medium by which this greatest of all
Christian gifts is effected upon men. Since the Spirit who is given
is life, the result of the gift of that Spirit is a new life, and we all
know what disastrous and debasing consequences have followed
from that dogma of regeneration through baptism.

"No doubt it is perfectly true that normally, in the early
Church, the Divine Spirit was given at baptism; but for one thing,
that general rule had exceptions, as in the case of Cornelius, and,
for another thing, though it was given at baptism it was not given
in baptism, but it was given through faith, of which in those days
baptism was the sequel and the sign."

THE VERBS OF THE SPIRIT

We return to the question itself: How and where does God
give Himself to us? Since much in the Christian life depends upon
this question of the Holy Spirit in the heart of the individual, let
us examine some of the verbs used in the New Testament in connection with His work in us. It seems to me that much of the difficulty

has been caused by failure to understand that the Holy Spirit does many different works in all who believe. Confusion of terms about these works has led to confusion about the underlying nature of His coming, and His work as a whole.

The Bible teaches that we are born of the Spirit, indwelt by the Spirit, baptized by the Spirit, sealed with the Spirit; that we may be filled with the Spirit and be anointed with the Spirit. If a careful study is made of these terms, much confusion will vanish. We will surrender ourselves to Him for the purposes which He has for us, and our lives will be filled with the joy and peace of believing and with the love which He sheds abroad in our hearts.

In this series of verbs, first in time and importance is that we are born of the Spirit into the family of God. This presupposes that we are by nature the children of wrath (Eph. 2:3), and that we become the children of God by faith in Christ Jesus (Gal. 3:26). One of the commonest theological errors of our day is the doctrine of the universal fatherhood of God and the universal brotherhood of man. A true Christian will oppose these errors, for they are at the root of many of Satan's triumphs over human hearts. The Bible teaches that there are two families and two fatherhoods. Men are born into this world as children of wrath and children of disobedience, and some of them even become children of the Devil. Jesus Christ said, "I speak of what I have seen with my father, and you do what you have heard from your father" (John 8:38). The Pharisees answered, "We were not born of fornication; we have one Father, even God" (8:41). Jesus answered, "If God were your Father, you would love me, for I proceeded forth and came from God; . . . you are of your father the Devil, and your will is to do your father's desires" (42, 44). How can anyone call himself a follower of Jesus Christ and then deny Him by believing in the universal fatherhood of God and the universal brotherhood of man?

NICODEMUS

How, then, does one get out of one family and into the other? In other words, how is one born again, born of the Spirit? Let us look at the Bible references which refer to this work of the Holy Spirit. A man named Nicodemus, a ruler of the Jews, came to Jesus by night and said to him, "Rabbi, we know that you are a teacher come from God, for no one can do these signs that you do, unless

God is with him" (John 3:2). Nicodemus' whole concept of Christ was wrong. That was why Jesus rebuked him by saying, "Truly, truly, I say to you, unless one is born anew, he cannot see the kingdom of God." Hundreds of teachers had come from God before Christ, and thousands of teachers have come from God since Christ, but the Lord Jesus Christ was certainly not a teacher come from God: He was God come to teach.

No man calls Jesus Lord—Jehovah—except by the Holy Spirit (1 Cor. 12:3), and this is why Nicodemus had such a low view of the person of Christ: he was a natural child of Adam and the Holy Spirit had not yet enabled him to perceive that Jesus Christ is God. So Christ told him that he must be born again.

A further proof that Nicodemus was not yet saved lies in the fact that he reacted to Christ's words in natural terms. Christ said that a man must be born of *hudor kai pneuma*—literally, of water and breath. The translators understood, of course, that the breath referred to the Holy Spirit, and so translated and interpreted the word *pneuma*. But the word "water" they translated literally. They should either have left the two symbols and translated the phrase, "Except a man be born of water and breath," or they should have translated both symbols to read, "Except a man be born of the Word and the Spirit." Our Lord's teaching was full of symbolism, and certainly all that we read concerning the new birth is high symbolism. How foolish that men should not comprehend these things! Some people actually believe that men are saved by the outward ritual of baptism. In the second chapter of John, when Jesus spoke of raising up a destroyed temple in three days, it was thought He meant a building; He was talking about the resurrection of His body. In the third chapter He spoke of birth; Nicodemus thought only of obstetrics: "Can [a man] enter a second time into his mother's womb and be born?" he asked.

To understand the symbols of the Bible, get a good concordance and look up all the verses which contain a given word. You will soon discover the spiritual meaning of any symbol. Under the symbolism of the new birth, the Lord was teaching that a man cannot save himself any more than he can bring himself into the world. The Bible is remarkably accurate in using natural birth to illustrate the new birth. We read in the Epistle of James, "Of his own will begat he us with the word of truth, that we should be a

kind of firstfruits of his creation" (Jas. 1:18). Here we see God as
the begetter, and we know from other passages that this was done
by the work of the Holy Spirit in the life of the individual. Our
Lord Himself taught Nicodemus that the Holy Spirit was the
divine agent in the work of salvation. There are many wonderful
symbols of the Word used in the Bible: lamp, light, hammer, fire,
mirror, sword, scalpel, milk, strong meat, and sweeter than honey
in the honeycomb. But Peter gives us a very daring illustration, in
which God likens the Bible to the male life germ. The Latin Vulgate
reveals this startling concept of salvation, for the word there used is
semen. The English reads, "Having been begotten again, not of
corruptible seed but of incorruptible [seed], by the Word of God,
which liveth and abideth forever" (1 Pet. 1:23).

NEW LIFE

When we put these passages together, we find this remarkable
analogy presented to us as follows: We who have become Christians supernaturally are the passive recipients of the new life of
salvation wrought in us by the effective work of God the Holy
Spirit. He first plants within the heart what we might call the ovum
of saving faith, for even our faith is not of ourselves, it is the gift
of God (Eph. 2:8). Then the Holy Spirit, the divine begetter,
pierces that saving faith with the seed of the Word, and, from
the contact of life with life, there is wrought within us a new life
which has no connection with ourselves by nature. God did not
use anything in Saul when He created Paul within him. God did
not use anything of Simon when He created the new Peter. God
did not use anything in Jacob when He created Israel within him.
God did not use anything of my own old Adamic nature when He
begot me from the dead. That is why we can say, "If any man is
in Christ there is a new creation" (as the margin of the Revised
Version puts it so well in 2 Cor. 5:17).

Thus we understand a part of our text in Romans. The Holy
Spirit has been given unto us in regeneration. Our new life is the
work of His divine begetting. A new creation has taken place, and
the scene of that new creation has been within.

Now it should be noted carefully that all of the people of
God from Abel (the first to die believing in God's Word about
the lamb which He provided) down to the last man who will ever

be saved are all born again by the same process. All who are thus saved are in the family of God. They have entered the new family by the new birth—the work of the Holy Spirit. Thus the Holy Spirit has been given (past tense) to every believer. But in this family of God, it should be noted, there are many groups. There is a difference between the patriarchs from Adam to Abraham and the group which we call Israel, who were saved under the covenant promise of God from Abraham to Christ. There is also a difference between those who were saved before Christ and those who have lived on this side of the cross. Those who are saved in our day are not only in the family of God; they are also in the Church, the body and bride of Christ. Entrance into the Church is by a separate work of the Holy Spirit in the life of each believer—a work distinct from the new birth. While the new birth takes us into the family of God, quite another work takes us into the body of Christ. The Lord by the Holy Spirit does something in us that He did not do in Abraham. He was saved by grace, and by grace alone, and he will be in Heaven even as we shall be in Heaven, though his relationship to Christ is slightly different from ours. This difference we shall see in our next chapter.

CHAPTER XVI

The Believer in Christ

And hope maketh not ashamed; because the love of God is shed abroad in our hearts by the Holy Spirit who is given unto us (Rom. 5:5).

W E HAVE seen that the Holy Spirit is a Person—the third member of the Godhead; that the verb is in the past tense; and, most importantly, that the recipients of this gift, the people called "us," are those individuals who have been made alive through faith in the blood of Jesus Christ.

It is false to think that the Holy Spirit has been given to every member of the human race. The Lord God has never poured out His Spirit upon the unsaved. There is a great illustration of this in the Old Testament ceremony of the cleansing of a leper by God's priests. The leper was brought before the priest, who took some of the blood of the trespass-offering and put it upon the tip of the leper's right ear, upon the thumb of his right hand, and upon the great toe of his right foot. Following this, the priest poured some of the anointing oil into the palm of his own left hand, and, after sprinkling some of it seven times before the Lord, he put a drop of the oil on top of the drop of blood on the man's ear, his thumb, and his toe (Lev. 14:14-17). A concordance will show that the oil was the symbol of the Holy Spirit, just as the blood of the lamb was the symbol of the atoning death of the Lord Jesus Christ. And the complete act shows us that as the oil was not put upon the flesh but upon the blood; so the Holy Spirit is not given to unregenerate men but only to those who have been cleansed through the redeeming work of the Savior. To think that every man has a spark of the divine within him is contrary to Scripture. To hold that the Holy Spirit dwells within all men is alien to the teaching of the Bible. The new birth must precede any other work of the Holy Spirit.

INTO CHRIST

How does any man get to be in Christ? The unthinking will hasten to answer, by the new birth. Much as I believe in and teach the necessity of the new birth, I do not think that we enter the body of Christ by that work of the Holy Spirit. Abraham was born again, and thus by faith was in the family of God but he was not in the body of Christ. All who preceded Christ and were made alive by the work of the Spirit were born of God, for otherwise they could not have been in His family. The new birth gives entrance into the family of God. Entrance into the body of Christ is obtained by quite another work of the Holy Spirit.

The verse which leads us to the heart of the subject is 1 Corinthians 12:13: "For by one Spirit we were all baptized into one body." Entrance into the body, then, is not by the regenerative work of the Spirit but by the baptism of the Spirit. No one may ask a believer whether he has been baptized with the Spirit. The very fact that a man is in the body of Christ demonstrates that he has been baptized by the Spirit, for there is no other way to enter the body. To call the baptism of the Holy Spirit a second work of grace is false to New Testament doctrine. I do not deny that there is a continuing work of the Holy Spirit, but that is not baptism.

Everyone who has been baptized by the Spirit is in the body; and everyone who is in the body of Christ has been baptized by the Spirit in order to get there. When these simple propositions are understood, there is no more confusion about getting the baptism or being baptized by the Spirit after one has been saved. For a Christian to ask the Lord to baptize him with the Spirit is exactly the same as a married man asking his wife if she will marry him. 'Tis done, and it cannot be twice done.

BAPTISM

To understand the meaning of baptism by the Holy Spirit, we must understand the meaning of the word "baptism" itself when used in connection with the work of the Holy Spirit. I refer here only to the baptism of the Holy Spirit, and my remarks have no connection with any mode of water baptism.

There is one Lord, one faith, one baptism, we read in Ephesians 4:5. Here we find the Godhead. The one Lord is God the Father; the one faith is the faith of the Lord Jesus Christ; and the one baptism is the baptism of the Holy Spirit.

Now, the root meaning of *baptizo* is "to plunge," "to dip," "to immerse." Obviously these definitions cannot be applied literally to the baptism of the Holy Spirit. But the difficulty has arisen from the fact that many fail to understand that there is more than one meaning for the original word for baptism.

In any language there are both literal and metaphorical meanings. The fact that the metaphor rises from the literal in no wise makes it necessary to think in literal terms of the metaphor. For example, the word "iron" means a certain metal; but who would think of metal in the phrase, "The iron entered into his soul"? We all know that iron there symbolizes tribulation. Iron also stands for courage, hardness, or strength of character; robustness of physical frame; firmness or obstinacy of will; harshness or severity of treatment. Thus iron can be used in any of these metaphorical senses.

A CHANGE OF IDENTITY

In the same manner the word "baptize" means, metaphorically, to change identity or to identify. In classical Greek comedy, one drunken slave is told by another that he is "baptized." He obviously has not been sprinkled, immersed, or poured upon. His identity has been changed. He has become beastlike, less than a man, and so is "baptized." A Greek historian uses the word to describe a beautiful field of grain, "baptized" by war so that it was changed to a field of carnage and death.

It might have been well if "baptize" had been everywhere translated instead of transliterated. Then we would read: "Go ye, therefore, and teach all nations, identifying them in the Name of the Father, and of the Son, and of the Holy Spirit" (Mt. 28:19). And "One Lord, one faith, one identification" (Eph. 4:5). Or, again, we would understand the words of the forerunner, John the Identifier, "I indeed identify you with water; but one mightier than I cometh, the latchet of whose shoes I am not worthy to unloose: he shall identify you with the Holy Wind and with fire" (Luke 3:16). This translation in no wise touches the argument of those who hold to a specific mode of water baptism.

THE BODY OF CHRIST

Let us now look at the word "body" into which we are identified when the Holy Spirit is given to us. Again, this word must be taken not in its literal but in its metaphorical sense. We are not baptized into the hands or feet of Christ, in the physical sense. We are identified with that great body of former sons of Adam who have been taken out of relationship with their first father and united to the Lord Jesus Christ as sons of the Heavenly Father by the work of the Holy Spirit who joins us to God's dear Son.

The dictionary gives thirty definitions of the word "body," each of which is carefully distinguished from the others. The use of the word here is figurative, coming from that marvelous phenomenon of which we usually take little notice; namely, that every action of our body is performed at the command of our head. Just so, to be in the body of Christ is to be under the command of our glorious Head.

An amazing example of physical dexterity is that recorded of the late Dr. Alexis Carrel, famous French physician, Nobel Prize winner in medicine, and head of Rockefeller Institute in New York. As a boy, Dr. Carrel decided to be a surgeon, and so prepared his hands to be flexible and supple. He placed the cover of a matchbox over the two smallest fingers of either hand and, with needle and thread, stitched together the edges of cigarette paper within the narrow confines of the matchboxes, and tied a knot to finish off the "operation." Later, as a surgeon, he amazed the medical world by the manipulative skill with which he worked in narrow recesses of the human body. Dr. Carrel's head had complete mastery over his fingers.

In the spiritual domain, we are frequently awkward because we do not allow our Head, the Lord Jesus, to control and dominate us so that we make every thought captive to obey Christ (2 Cor. 10:5). The world will never look at clumsy handlers of the problems of life, but it will stop in awe before the life that allows itself to be trained to proficiency in the craft of Christian living. Men did not admire the fingers but the head of Dr. Carrel: men will not admire the Christian but the Lord Jesus when they see your good works, and will glorify your Father which is in Heaven (Mt. 5:16).

This, then, is the relationship into which we are identified by the baptism of the Holy Spirit. We grow up into "the head, even Christ, from whom the whole body fitly joined together and compacted by that which every joint supplieth, according to the effectual working in the measure of every part, maketh increase of the body unto the edifying of itself in love" (Eph. 4:16). Phillips has paraphrased this, "We are not meant to remain as children at the mercy of every chance wind of teaching and the jockeying of men who are expert in the crafty presentation of lies. But we are meant to hold firmly to the truth in love, and to grow up in every way into Christ, the Head. For it is from the Head that the whole Body, as a harmonious structure knit together by the joints with which it is provided, grows by the proper functioning of individual parts to its full maturity in love."

NO SECOND WORK

Now, it is not the physical body of Christ into which we are identified by the Spirit, but into that sovereign intelligence which articulates lives. This is a great truth, but it is not the whole truth concerning the work of the Holy Spirit in placing us in Christ. We have shown enough, however, to demonstrate that every believer in Christ is thereby in the body of Christ, and therefore the baptism of the Holy Spirit has taken place for him. It is absolutely impossible to speak correctly of a baptism of the Holy Spirit in terms of something that is to be a separate, subsequent experience.

"But," someone may ask, "what about Paul's arrival at Ephesus and the second baptism of the disciples there?" For when he came he asked the believers, "Did you receive the Holy Spirit when you believed?" (Acts 19:2). Alas, how that question has been mishandled in our day! For there are those who ask it today of Christians, and think that a second work of grace must be performed in the life of a believer. Notice that the people of Ephesus answered that they had never even heard that there was a Holy Spirit. When Paul asked them about their baptism, they replied that they had been baptized with the baptism of John, the forerunner. Paul then explained what had happened in the meantime, and the people were rebaptized in the name of the Lord Jesus.

Perhaps an illustration from our own American history will make clear what took place in Ephesus. During the latter part of the eighteenth century, many colonists left Virginia and started through the mountains to the valley that lay far to the west. Some were forced to stay in the mountains, either through fear of Indians or because the death of a horse or the breaking down of a wagon made it impossible for them to take their goods farther. Twenty years passed, during which they saw no white men. Finally, a group of travelers made their way through the region where these isolated settlers were living. Naturally there was much conversation about the outside world. The travelers might have asked the mountaineers what they thought about the Republic and the policies of the Congress. The isolated ones would have answered, "We have not so much as heard that there is a Congress or a Republic." Then they would have gone on to say that they thought of themselves as loyal subjects of the British King, and that they had not so much as heard that there was a George Washington, a Revolutionary War, or the establishment of the Republic. But when they were told all that had happened, they entered into an understanding of their new status, and became American citizens in that hour by knowledge, as they had been for some time in fact.

It is sometimes objected that the disciples in Samaria received the Holy Spirit some time after their regeneration (Acts 8:16, 17). True, but these people were in a transition period. They had listened to Christ Himself after being brought to Him by the woman at the well. They were not yet in the Church, the body of Christ, because it did not exist before Pentecost. They therefore needed this subsequent experience of receiving the Holy Spirit. They are not in the same category with those who come to Christ in our generation and receive salvation and the Holy Spirit at the moment they are born again.

Likewise, many of the children of Israel, who traveled to Jerusalem in the days of John the Baptist, heard and followed him, and were baptized by him. Then they went back to their remote homes, and during the ensuing years were ignorant that Jesus Christ had been manifested, had died and been raised from the dead, had ascended into Heaven and had sent forth the Holy Spirit. But as soon as they were told by Paul, they realized their new status and were identified with the infant Church, becoming members of that body by the work of the Holy Spirit.

But we today are the immediate objects of the full work of the Holy Spirit. At the same moment, simultaneously and instantaneously, we are born of the Spirit into the family of God, and baptized by the Spirit into the body of Christ. The Holy Spirit has been given to every believer. And, strong and secure in that fact, we live our Christian life from day to day.

CHAPTER XVII

Christ in the Believer

And hope maketh not ashamed; because the love of God is shed abroad in our hearts by the Holy Spirit who is given unto us (Rom. 5:5).

HERE is one of the most important texts in the Bible. It states that the Holy Spirit *has been given* to us. The group receiving this gift is limited to those who have been made alive through faith in the blood of Christ. The gift has many phases, and many of the works of the Holy Spirit are simultaneous and instantaneous. Let me explain this by an analogy.

MANY CHANGES IN A MOMENT

When a young woman comes into my church to be married, several changes take place when I say, "By the authority committed to me under the laws of the State of Pennsylvania and in the name of the Father, the Son, and the Holy Spirit, I now pronounce you man and wife." For example, she came in with one name and she goes out with another. She also came in with one legal status and she goes out with another. If she owned a house and lot, she could have sold it before the wedding with no signature but her own. But, as soon as I pronounce her married, she can no longer sell property without securing her husband's signature. She is bound to him by law. But there are still other changes. There is a psychological change: she knows and feels a subtle difference between being single and married. There is also a social change: now that she has a home of her own, she is expected to be hospitable, and to reciprocate social favors. Which change takes place first? The answer is that all occur at the same moment. The name change, legal change, psychological change, social change, all occur instantaneously and simultaneously.

So it is when God quickens our souls and makes us alive in Christ. At that moment our bodies become temples of the Holy

Spirit, we are born of the Spirit into the family of God, and baptized by the Spirit into the body of Christ, and we are sealed with the Holy Spirit unto the day of redemption. All these things take place simultaneously and instantaneously.

None of these is what some people call a second work of grace. There is a further work of the Holy Spirit, which in the Scriptures is called the filling of the Spirit, but this is not to be confused with the permanent works of the Spirit which are done once and forever at the moment one believes in Christ as Savior.

THE TEMPLE OF THE SPIRIT

We have looked in detail at the work of the Spirit in regeneration, and in baptizing or identifying the believer into the body of Christ. Let us now consider that the Holy Spirit has been given to us in order to possess us. We are children of the dust that became Adam when God breathed into it the breath of life. All that we inherit from our parents is the nature of Adam. We are children of the flesh. That which is born of the flesh is flesh, and it can never be anything else. But, the moment we are born of the Spirit into the family of God, our bodies become the temple of the Holy Spirit. You will note a seeming grammatical error in the last sentence, but it is a correct theological truth. Our bodies become not temples but the temple of the Holy Spirit. For it takes all true believers of all ages to house the Holy Spirit for the completion of the work which He intends to do through those who form the true Church.

God will not be thwarted in His plans. He created man in His own image and for a great, eternal purpose, and that purpose will be fulfilled to the last detail. In the preceding chapter we pointed out that the believer was placed in Christ, but here we see that Christ comes to dwell in us. There is a great difference between my being in Christ and Christ living in me. I am in Christ by identification, the baptism of the Holy Spirit, which means that I am identified with Him and in Him, to be dominated by Him as He is to dominate all believers. But the truth we emphasize here is that each believer is to be possessed by the power and presence of the Holy Spirit so that the infinite purpose of God may be worked out within the compass of that believer's life and personality.

In the epistle to the Ephesians Paul prays for the Ephesian believers (and, of course, for all believers) that God would grant them according to the riches of His glory, to be strengthened with might by His Spirit in the inner man; that Christ might dwell in their hearts by faith; that they, being rooted and grounded in love, might be able to comprehend with all saints what is the breadth, and length, and depth, and height, and to know the love of Christ which passeth knowledge; that they might be filled with all the fullness of God (Eph. 3:16-19). When the translators of our King James Version reached this passage they were evidently afraid to render it in all its glorious fullness because of the seeming impossibility of the statement. The correct translation is "that you might be filled *unto* all the fullness of God."

ALL THE FULLNESS

Let me illustrate the difference between *with* and *unto*. While I was preparing this chapter, I was preaching on the Pacific Coast, and frequently had opportunity to look out over the broad expanse of our largest ocean. The glorious stretches of shore and sky and sea quicken and thrill our imagination as our littleness is placed alongside that unending expanse. Now, suppose I dip a pint jar into the water and fill it. Can I fill that jar unto all the fullness of the Pacific Ocean? If I carry my jar to someone in Kansas who has never seen the ocean and tell him that I have it in my jar, he will look in vain to see what the ocean really is. All I can show him is a pint of seawater. There will be none of the mighty sweep of distance, the power of waves, the swelling of ocean surfaces, the wonders of its depths. I cannot put into a bottle the combing breakers or the vast reaches of the sea.

Such a sampling might be likened to the verse we are looking at if it were to be rendered merely that God proposes to fill us with His fullness. But if it were possible for me to put the whole of the ocean into the bottle, then we could understand what God plans to do with those whom He has redeemed. He does not intend to make us little samples of Deity. He does not look upon us as little beings to display pints of His power. The whole teaching of the Bible is that He plans to exalt us to the throne of the government of the universe with Himself, and to increase and enlarge our capacities forever and ever. "This is life eternal, that they might know thee" (John 17:3), and when we reach eternity, we shall discover that He is still expanding our capacity, still filling us with Himself, and that He will continue to do so forever.

We are to be filled unto all the fullness of God. And this infilling begins at the moment of salvation when He puts Himself within us, as a whole oak tree is in a tiny acorn. Even now the Lord God Almighty by His Holy Spirit dwells within a small portion of the population of this earth. That elect company, chosen in Christ before the foundation of the world, has become His temple. In this age He does not dwell in buildings but in the hearts of true believers. The Holy Spirit has been given, as our text says, and He dwells within us.

CHRISTIAN LIVING

The Lord is laying the groundwork in this part of the epistle for the great ethical teachings that come at the end. The only way to produce a Christian life is through the life of God as set forth in Christian doctrine and experience. Thus the first part of the epistle is doctrinal and the latter part is ethical. This is always God's method. In the twelfth chapter the great exhortation to Christian living is the doctrine here set forth, which makes such living possible. "I appeal to you therefore, brethren, by the mercies of God, to present your bodies as a living sacrifice, holy and acceptable to God, which is your spiritual worship" (Rom. 12:1).

Two great passages in the epistles to the Corinthians also draw conclusions from our text and serve to illustrate it. We read: "Do you not know that your bodies are members of Christ? Shall I therefore take the members of Christ and make them members of a prostitute? Never! Do you not know that your body is a temple of the Holy Spirit within you, which you have from God? You are not your own; so glorify God in your body" (1 Cor. 6:15, 19, 20).

And again, "Do not be mismated with unbelievers. For what partnership have righteousness and iniquity? Or what fellowship has light with darkness? What accord has Christ with Belial? Or what has a believer in common with an unbeliever? What agreement has the temple of God with idols? For we are the temple of the living God; as God said, 'I will live in them and move among them, and I will be their God, and they shall be my people. Therefore come out from them and be separate from them, says the Lord, and touch nothing unclean; then I will welcome you, and I will be a father to you, and you shall be my sons and daughters, says the Lord Almighty' " (2 Cor. 6:14-18).

Note that the entire appeal to holiness of living and separation from the world is based on the truth that the Holy Spirit has been given to us. God points out to His little flock of true believers that He has put a difference between them and the citizens of the world. In the passage in Second Corinthians, God contrasts believers to those who are not saved. His own are righteousness, light, Christ, believers, temples of God. The worldlings are unrighteousness, darkness, Satan, unbelievers, and idols. Because of this oppositeness of name and nature, the Lord commands believers to separate from unbelievers; there should be no joining of their lives, whether in marriage or any other union. Not only should there be no marriage between peoples of different religions, but also people who take communion in a church that is faithful to God should not be joined to those who take communion from the same table but who do not possess new life in Christ. The believer must see that all of his unions are with those of like precious faith. For those who are not saved, the believer can only bear witness in Christ, testify against them and their destiny, and invite them to come out of death into life.

The Holy Spirit has been given unto us. Thus all things become new in our lives. This does not mean that we are to wear some sort of uniform and behave differently from the world in outward life. It means that the Lord will be our life, that Christ will be formed within us, and that He will so direct and order our lives that all things will be made new, day by day and moment by moment. This presence of the Holy Spirit within us will not make us cantankerous and narrow, but will give us the wide vision of the sons of God, and so fill our lives with the love of God that people will take knowledge of us, as they did of the early disciples, that we have been with Jesus Christ and have learned from Him. Today, those who live around us cannot think of us as having lived with Jesus in the days when He walked in Galilee, but they can see that there is a great difference between our lives and theirs. And they should realize that it is the life of Christ growing within us, formed within us by the Holy Spirit, that makes the difference. It will not be merely a difference of participation in or abstinence from certain practices, but the inward presence of the positive life of the love of God within us.

A POSITIVE TESTIMONY

The following story will illustrate the fact that the outworking of the life of the Spirit does not result merely in abstention from worldly practices. In a certain city in the west, there is a woman who has become famous in Christian circles because of her testimony for Christ. She has transformed the life of a great church and has led dozens of young people into full-time Christian service. She dresses in style comparable to that of the most worldly people. In a nearby town was a godly shoemaker who, though making good money, lived on the slenderest budget in order to give to Christian work. One evening he attended a banquet where the lady was the speaker. He looked at her splendid coiffure, her lovely gown, her well-manicured and lacquered fingernails. Afterward, he asked her why she dressed as she did. Immediately she asked him why he was wearing a necktie. Taken aback, he stammered that it was the custom, and that if he did not wear a necktie people would think he was queer. She replied that she lived and moved among people who dressed as she did. If she did not dress somewhat as they did, she would be conspicuous, they would think her queer, and they would not listen to her presentation of the gospel. He nodded and turned away without further comment.

How important it is for Christians not to judge one another in such trivial things! Each of us must answer to God for the way we dress, walk, talk, act, live, think, and manifest the love of the Lord Jesus Christ to those around us who are dead in trespasses and sins. We must never set our own standards as divine, or binding on others.

The Holy Spirit has been given unto us. We must let Him control us and manifest Christ in us. God never made two blades of grass alike, two leaves alike, or two grains of sand alike. We may be sure also that He never made two Christians alike, and that He has His children in every sphere and walk of life, forming Christ in them so that all around may see His power.

WORKING OUT SALVATION

God has given us His Holy Spirit. This fact makes it possible for us to please Him, to walk in His ways, and to solve our daily problems. This truth also explains one of the most misquoted and misapplied passages in the Bible: "Therefore, my beloved, as you have always obeyed, so now, not only as in my presence but much more in my absence, work out your own salvation with fear and trembling" (Phil. 2:12). Some have foolishly thought this verse taught that people were to work for salvation, but such is not the teaching of Scripture. One of the elementary principles of Bible study is that no one verse may be used to contradict the teaching of other verses. You may be sure that you have not grasped the meaning of a verse if it seems to contradict any other verse in Scripture.

An understanding of the great scandal in the church at Philippi will explain the meaning of "work out your own salvation." Two women, Euodias and Syntyche, were not speaking to each other, and the rift between them was involving others within the church so that division threatened. The leaders of the church sent word to Paul who answered with a great call to Christian unity. In the course of his reply he used the word "salvation" three times, and in each case with a different meaning. First, he speaks of his own salvation in his court trial before Caesar. There is no question of salvation from sin or from Hell, or salvation for Heaven. Its meaning here has nothing to do with theological salvation. The second time he uses the word, he refers to the difference between believers in Christ and the unbelievers who were the cause of their persecution. The fact that the believers were hated in the world was proof that they were saved and the persecutors were lost. The third time, Paul uses the word with reference to the antagonism between the two women and says, in reality, "Work out your own solution to that problem with fear and trembling, because God is working in you both to will and to do of his own good pleasure; but do all things in the course of working out this solution, without murmuring and without disputing" (Phil. 2:12-14).

THE INDWELLING PRESENCE

The power by which the church can solve its problems is the indwelling presence of God, by the Holy Spirit who has been given to all believers. This is why we as believers do not need the Church to make our decisions or interpretations for us. The Church of Jesus Christ is not an authority but a recipient. Do not let anyone draw you aside by specious reasoning or by pointing to divisions. Those divisions are but indications that not all men have fully yielded to the indwelling life of the Holy Spirit. There are no divergences at all between true believers on the person and work of Christ. There is no Christian who does not agree that Jesus Christ is God, born without a human father, raised from the dead in the same body in which He died, ascended into Heaven, and sat on the throne of God the Father. If in the churches there are those who deny any of these truths, such are tares and not wheat. All who are born again have the Holy Spirit dwelling within them, and are in agreement upon the fundamentals of the Christian faith and life. And we are being called to a closer and closer unity day by day. This oneness to which we are being called is not organization but union within the organism of believers.

And the day will finally come when the whole body of believers from Abel, the first to die on this earth, down to the last man to die or be transformed by the Lord will gather with God in Heaven and associate with Him in the government of the universe forever. And because He chose us and gave us His Holy Spirit to dwell within us so that we might manifest Him here in the days of conflict, we shall be one with Him in that day, manifesting His glory forever.

CHAPTER XVIII

A Finished Work

And hope maketh not ashamed; because the love of God is shed abroad in our hearts by the Holy Spirit who is given unto us (Rom. 5:5).

THE Holy Spirit has been given to us. This is the key to all that follows.

Charles Wesley exults in this truth thus:

> Away with our fears,
> Our troubles and tears:
> The Spirit is come,
> The witness of Jesus returned to His home.
>
> The pledge of our Lord
> To His Heaven restored
> Is sent from the sky,
> And tells us our Head is exalted on high.
>
> Our Advocate there
> By His blood and His prayer
> The gift hath obtained,
> For us He hath prayed, and the Comforter gained.

Yes, the Holy Spirit has been given to that select company who have turned from confidence and trust in themselves to put their faith and hope in the Savior, the Lord Jesus Christ. While here on earth the Lord promised that he would ascend into Heaven, and would send the Holy Spirit to dwell within the hearts of His people. The Holy Spirit came, and we were born of the Spirit into the family of God; we were baptized of the Spirit into the body of Christ; our bodies became the temples of the Holy Spirit. All these works of the Holy Spirit simultaneously and instantaneously became ours when we were saved: We had been dead in trespasses and sins; we were quickened by the Holy Spirit. We had been identified with Adam and the world; we were identified by the Spirit as part of the body of Christ. Our bodies had been the temples of idols; they became the dwelling place of the Lord Jesus Christ by His Spirit.

Finally, we discover from the study of the Word of God that, at that same moment, we were sealed with the Holy Spirit. This doctrine is very important, for it is our guarantee that the promise of God was not temporary. Neither was it contingent on anything within ourselves, but it was all of grace, and, when the Holy Spirit came to us, He came once, for all, and forever.

THE INDWELLING SPIRIT

Some have thought that God would or could remove His Spirit after He had once made us alive. Such an idea is never found in the Scriptures. It is true that in the great Psalm of repentance erring King David cried out, "Cast me not away from thy presence, and take not thy Holy Spirit from me" (Ps. 51:11). It is very unfortunate that this verse has been included in the liturgy of the Church of England, for multitudes of people chant that prayer every Sunday, and believe that it is possible for God to take His Holy Spirit from those in this age who have believed in Him. David lived in the Old Testament dispensation. The presence of God was in the Holy of Holies in the tabernacle at Jerusalem. When David prayed, "Cast me not away from Thy presence," he was saying, "Do not exile me from Jerusalem." And when he prayed, "Take not thy Holy Spirit from me," he was praying that the special power which had been put upon him would not be removed.

To the twelve disciples the Lord Jesus Christ said of the Holy Spirit, "He dwells with you and will be in you" (John 14:17). The prepositions are most revealing. He dwelt *with* the men of the Old Testament but He dwells *within* the men of grace.

When the Holy Spirit comes upon an individual today, making him alive in Christ, dwelling in his body, and joining him to the living Christ, it is a complete work, a finished work. True, afterwards He fills with greater power those who are yielded to Him, and He can be grieved and withdraw that special filling from the believer. The disciples were identified with the Lord Jesus Christ on the day of Pentecost, and were filled with the Holy Spirit, and these same men were again filled with the Holy Spirit a few days later. The obvious inference is that in the interim they had lived in such a manner as to be partly filled with themselves, and it became necessary for the Lord to fill them again with Himself. In Acts 2:4, "They were all filled with the Holy Spirit"; after the first warnings of the Sanhedrin against preaching in the name of Jesus, the disciples met and prayed; and we read that "when they had prayed, the place was shaken where they were assembled together; and they were all filled with the Holy Spirit" (Acts 4:31).

POWER FOR SERVICE

The difference between the simultaneous quickening, indwelling, and permanent placement in Christ on the one hand, and the continuous and repeated fillings of the Spirit must be understood if we are to be kept from fear of the loss of salvation, and if we are to be empowered day by day for Christian life and service.

Wesley understood well the difference between the permanent work of the Spirit and the filling of the Spirit. Some of his followers have twisted his words beyond all recognition and made them mean something which the Bible certainly never teaches and which Wesley never taught. Here are lines from Wesley's hymns which show that he knew the Holy Spirit had already come to dwell permanently within the believer, and that it was impossible for the believer to be abandoned by the Spirit.

> God, the everlasting God,
> Makes with mortals His abode . . .
>
> Never will He thence depart,
> Inmate of a humble heart . . .

And again:

> The Holy Ghost, if I depart,
>   The Comforter shall surely come,
> Shall make the contrite sinner's heart
>   His loved, His everlasting home.

In some of his other hymns, Wesley cried out for the coming of the Holy Spirit in power, but both truths are biblical, and one does not deny the other. Later in the epistle to the Romans, God states that His gifts and callings are without repentance (11:29). This means that God is not an Indian giver—giving and taking back again. Salvation does not depend upon the whim of an individual Christian but upon the justifying work of God. The Holy Spirit is implanted once and for all; and when we are placed in Christ by the Holy Spirit, the blessed third person of the Godhead puts the seal of certainty upon us and shuts us into Christ. We are not only saved but safe.

SEALED

In modern times the use of the seal has diminished until now only official documents are marked with a seal. If you get a United States passport to travel, the seal of the nation is crushed into the fabric of the paper so that it is impossible to eradicate or alter it. Corporations' seals are affixed to legal documents. A notary confirms the oath of an affidavit with his seal. In ancient times, however, each man carried his own seal with him at all times. Since most people could not write, the seal was affixed as the mark of the individual's responsibility. Today the signature takes the place of the seal. Add together everything that is confirmed by an official seal and a personal signature, and you get the idea of the biblical significance of the seal. Then, turn to the epistle to the Ephesians and read the great fact bound up with exhortation to holy living: "Do not grieve the Holy Spirit of God, in whom you were sealed for the day of redemption" (Eph. 4:30).

This is one of the most comforting and strengthening truths in the Word of God. The Holy Spirit has done so much in saving us that we should live in gratitude. Likewise, the love of Christ deserves our gratitude: "Hereby perceive we the love of God, because he laid down his life for us" (1 John 3:16). "Herein is love, not that we loved God, but that he loved us, and sent his Son to be the propitiation for our sins" (1 John 4:10). And, "We love him, because he first loved us" (1 John 4:19). When we comprehend that our redemption began in the heart of God, and that the Lord Jesus Christ performed the work of satisfaction for our sins because His name and nature are love, we are moved to love Him and live for Him. "The love of Christ constraineth us; because we thus judge, that if one died for all, then were all dead; and that he died for all, that they which live should not henceforth live unto themselves, but unto him who died for them, and rose again" (2 Cor. 5:14, 15).

This constraining love must draw us to live so as not to grieve the Holy Spirit, who has sealed us for the day of redemption. Learn this well: we are not only saved, we are also safe. Christ paid the price of our sins, and the Holy Spirit maintains us in our sure position as children of God: brought out of darkness, placed in the light of eternal life, and sealed; that is, shut in, so that we can never get out. Such love demands our love and yieldedness.

Some Christians (and we do not doubt their sincerity) are almost incurably addicted to the doctrine that salvation is by something that we do ourselves. We who follow the Word of God believe that any teaching or system that places the emphasis on what man does for God is false. The truth is that God has done everything for us; we are the recipients of pure grace and should live lives of love in return for the grace that has been given to us. Perhaps those people who tremble, even while standing on the rock Christ Jesus, would read our text: "Grieve not the Holy Spirit wherewith ye are sealed until the day when you break the seal and take yourself out of the love of God." Such an idea is alien to the whole revelation of God. God never started anything that He does not intend to finish. "He that hath begun a good work in you will keep on perfecting it until the day of Jesus Christ" (Phil. 1:6). "The path of the justified ones is as a shining light that shineth more and more unto the perfect day" (Prov. 4:18).

The presence of the Holy Spirit within the believer is the seal and guarantee of security. While a shipment is in transit, men use a seal as a mark of protection against tampering. The government places a seal upon a package to safeguard it until customs officers have inspected it. God has placed the Holy Spirit upon us as the seal of our safety until the day of redemption. This great act is prefigured in the Old Testament. When God planned to destroy the world with the flood, He determined to save Noah and his family within the ark. We read that God appeared to Noah under His name of God the Creator, and told him to take two animals of every kind into the ark for the preservation of the species. Then God appeared unto Noah under His name Jehovah, the Redeemer, and told him to take seven of each of the clean animals to use as blood sacrifice for sin. Then follows this beautiful verse: "And they that went in, went in male and female of all flesh, as *God* had commanded him: and *Jehovah* shut him in" (Gen. 7:16). Thus, when we entered into Christ, the Creator wrought within us the new

birth; when we were safe in Christ, the Redeemer shut us into Christ
by placing upon us the seal of the Holy Spirit. Thus we are saved
and safe.

THE DOWN PAYMENT

Yet other verses in the epistle to the Ephesians explain how
God has given us the Holy Spirit as the seal. "In him you also, who
have heard the word of truth, the gospel of your salvation, and have
believed in him, were sealed with the promised Holy Spirit, which
is the guarantee of our inheritance until we acquire possession of
it, to the praise of his glory" (Eph. 1:13, 14).

Sometimes it is difficult to understand certain passages in the
Bible, perhaps because we have heard them so often that they slip
through our minds without making an impression. In other cases,
people are unacquainted with the Bible and so do not understand
some of the theological teaching or the archaic form of the old
English words. After World War I, I was living in Brussels, Belgium,
in a home in the *Quartier Louise*. Each day I spent four times
twenty minutes on the street-car, going to and from my office. The
idea occurred to me to get a room close by my office where there
were nice residential streets, and modern houses which displayed
signs of rooms for rent. One day I rang the bell at a house that exhibited such a sign. The room was just what I wanted. The size,
location, and price were right. In French, I told the landlady that
I would take the room and asked if I might move in in about ten
days since my rent was paid that far ahead in the house where I
was then living. She consented and then hesitantly asked me a question, using a word that I did not understand. She said, *"Est-ce que
Monsieur voudrait verser des arrhes?"* I repeated the line question-
ingly, *"Verser des arrhes?"* She replied to the effect that she was sure
that I was honest and that I intended to return in ten days, but if she
took the sign out of the window and I did not return, she would
lose ten days' advertising. But if I would be willing to pay something
down on account. . . . I understood, and gave her enough francs
to satisfy her. I went back to my office and said to one of my fellow
workers, "What does it mean . . . *verser des arrhes?*" He replied, "It
is in the first chapter of Ephesians." I looked it up and discovered
that God tells us that when He saved us He gave us the Holy Spirit,
sealing us into Christ by Him, as the earnest, the pledge, the down

payment of our inheritance. Phillips paraphrases it, "And after you gave your confidence to Him you were, so to speak, stamped with the promised Holy Spirit as a guarantee of purchase, until the day when God completes the redemption of what He has paid for as His own, and that will again be to the praise of His glory."

THE FOUNDATION OF GOD

Thus, the Holy Spirit has been given to us as the seal which locks us in Christ eternally; He is the pledge or guarantee of complete and final salvation. All of this, however, speaks of the work, as it affects us. Another verse speaks of this truth in relation to God. We read, "The foundation of God standeth sure, having this seal, The Lord knoweth them that are his. And, Let every one that nameth the name of Christ depart from iniquity" (2 Tim. 2:19). Here is an amazing thought. We can understand what is meant by the foundation of a building, and we can understand that money from a trust can become the foundation on which works of charity are established, but how shall we comprehend the foundation of God? It clearly means that if you do away with the certainty of salvation, you do away with the very nature of God. From the point of view of the biblical revelation which God has made concerning Himself, it is impossible to think of God apart from the security of the believer. For the believer is a child of God by the work of God the Holy Spirit, who has placed him in Christ and who dwells in the believer. Therefore, if it were possible for a believer to get out of Christ, the Holy Spirit would have done a slipshod work. God would have started something that He could not finish. Salvation would be a matter of chance. He has bound all the redeemed to Himself and has put upon them the brand of His ownership, the pledge of their future redemption.

CHAPTER XIX

Love Poured Out

And hope maketh not ashamed; because the love of God is shed abroad in our hearts by the Holy Spirit who is given unto us (Rom. 5:5).

WE NOW go back one clause in our text, and note that the Holy Spirit has poured into our hearts the love of God. In Galatians we read of the ninefold fruit of the Spirit, and the first named is love. All other fruit comes from this. Paul seemingly makes an error of grammar, but we shall see that it reveals further wonders. "The fruit of the Spirit is love, joy, peace, longsuffering, gentleness, goodness, faith, meekness, self-control" (Gal. 5:22). But should he not have said, "The fruits of the Spirit are. . . .?" Certainly it would not be proper to say, "The fruit of California is apples, oranges, figs, dates, prunes, *etc.*" But God is teaching us that the fruit which He grows in our lives comes in a cluster like grapes.

Of the first fruit, which is love, Maclaren has written, "After all is said and done, the love of God, eternal, self-originated, the source of all Christian experiences because of the work of Christ which originates them all, is the root fact of the universe and the guarantee that our highest anticipations and desires are not unsubstantial visions," but they are realities seen with the eye of faith and sure of accomplishment because they are from God. God is love; therefore the man who trusts Him will not be disappointed.

BALANCE

Some of my readers may become a little impatient at the emphasis which I am about to place upon the importance of Christian living. But there is great need for a change of emphasis in Christian teaching, as the following anecdote will illustrate. After the first world war I ministered in several country parishes in the mountains of southeastern France while attending the university at Grenoble. Many peasants carried their burdens in a sack with pockets at both ends, called a *besace*, that was thrown over the shoulder. If divided evenly, the load was quite easy to carry. One day I saw a small boy carrying a *besace* that had too much weight in the rear pocket. He tried to shift it, but it dragged him backward. Finally, his grandmother shouted at him in the provincial dialect, "Have you no sense, you galoot? Will you let your burden choke you by not dividing it?" And this is happening to Christians today.

There are two parts to Christian teaching. There is the message of evangelism: what Christ has done by dying for us on the cross; and there is the message of the work of the Holy Spirit in daily life. Many churches offer little more than the message of evangelism; it is all well and good to talk about the glory of the cross, and to set forth the wonder of how Christ took our place and died in our stead. But all this was for a present purpose, and that purpose is the life of Christ within us. To this end Paul wrote, "My little children, of whom I travail in birth again until Christ be formed in you" (Gal. 4:19); and again, "Would to God you could bear with me a little in my folly; and indeed bear with me. For I am jealous over you with a godly jealousy; for I have espoused you to one husband, that I may present you as a chaste virgin to Christ" (2 Cor. 11:1, 2). We must shift the weight in our *besace* and put proper emphasis on Christian living. Otherwise, preaching only salvation will throw the believer off balance and his Christian life will be distorted.

A NEW LIFE

Maclaren well says, "The fact that so many of us seem to imagine that the whole Gospel lies in this, that 'He died for our sins according to the Scriptures,' and have relegated the teaching that He, by His Spirit, lives in us, if we are His disciples, to a less prominent place, has done enormous harm, not only to the type of Christian life, but also to the conception of what Christianity is, both amongst those who receive it, and amongst those who do not accept it, making it out to be nothing more than a means of escape from the consequences of our transgression, instead of recognizing it for what it is, the impartation of a new life which will flower into all beauty, and bear fruit in all goodness."

Let us understand, then, that God reached down and redeemed us from the dung heap of this earth for the purpose of forming Christ within us and has left us in the midst of this world to reveal the power and life of Christ. The Lord Jesus ascended into

Heaven, but at Pentecost He sent the Holy Spirit, not only that millions of believers might be saved out of this present evil world but also that they might live in it as lights, holding forth the Word of life.

Many people make the mistake of believing the old hymn, "The Light of the World is Jesus," but those who know their Bibles know that the Lord Jesus is not the light of the world in this present age. He said, "As long as I am in the world I am the light of the world" (John 9:5). But the day came when the Lord Jesus Christ ascended to Heaven: it was as though the sun had gone down, and gross darkness settled over the earth once more. But one glimmer of light was left. It was the first pale sliver of the new moon, the true Church. It was intended to grow and glow and reflect the light of the absent sun. The world lies in darkness when the sun has set, but by looking up at the moon, we can tell that the sun is still shining. Thus the Lord Jesus meant the true body of His followers to be on this earth. Although He knew that as soon as He departed from the earth darkness would set in, and that this darkness would continue, He said to those who believed in Him, "Ye are the light of the world. A city that is set on a hill cannot be hid" (Mt. 5:14). Is it any wonder that the world is in darkness today when the Church seeks to glow in her own light instead of reflecting her absent Lord?

CHRISTIAN EXPERIENCE

At this stage we are brought face to face with our own Christian experience; if we are yielded to the touch of the Holy Spirit, He will press the point to the center of our conviction and the throttle of our wills. Is the love of God for us suffusing our hearts, filling our beings, and flooding every part of our lives? For, make no mistake about it, the apostle speaks here as though this flooding presence of the Holy Spirit, pouring the love of God into our hearts and bringing us to supreme confidence in Christ and to absolute certainty of our salvation, is the present condition of every one who has trusted in Christ. This should cause many Christians to rush to the Word of God to see what their resources are, and to bare their hearts before the power of the Holy Spirit that He may flush out debris that has clogged the channels of living, and bring the smooth flow of love to its highest level.

In many parts of our country agriculture is carried on by irrigation since ordinary rainfall does not suffice, or is seasonal. It is of the highest importance that the channels be kept open or the land will revert to its arid condition and the crops will fail. Thus it is in the hearts of believers. Indeed, the traveler knows well that great valleys once famed for teeming populations drew their life from the rich soil; but today these, like the valleys of the Euphrates and Tigris, are half desert and half arable. The archaeologist has traced systems of canals that in ancient times carried water to far fields. But the dams were allowed to fall into disrepair; the channels filled with silt; and the breaking down of the flooding system brought dryness and death. How many Christians confess that this is their experience in spiritual things!

Maclaren, who is at his best when expounding passages on the flowing love of God, writes: "Here again the apostle takes for granted that in every Christian heart there is, by a divine operation, the presence of the love, and of the consciousness of the love, of God. . . . This is the ideal of a Christian life; it is meant that it should be so, and should be so continuously. The stream that is poured out is intended to run summer and winter, not to be dried up in drought, nor made turbid and noisy in flood, but with equable flow throughout. I fear that the experience of most good people is rather like one of those tropical wadies . . . in Eastern lands [he might have said in Southern California] where there are alternate times of spate and times of drought; and instead of a flashing stream, pouring life everywhere, and full to the top of its banks, there are for long periods dismal stretches of white sun-baked stones and a chaos of tumbled rocks with not a drop of water in the channel. The Spirit pours God's love into men's spirits, but there may be dams and barriers, so that no drop of water comes into the empty heart."

THE WESLEYS' HYMNS

In the light of this, I believe we can understand the hearts of John and Charles Wesley. They were objects of the flow of the river of God's love in their hearts, and lived in that all-mastering love. Then something happened which lessened the flow, and they rushed back to God, crying out in agony for the flood to flow again. Some of their most poignant hymns are cries to God for the return of the full flow of the Spirit of love. In the light of the Word of God we must agree that they were quite right when they said that the Holy Spirit had already made them alive, and had taken up His abode within them never to depart; and that they were resting in Him. They were sure that He was there. But, because He was not at full flood, they cried out for that fullness. Some dryness had come into their souls, and they were gasping like fish out of water, as Christians should, until all was right again and the Holy Spirit was flooding their souls. Thus Charles Wesley wrote:

> I want the Spirit of power within,
>   Of love, and of a healthful mind:
> A power to conquer inbred sin;
>   Of love, to Thee and all mankind:
> Of health, that pain and death defies,
>   Most vigorous when the body dies.
>
> When shall I hear the inward voice
>   Which only faithful souls can hear!
> Pardon, and peace, and Heavenly joys
>   Attend the promised Comforter:
> O come! and righteousness divine,
>   And Christ, and all with Christ, are mine.
>
> O that the Comforter would come!
>   Nor visit as a transient guest,
> But fix in me His constant home,
>   And take possession of my breast.
> And fix in me His loved abode,
>   The temple of indwelling God.
>
> Come Holy Ghost, my heart inspire!
>   Attest that I am born again;
> Come, and baptize me now with fire,
>   Nor let Thy former gifts be vain;
> I cannot rest in sins forgiven;
>   Where is the earnest of my Heaven?
>
> Where the indubitable seal
>   That ascertains the kingdom mine?
> The powerful stamp I long to feel,
>   The signature of love divine:
> O shed it in my heart abroad,
>   Fullness of love, of Heaven, of God.

It is evident from a close study of that hymn that the Wesleys knew that the Holy Spirit *has been* given to believers. Charles

Wesley was born again, and he knew it; but in the fourth stanza he cried out for the attestation of the fact. The crux of what he was saying is the third line of the last stanza: "The powerful stamp I long to feel." The true Christian should long to feel this powerful stamp of the presence of God, impressing his soul with the love of Christ.

PRACTICAL POSSESSION

All my life I have heard preachers tell audiences that salvation depends not on feeling but on faith. Theologically that is true, but practically we desire feeling as evidence of the presence of God. It would not be enough for the executor of an estate to tell me that someone had left me a fortune. I would immediately ask, "When can I begin to spend it?" If he should argue that the proof of possession was not in spending the money but faith in the bankers' word that the account was mine, it would still not satisfy me. A fortune is worth nothing if the heir does not actually possess it.

Likewise, it is all right to know that I am saved and that nothing can separate me from the love of God. But I want more than that, and God wants me to have more than that. The Bible shows me everywhere that God the Father is more eager for me to enter into full possession of my resources in Christ than I am to possess them. True, my salvation depends one hundred per cent upon the work of God, and I am to accept it by faith and believe His promise. But I want to experience possession. The man who inherits the fortune wants to spend it. The man who has built a new house wants to live in it. The one who has bought a new automobile wants to drive it. The girl who has a new dress wants to wear it. The scholar who has received a new book wants to read it. The child who has been given a new toy wants to play with it. The hungry man who has been invited to dinner wants to sit down and eat. And just as all of these hungers and thirsts need fulfillment, so the true child of God must hunger and thirst after righteousness.

HUNGER AND THIRST

This may seem a paradox, for it might be maintained that one who has found Christ is fully satisfied and therefore can never hunger or thirst again. The late Arthur Pink of Australia wrote, on our Savior's precious words in the Beatitudes: "'Blessed are the pure in heart, Blessed are they that hunger and thirst after righteousness.' Like the previous ones, this fourth Beatitude describes a dual experience: an initial and a continuous, that which begins in the unconverted, but is perpetuated in the saved sinner. There is a repeated exercise of this grace, felt at varying intervals. The one who longed to be saved by Christ now yearns to be made like Him. Looked at in its widest aspect, this hungering and thirsting refers to that panting of the renewed heart after God (Ps. 42:1), that yearning for a closer walk with Him, that longing for a more perfect conformity to the image of His Son. It tells of those aspirations of the new nature for divine blessings which alone can strengthen, sustain, and satisfy it. Our text presents such a paradox that it is evident that no carnal mind ever invented it. Can one, who has been brought into vital union with Him who is the Bread of life and in whom all fullness dwells, be found still hungering and thirsting? Yes, such is the experience of the renewed heart. Mark carefully the tense of the verb: it is not 'Blessed are they which have hungered,' but 'Blessed are they which do hunger and thirst.' This has ever been the experience of God's saints."

Although the unsaved man never seeks God, as we saw in the third chapter of Romans, God constantly calls the redeemed to seek Him to experience the deepening processes of the Christian life, and enjoy the provision which God has made for His children. He wants us to know that the Holy Spirit is constantly pouring the love of God into our hearts. Therefore, in seeking to avoid the false doctrine of a second work of grace for "it," instead of for Christ—we must take care not to miss the truth that we need to move toward God. Let us not fail to get the third, the hundredth, and the thousandth blessing because we are afraid of a false theological teaching.

When we are saved, the resources of God are bestowed upon us. We lay hold upon them in the first, fresh moments of salvation with great joy. Then we turn our eyes away from Christ, and our joy ebbs. This happened to the Wesleys, and happens to all of us. But the Wesleys were in almost a frenzy of desire when their joy was down even slightly. And well they should have been. It is, of course, impossible for a Christian to spend his life crying out to God: "Fill me, fill me, fill me, fill me!" For there is work to be done, a life to be lived, and a time of sleep, the awakening from which will be under the control of stray thoughts. If we do not constantly rush back to the Lord to plunge into the flooding love that He pours into our hearts, we shall grow cold and callous. It happens in every Christian life. It happens in the best and most powerful Christian lives for periods of a few moments or hours. It happens in multitudes of good and oft-used Christians for days at a time. Alas, in some Christians for months or even years life is parched and empty because they have not sought to be filled and suffused with the outpoured love of God.

If you will bow before the Lord in this moment, He will break down the barriers. Say to Him, "Lord, cleanse me from every sin; remove every barrier to the flooding of Thy love. May the Spirit who dwells within me rule and overrule in all things. Come as a rushing mighty wind. Come as a flood. Come as a fire. Come as Thou wilt, O Lord, but come . . . come . . . come!"

CHAPTER XX

Anchored within the Veil

And hope maketh not ashamed; because the love of God is shed abroad in our hearts by the Holy Spirit who is given unto us (Rom. 5:5).

ONE of the most important by-products of the work of the Holy Spirit is full assurance of faith, in a hope that never disappoints us. Reversing the order of this verse, the truth is seen as follows: The Holy Spirit has been given unto us, and with Him the love of God keeps on pouring into our hearts, and so we have a hope that will never be deceived.

Let us look at several other versions of the phrase, "Hope maketh not ashamed." The Revised Version has it, "Hope putteth not to shame." The Roman Catholic Confraternity says, "Hope does not disappoint." Segond renders it, "Hope does not deceive." Phillips' paraphrase speaks of "A steady hope that will never disappoint us."

HOPE FREQUENTLY DISAPPOINTS

First of all, let us face the fact that, at least at times, most things in life have a sour taste. The great hymn, "In the Cross of Christ I Glory," speaks of being overtaken by the woes of life, of being deceived by hopes, and annoyed by fears. Now, the opposite of hope is despair. This word is very interesting to a philologist, because it comes from the French *désespoir*, which is the word *espoir, hope,* with the negative prefix. So etymologically the word "despair" means no hope. It is the exact synonym of hopelessness. Shakespeare wrote of it as "grim and comfortless despair." Bunyan told of the "castle called Doubting Castle, the owner whereof was Giant Despair."

Whether or not events in life move from hope to hopelessness, there can be no doubt that hope frequently disappoints the one who has rested in hope. In Proverbs we are told, "Hope deferred maketh the heart sick" (13:12). Cicero coined the phrase that has become proverbial, "While there's life there's hope"; but Thomas Shadwell said, "Hope is a very thin diet."

The marvel of the Christian faith is that its hope is entirely different from the hopes that arise from man's doings and promises. Dryden looked upon all life as nothing more than disappointment to the hopes to which men cling, and wrote:

> When I consider life, 'tis all a cheat,
> Yet, fooled with hope, men favor the deceit;
> Trust on, and think tomorrow will repay.
> Tomorrow's falser than the former day;
> Lies worst, and while it says we shall be blest
> With some new joys, cuts off what we possessed.

HOPE AND FEAR INSEPARABLE

It is evident that these sorrowful and cynical statements describe only the evanescent hopes of men in their dealings one with another and with life. The point of our text is that the hope which comes from the love of God, which keeps on pouring into our hearts by the presence of the Holy Spirit whom God has given to all believers, is totally different from human hopes. François de la Rochefoucauld, a French man of letters who had deep insight into many moral problems, wrote in *Maxims*, "Hope and fear are inseparable." Let us examine this statement; it will furnish the background for the contrast between hope that ends in despair, and the hope that is never disappointed, that cannot bring confusion, and that has no fear.

The first hopes of life come to us as children. But we soon learn that we do not get everything we want, and that the things we do get do not bring the joy that we thought they would. In school days, we hope to get high marks in examinations but we fear that we will not. We hope to make the football team and fear that we will not. If we do become champions, we soon are disappointed in other fields. A young man gets the job he wants but someone else gets the girl he wanted to marry, or it is the other way around. A girl is asked in marriage and consents, but she knows she must take him for worse as well as for better. She sees the disappointments of many of her friends, and many marriages ending in tragedy. She sees the husband of a friend or relative change from a seemingly strong character to become the victim of an evil habit, of liquor or lust or some other fungus of the heart. Her hopes always have a slight tremor, and her smile will have one or two tears. This is life. Worldly hope and fear are inseparable.

The young couple look down, smiling and tearful, upon their first child. They have great hopes for the child, but with the hopes are fears. Will he live? Will he be strong in body? Will his mind be bright? Will he get into trouble and bring them heartache? The child is a bundle of hopes and fears. Hope and fear are inseparable.

And thus it is through all life down to the last sickness and death. Business life, social life, personal life; the life of the body, the mind, and the spirit; every aspect of life presents a combination of hopes and fears. This is true not only for everyone who is not a Christian but it is also true for the Christian in all phases of his life that are not centered in God. For the believer, all phases of life should be bound up in God. But on the practical level, Christians need fuller assurance. And so God weans us day by day from confidence in the things of earth to confidence in those invisible things which cannot deceive and never disappoint.

CHRISTIAN HOPE

The Christian's hope has not the slightest admixture of fear because it rests on the nature and character of the one Being in the universe who cannot deceive those who put their trust in Him.

First, because our God is eternal, our hopes cannot put us to shame or disappoint us. You might have a financial problem and work it out with a banker so that everything will come out right; but the day before you are to get your money, the banker drops dead, or is taken with a lingering sickness. Your hopes are disappointed and you cannot arrange with anyone else for the loan. On the other hand, if you have a problem with God, such factors will never enter for God is eternal and He cannot become ill. An interesting illustration of this attitude toward the unchangeable God is in the Hebrew text of the Book of Habakkuk. In the first chapter of that prophecy the writer discusses the problem of evil and asks God how it is possible for a man to live in a world of iniquity. God answers by telling him to look away to the cross of Christ. But a second question arises: How can God look upon sin? The King James Version translates it as follows: "Art thou not from everlasting, O Lord my God, mine Holy One? we shall not die" (Hab.

1:12). The Hebrew is quite different. Evidently the translators were afraid of what they saw, and, by trying to "correct it," they spoiled it. For the Hebrew reads: "Art thou not from everlasting, O Lord, my God, mine Holy One? *Thou* shalt not die." Since God cannot die, the translators rendered it "We shall not die." But it is actually "Thou shalt not die." In other words, Thou art the eternal God. We need not fear what may come to pass in this wicked world because we are joined to Thee. Whatever comes, it has been conceived in His eternal mind and permitted for His eternal purposes. Therefore, when we are joined to God, our hopes are eternal and cannot be disappointed. Our trust in Him will never be confounded. He is the eternal God. And it is written, "The eternal God is thy refuge, and underneath are the everlasting arms" (Deut. 33:27).

GOD UNCHANGEABLE

Again, we may note that because our God is unchangeable our hopes cannot put us to shame or disappoint us. In earthly affairs hearts are broken because of the fickleness or changeableness of someone in whom confidence and love have been placed. Early in my ministry I learned of a young woman who was slowly dying. She had been in robust health and joyous spirits, preparing to be married. Her trousseau was ready and the wedding invitations had been mailed. Then, one night, her fiancé eloped with another girl. The jilted girl slowly pined away; her health and life were ruined, and she went to a premature grave. She had had hopes, but they deceived and disappointed her. It can never be so with our God, because the hopes which we have in and from Him are unchangeable. God is not a man that He should lie. He is the unchangeable God. There is no variableness in our God, neither shadow cast by turning (Jas. 1:17). When God wished to attest a thing was true, He swore by Himself because He could swear by none greater. And so by two immutable, unchangeable things in which it was impossible for God to lie, He confirmed the truth to us who have fled for refuge to lay hold upon the hope that is set before us (Heb. 6:18).

This passage of Scripture in Hebrews 6 inspired one of our greatest hymns.

My hope is built on nothing less
   Than Jesus' blood and righteousness;
I dare not trust the sweetest frame,
   But wholly lean on Jesus' name.

On Christ, the solid rock, I stand;
All other ground is sinking sand.

When darkness veils His lovely face,
   I rest on His unchanging grace.
In every high and stormy gale
   My anchor holds within the veil.

His oath, His covenant, His blood,
   Support me in the whelming flood;
When all around my soul gives way
   He then is all my hope and stay.

WITHIN THE VEIL

The poet says, "My anchor holds within the veil." The text in Romans states: "Hope does not disappoint us." Hebrews says that we are to have "strong encouragement, who have fled for refuge to lay hold on the hope set before us; which we have as an anchor of the soul, a hope both sure and steadfast and entering into that which is within the veil; whither as a forerunner Jesus entered for us, having become a high priest forever after the order of Melchizedek" (Heb. 6:18-20).

This picture of a high priest entering within the veil takes us back to the Jewish tabernacle. Out under the sky was the altar where the lambs were killed. A few feet toward the north was a laver, filled with water, where the priests washed their feet, after offering the blood sacrifice for sin. Beyond this was the first curtain of the tabernacle, and beyond that curtain were the table of showbread, the seven-pronged candlestick, and the altar of incense. Finally there was the second curtain or veil, which was torn in two when our Lord Jesus Christ died on the cross.

This veil was never passed except on the day of atonement, and only after the high priest had offered two sacrifices—one for his own sins and one for the sins of the people. Within the veil was the ark of the covenant, a box made of wood and overlaid with gold. Within the box were the original tables of stone on which God wrote the law. He replaced the first set of tables which Moses broke. Above this box was the pillar of cloud by day and the pillar of fire by night. Between the law transgressed by man, and the cloud of God's holiness and justice, lay the lid of the box also made of wood overlaid with gold and ornamented with two statues of cherubim, the highest order of angels, with their wings stretching out to overshadow the cover of the box. Here, between the wings of the cherubim from one side to the other, and between the law below and the glory above, the high priest placed the blood of the sacrifice.

ANCHORED

How does our anchorage fit into this picture? We must consider the image which God has given us: a boat outside the tabernacle area. The Lord took the anchor and, dragging the chain after Him, went in to anchor us securely that we might not only be saved but safe. He passed the first altar, representing His death on the cross. Surely this is a good place to anchor our hopes so that we shall not be disappointed, deceived or ashamed? But no! There is more than the Savior's atonement, wonderful as that is; for when the Lord Jesus died He rose from the dead and ascended into Heaven. He walked on to the laver where the priests received their cleansing. Surely this would be a good place for Him to cast the anchor? Would we not be safe and secure if we knew we were cleansed from the penalty and power of sin? But it is not enough. On He went into the holy place where we see the table of shew-bread. Surely if we feed upon Christ, saved, safe, and satisfied, this will be enough? But no! He passed the seven-branched candelabra, where He shed the light of His illumination upon us. If we are flooded with His light, have we not all we need? But no! Still drawing the anchor of our hopes with Him, He reached the altar of incense where we worship the true and living God in Spirit and in truth. If His Spirit and truth are within us and we are brought to true worship, have we not reached the reason for our salvation? But no! Coming to the second veil He tore it aside to expose the throne and heart of God to our gaze. This was the veil of His very flesh, and He opened the way for us at the price of His own sacrifice for sin. Here is revealed the glory of God, overshadowing the holiness of God and revealing the love of God. Here He brought His anchor, and cast it securely into that which is within the veil, and there our anchor holds.

FULL ACCEPTANCE

He has brought with Him to this place all that He did in dying upon the cross. The Lord God takes it and holds it close to Himself. Not only has the Savior died, but the Heavenly Father has also accepted His death as the full payment for our sins. This is the whole point of the story. Our salvation does not depend merely upon the death of the Savior, but upon the Father's acceptance of that death. This is why our hopes cannot be disappointed and need never be ashamed. Our God is eternal and unchangeable. Our God has accepted the payment of Christ in full for our sins, and henceforth not even God Himself can demand payment from a Christian. It would be impossible for God to condemn me in any way, or you either, if you have believed in Jesus Christ. It would be impossible for God to send me to any place of suffering for my sins. It would be impossible for God to put any punishment upon me. He has accepted the death of Christ as payment in full.

The most important thing which can be said about the death of Jesus Christ is that God is satisfied with the payment.

CHAPTER XXI

Christ Died for the Ungodly

For when we were yet without strength, in due time Christ died for the ungodly (Rom. 5:6).

I RECOGNIZE clearly that salvation does not depend upon feeling, but I recognize just as clearly that it is impossible to be born again without feeling it in every part of our being. A man who has been wounded in battle is brought unconscious into a hospital. The surgeon pours blood plasma into his veins and, little by little, consciousness returns. His eyelids flutter, he begins to comprehend the sounds that are around him, his mind awakens as his eyes open, and he takes in his surroundings. Even in his great weakness he knows he is alive. Thus the divine love is diffused throughout the being of each child of God, after he has been quickened by the new birth.

THE LOVE OF GOD

But there is something more. The love that is felt and known within is a pure stream which has its source in God Himself. Believing, as we do, in the verbal inspiration of the Scriptures, we must look with great care at every syllable of Romans 5:6. Such examination will pay rich dividends.

The first word, "for," is a conjunction, introducing the basis for what has gone before. Let us go back to our illustration of the wounded man. In battle he is suddenly wounded. He drags himself to a sheltered spot and awaits help. He becomes unconscious, and the next thing he knows is the warm feeling of returning life. Plasma is flowing into his veins and life is pulsing within him. "How did all this come about?" he asks. We answer thus: "For someone in America donated blood for you." "For" explains the fact that the flowing warmth of life has its source in an act that was done far away, and long before the transfusion. Thus, in our text, we have a strong hope that can never deceive us because of the inward flowing of the love of God from the outward historical fact of the death of Jesus Christ for us.

Thus the love of God is something that acts within us and comes to us through a historical fact. But, we ask, why did God send His Son to die for us? The answer, once more, is that God is love. But someone may ask further, why did God love us? There is no answer to that question. If you seek to look beyond God, you are foolish, for beyond Him there is nothing.

THE ETERNAL GOD

The child sometimes asks, "Mother, who made God?" The wise mother answers, "My child, no one made God. God is. God always has been. God always will be. He is what we call eternal." Thus it is with the love of God. The love of God is God. You cannot explain the infinite. If you seek to reduce it to the level of human understanding, you will fail. You cannot explain the sun by a candle, the ocean by a drop of sea water, the stars by a handful of sand, a bird by a feather, a forest by a leaf, or sorrow by one tear. You cannot even explain human love by the gesture of a father when he catches his child to his heart. If you cannot explain these visible things or these human emotions, how will you explain things which are invisible and emotions which are divine? The answer is, you cannot.

A friend of mine once sought to describe the rainbow to a person born blind. She described the colors from red to violet, and likened them to the notes of the musical scale. She took the blind person to the underside of a stone bridge and let her feel the curve of that great arch and explained the magnitude of the arch of the rainbow. Then, she asked her friend whether she now understood this wondrous beauty. With great hesitancy the blind woman answered, "Well, I think that . . . it is something . . . heavy . . . ?"

GOD'S LOVE REVEALED

And thus it will be if I attempt to explain to you the source of the love of God. The love of God is God. His name is love, His nature is love. He is love. You may put all of the throbs of the human heart into one great throb, and you have not touched the fringe of the love of God. But how is the love of God revealed? First, we read that Christ died for us who were "yet without strength," and "ungodly." Then in verse eight we note that His intervention took place "while we were yet sinners." Let us look more closely at these details for they form the background for the display of the love of God the Father and the Son.

Christ died for us when we were "yet without strength." The American Standard and Confraternity translations both render the passage to show that this dying love of God was manifested for us when we were yet "weak." The Revised Standard Version, Williams, and Goodspeed all state that this death of Christ came to pass when we were "helpless." Phillips renders it "powerless." The lexicons illumine the meaning of the original word. "Weak, infirm, feeble," says Thayer, "unable to achieve anything great, destitute of power among men, sluggish in doing right." In the New Testament the word is used to describe religious systems which existed before our Lord's time as having no power to promote righteousness and salvation.

IMPOSSIBILITIES

When we put these ideas together, we get a picture of what man is in himself. It is impossible for man to do anything for himself. When we use the word "impossible," we must realize that there are two types of impossibilities. Some things are impossible conditionally; other things are impossible unconditionally. For example, you might say of a man who is paralyzed, "It is impossible for him to walk downtown unless his body is healed." You might then continue, "It is impossible for you to fly unless you are equipped with wings." You might say that it would be impossible for you to fly to the moon, and you would mean that it would be impossible unless you had a body which did not need air. And if you had such a body, you might say that, though you could fly to the moon, you could not fly to the sun, and then you would add that it would be impossible unless you were equipped with a body which did not need air and was not combustible. You may extend that series of impossibilities until you exhaust your imagination, but you can see that "unless" would alter the premises and make the conclusion a possibility.

Then there are unconditional impossibilities. It is impossible for anything to be true and false at the same time. It is impossible for something to exist and not exist at the same time. The Bible states that it is impossible for God to lie (Heb. 6:18). And when the Bible teaches that man is helpless, it means that he can do nothing for himself that will satisfy God.

It is interesting to note that the word "impotent" comes from the same Latin root as "impossible." Man is impotent, powerless, helpless. It is impossible for him to do anything for himself. Rudolf Kittel, the great German lexicographer, says that three words whose ideas are closely related are *man, the flesh,* and *helpless.* David the Psalmist said, "What is man, that thou art mindful of him? and the son of man, that thou visitest him? (Ps. 8:4).

MAN'S HELPLESSNESS

Man's helplessness, his inability to do anything for himself, is at the basis of the divine revelation concerning salvation. Let us look at several verses which enlarge upon this truth. First, our Lord said, "Except a man be born again, he cannot see the kingdom of God" (John 3:3). Note well, it does not say that man *does not* see the kingdom of God, but that he *cannot* see it. Our Lord is saying in unequivocal terms that man who has not been born again is incapable of comprehending and receiving the things of the Spirit of God.

Turn the pages of the Gospel of John and hear our Lord saying again, "Why do ye not understand my speech? even because ye *cannot* hear my word" (John 8:43). He was speaking to Pharisees who opposed His every utterance. His simplest statements were perverted, distorted, and rejected. The Lord declared that the reason for their attitude was that they were spiritually deaf. They *could* not hear His Word. It was impossible for the Word to reach the inner ear of their consciousness.

In the same Gospel the Lord announced His departure to His disciples. At the same time He told them that He would be replaced on earth by the Holy Spirit. His words are filled with great comfort for the believer, but they include a terrible indictment of the unregenerate man. In John 14, Jesus says, "And I will pray the Father, and he shall give you another Comforter, that he may abide with you forever: [and now note well the following] even the Spirit of truth; whom the world *cannot* receive, because it seeth him not, neither knoweth him" (John 14:16, 17). Once more we have the flat statement that the world *cannot* receive the Holy Spirit. The reason is that man is dead in trespasses and sins.

We now turn to Romans 8 for a statement that fits into the pattern of our text: "The carnal mind is enmity against God; for it is not subject to the law of God, neither indeed can be. So then they that are in the flesh cannot please God" (Rom. 8:7, 8). God declares that the unsaved man is not only not subject to the law of God, but also he cannot be subject to the law of God. Man's nature is sinful, and sin cannot be subject to God. All things subject to God are holy. Since sin and holiness are opposites, it is impossible for the sinful mind of man to be subject to the law of God. It is well to pause a moment because here natural religion diverges from supernatural religion. When the Council of Trent met in 1564, they set forth that "God does not ask the impossible." But the very heart of the biblical revelation is that God does ask the impossible. When man admits his helplessness, God intervenes and does the impossible, provides the impossible, and fulfils the impossible within the life of man.

SPIRITUAL DISCERNMENT

The latter half of this quotation from the eighth chapter of Romans is, "So then they that are in the flesh cannot please God." Those who are "in the flesh," of course, are the opposite of those who are "in Christ." Those who are in Christ have been made acceptable in the Beloved; but those who are in the flesh cannot please God. When the Lord Jesus came into the world the Father spoke from Heaven, saying, "This is my beloved Son, in whom I am well pleased" (Mt. 3:17). Unless we are in Christ it is impossible to please God. Men may argue about pleasing God by good works, offerings, sacrifices, forms, and ceremonies; but over against every effort stands this flat declaration, "They that are in the flesh cannot please God."

In the first Corinthian epistle we read, "The natural man receiveth not the things of the Spirit of God, for they are foolishness unto him; neither can he know them, because they are spiritually discerned" (1 Cor. 2:14). Here, again, is a direct statement that man is helpless. He cannot know spiritual things because they are spiritually discerned, and he cannot have spiritual discernment until he has the Spirit, and he cannot have the Spirit until he has been born of the Spirit.

Through Peter, the Holy Spirit also speaks of man's total

inability to please God. He describes unsaved men as beasts who
will perish in their own corruption, and says of them, "Having eyes
full of adultery, and that cannot cease from sin . . . an heart they
have exercised with covetous practices; cursed children" (2 Pet.
2:14). Certainly no man would dare to say this on his own authority.
But no Christian would dare to contradict it. God says the unsaved
man cannot cease from sin. In Proverbs 21:4 we are told that the
plowing of the wicked is sin. This is readily comprehensible in the
light of all the truth of God. The homemaking of the unsaved woman
is sin; the schoolteaching of the unsaved schoolteacher is sin; steno-
graphic work, bookkeeping, carpentering, millwork of the unsaved is
sin; yes, the breathing of the unsaved man is sin. For just as the
farmer who is not a believer turns over God's soil, and plants the
seed with life which God has placed in it, and relies upon God's
sunshine and air to bring the seed to fruition in order that his sinful
way of life may be continued; so the man who breathes is taking
God's air to keep his wicked heart pumping. This is arrant sin.

Put together these six passages, and you will discover that the
unsaved man cannot see the kingdom of God; he cannot hear the
Word of God; he cannot receive the Holy Spirit; he cannot be
subject to the law of God; he cannot please God; he cannot know
the things of the Spirit; and he cannot cease from sin. What an
indictment the Word of God makes against the unregenerate man!
And it is all summed up in our text—he is helpless, without strength,
weak, powerless, destitute. At the same time none of this minimizes
man's responsibility before God. Although spiritually dead, he is
accountable to God. Both the Word of God and conscience tell us
that we are answerable.

CHRIST DIED

How, then, does all this contribute to the argument that our
hope can never deceive us? We turn now to the rest of this text
in Romans 5: "For when we were yet without strength, in due time
Christ died for the ungodly." We will not dispute the fact that we
are ungodly. If you argue the matter, you cannot be saved. If
Scripture teaches anything, it is that God will not argue with man
over His verdict about man's being. God is the Creator and man
is the creature. God declared that the creature is not like the
Creator, and that is all there is to it. But as soon as I accept the

fact that I am ungodly by nature, I accept the consequent fact that Christ died for me. And as soon as I acknowledge that Christ died for me personally, I know that my sins have been dealt with and I have all confidence toward God. When my sins rise up before me, I have but one answer: Christ died.

In the seventeenth century, Bishop Beveridge wrote, "I cannot pray, except I sin; I cannot preach, but I sin; I cannot administer, nor receive the holy sacrament, but I sin. My very repentance needs to be repented of: and the tears I shed need washing in the blood of Christ."

But since there is cleansing for me because Christ died, my hope is anchored within the veil and nothing can turn me from confidence in God. When I discover sin within me, I remember that He knew about that flaw before the foundation of the world, and chose me in spite of what He knew I would be. Nothing in my life astonishes Him. God knows the material out of which He made us. Souls made of dust can never be other than dirty. He did not attempt to reform us; but He planned to die for us to give us new life. He did not plan to alter or patch us; His purpose was to create us anew in Christ and to give us His own life through Him. Here, then, is our sure and steadfast hope. Christ has died. He has died for the ungodly. He has died for the weak, the helpless, the powerless, the infirm, the sinner. He has died for those who were dead.

Out of His death has come life for us. We have obeyed the call of the Spirit and have learned that we are the objects of His love; since He found no merit in us but knew what we were before He saved us, we are confident our being beloved is an unchangeable attitude from the Father because of the very nature of His being. When God spoke the Word of creation, His sovereign power brought forth the universe. When God spoke the Word of redemption, His perfect love brought it to accomplishment. What He has promised, He has performed. Christ has died; we are saved, safe and alive forevermore.

CHAPTER XXII

In Due Time

For when we were yet without strength, in due time Christ died for the ungodly (Rom. 5:6).

THE chain of logic in Romans 5:1-6 is that, having been saved, the believer has all the blessings which flow from salvation. Not the least of these is a fixed and steadfast hope which is constantly renewed by the flow of divine love poured into his life. Not only is there this subjective knowledge or feeling of the love of God that brings the fresh supply of hope, but also there is the objective, historic fact of the death of the Lord Jesus Christ. That death occurred "in due time." In the American Standard Version it is "in due season"; in the Revised Standard Version, "at the right time"; Williams, "at the proper time"; Goodspeed, "at the decisive time"; the Confraternity, "at the set time"; while in the French of Ségond, which I like best of all, "at the appointed time."

GOD'S WAYS NOT OURS

Time is a word for creatures. God is outside of time. Recognition of that fact will be one of the great landmarks in your spiritual life. You will take many rapid steps forward in Christian experience and in comprehension of spiritual things when you take God out of time and place Him in His true habitat—eternity. "For my thoughts are not your thoughts, neither are your ways my ways, saith the Lord, For as the heavens are higher than the earth, so are my ways higher than your ways, and my thoughts than your thoughts" (Isa. 55:8, 9). This is one of the great key passages of the Bible. Understand it, and much else will be clear to you. Reject it, and you condemn yourself to wander in a maze.

Some may believe that it is very easy to comprehend that God's ways are not our ways, but, when we come to practical applications, we discover that many people wish to reduce God to their status. We are creatures of time. We cannot contemplate life without thought of the past, and we live in awareness of the present.

Being creatures of anticipation, we are bound up with thoughts of things to come. Most of us are occupied with present work in order to pay future accounts and assure the continuity of life. Thus, we are victims of experience. In our environment we find the same continuity. Night succeeds day; seasons roll in accustomed sequence; rivers rise and fall with the swell of rains, and carry eroding mountains to the sea. The scars of the ages are deep set on earth's body and the bones of past ages come to the surface with the passage of the years.

> Time, like an ever-rolling stream,
> Bears all its sons away;
> They fly, forgotten, as a dream
> Dies at the opening day.

ACCORDING TO PLAN

We confess the fact of our own creaturehood, living in time, carried away by time, and moving toward the unknown unless we know God as revealed in His Word. It is evident, therefore, that when we say that Christ died in due time, we are linking that death to ourselves, and ourselves to God. We must reject Goodspeed's idea that Christ died at the decisive moment. God does not make decisions as man makes them. To make a decision implies variableness, previous indecision, or ignorance; at the least, existence of a problem not yet previously considered. But God's decisions are eternal decrees, unchanging and unchangeable. That is why we can rest upon Him; there is no change or variation within His being. All things originated in Him. We must avoid the pitfall inherent in the etymology of our English word "foreknowledge," or we shall think of it as advance knowledge, as though God had merely advance information of something that another will than His was going to perform. The Greek word *prognosis*, twice used in the New Testament and translated "foreknowledge," is given in Thayer's lexicon as "prearrangement."

Certainly the death of Christ was "at the proper time," and "at the right time," for God and all His works are perfect. I believe that by far the best translation is that of the French version, which later appeared in the Confraternity version in English. Christ died "at the appointed time." Christ died "at the set time." Everything was according to plan and occurred at the proper time.

The best way to interpret Scripture is to study Scripture. As we read the New Testament we may be astonished to see the number of verses which express further points in connection with the thesis that Christ died according to plan, and at a set time. In Revelation 13:8 we read that Christ was "the Lamb slain from the foundation of the world." In Ephesians we read that the believers were chosen by God in Christ "before the foundation of the world" (1:4), and all this was "according to the purpose of him who worketh all things after the counsel of his own will" (1:11). In Galatians we are told, "But when the fulness of the time was come, God sent forth his Son, made of a woman, made under the law, to redeem them that were under the law" (4:4, 5). Here the time element is linked to the past. The coming of Christ to die was revealed in prophecy. Thus Paul defined the essence of the gospel as "Christ died for our sins according to the scriptures" (1 Cor. 15:3).

BEFORE ALL TIME

On the day of Pentecost Peter referred to this double element of a set time and Scripture fulfillment with reference to the death of Christ. "Men of Israel," he said, "hear these words: Jesus of Nazareth, a man attested to you by God with mighty works and wonders and signs which God did through him in your midst, as you yourselves know—this Jesus, delivered up according to the definite plan and foreknowledge of God, you crucified and killed by the hands of lawless men" (Acts 2:22, 23).

In his first epistle Peter again correlates time and the Scriptures in connection with the death of our Lord. He writes: "You know that you were ransomed from the futile ways inherited from your fathers, not with perishable things such as silver or gold, but with the precious blood of Christ, like that of a lamb without blemish or spot. He was destined before the foundation of the world but was made manifest at the end of the times for your sake" (1 Peter 1:18-20).

Likewise in the epistle to the Hebrews we find time, the Scriptures, and the death of Christ linked together. The writer draws the contrast between the priest who offered a daily sacrifice—a thing now abominable in the sight of God—and the Lord Jesus as the great high priest who offered but one sacrifice. We read: "For Christ has entered, not into a sanctuary made with hands, a copy of the true one, but into heaven itself, now to appear in the presence of God on our behalf. Nor was it to offer himself repeatedly, as the high priest enters the Holy Place yearly with blood not his own; for then he would have had to suffer repeatedly since the foundation of the world [*kosmos*]. But as it is, he has appeared once for all at the end of the age [*aion*] to put away sin by the sacrifice of himself" (Heb. 9:24-26).

Putting these passages together, we draw the following important conclusions: (1) The death of Christ was eternally determined and planned by God. (2) In Old Testament times the plan to send Christ and sacrifice Him for the sins of men was set forth in some detail. (3) When Jesus Christ came to earth, He came on a time schedule fixed by God. (4) These three things being true, it follows that everything planned by God, and set forth by Him in the Scriptures, has been fully accomplished by the death of Jesus Christ. Let us look at these conclusions in further detail.

PLANNED IN ETERNITY

First, the death of Christ was planned in eternity before the foundation of the world. In the counsels of the Godhead, the members of the Trinity determined that Jesus Christ should come to earth and assume a human form for the distinct purpose of allowing Himself to be killed. The fact that men would be the instruments would not detract from the actual cause of His death; namely, that God the Father put God the Son to death. Look at that sentence closely. It is doubtful if a more important sentence could be written in this book. Some have tried to make capital of the fact that the Jews delivered Christ to the Roman authorities, but this is relatively unimportant. Others remind us that Gentiles drove the nails which crucified Christ—again, relatively unimportant. The paramount fact about the death of Jesus Christ is that God the Father put Him to death. We read in Isaiah, "For it pleased Jehovah [the Father] to bruise him [God the Son]; he [from heaven] hath put him [on earth] to grief" (Isa. 53:10).

The New Testament counterparts of this verse tell us that God made Christ to be sin for us, He who knew no sin, that we might be made the righteousness of God in Him (2 Cor. 5:21). And, Christ was delivered by the determinate counsel and prearrangement of God (Acts 2:23). When we comprehend that God the

Father put God the Son to death, we understand that the death of Christ was the payment by the love of God to the justice of God, and this payment was satisfaction to God for the sins of men.

Several years ago, while crossing the Atlantic Ocean, I preached at the Sunday service. Later, a group of college students came to tea, and we discussed faith and the atonement. In the course of the conversation I used the illustration of a judge whose son came before him accused of reckless driving. The charge was abundantly proved, and the judge fined the young man the full amount permitted under the law. After the fine was assessed, the judge adjourned court, came down from the bench, and paid his son's fine. A girl, who was spokesman for the group, interjected, "But God cannot get down off the bench!" I replied, "You have given me one of the best illustrations of the incarnation that I will ever have. For Jesus Christ was no more or less than God come down off the bench to pay the fine which He had imposed upon us."

IN THE OLD TESTAMENT

Second, this doctrine is set forth in detail in the Old Testament. Prick almost any verse in the Old Testament and you will find that it bleeds for the death of Christ everywhere. Even in the midst of the first curse upon sin God announced that He would send a Redeemer, and that the seed of the woman would bruise the serpent's head (Gen. 3:15). The woman is Israel, and the seed is the Lord Jesus Christ. A substitute lamb was provided to purge the iniquities of the sinner. The place—Jerusalem—was determined where the lambs should be killed, and a curse was pronounced on anyone who offered a sacrifice outside of Jerusalem (Lev. 17).

It is not necessary to trace in detail the Old Testament teaching, but scores of prophecies were fulfilled in the coming and death of the Lord Jesus Christ. In Micah 5:2, Bethlehem is named as His birthplace. His virgin birth was foretold in Isaiah 7:14. His death by crucifixion was prophesied in Psalm 22, and this centuries before the founding of Rome and the invention of crucifixion. The lives of Abraham and Isaac show many parallels with the coming of God's Isaac. Abraham and Sarah had a child, not virgin born but supernaturally born, which was sufficient for the pageant that pictured our Lord's birth. Abraham offered up "his only begotten son" (Heb. 11:17). And the doctrinal meaning of salvation by the shed-

ding of the blood of a substitute is set forth in such detail
can say, "He was wounded for my transgressions; he was
for my iniquities; the chastisement of my peace was upon h
by his stripes I am healed. I like a sheep had gone astray; ... ᴴᴬᵁ
turned to my own way; but Jehovah laid upon him the total of
my iniquity" (Isa. 53:5, 6).

A TIME SCHEDULE

Third, we find that all this was in accord with a definite time
schedule. Daniel had some knowledge of the plan of God, and he
prayed and asked for more. God sent the angel Gabriel who gave
him a divine revelation to set down for our guidance and knowledge. The angel said to Daniel, "Seventy weeks are determined
upon thy people . . ." The word here translated "weeks" is a time
word that refers to periods of seven years. We use "decade" for a
period of ten years. If we use "heptad" for seven years, the passage
will become simple. "Seventy heptads are decreed upon thy people
[Israel], and upon thy holy city [Jerusalem], to finish the transgression, and to make an end of sins, to make reconciliation for
iniquity, and to bring in everlasting righteousness, and to seal up
the vision and prophecy, and to anoint the most holy" (Dan. 9:24).
Here is announced a period of seventy times seven years, or 490
years. But this total is divided into three sections: "Know therefore
and discern that from the going forth of the command to restore
and to build Jerusalem unto the Messiah the Prince, shall be seven
heptads, and sixty-two heptads; the street shall be built again, and
the wall, even in troublous times."

We note that the total of seventy times seven years is divided
into three periods. Two of these periods are seven times seven, or
49 years; 62 times seven, or 434 years. Now these two figures together make 69 times seven, or 483 years. But this leaves seven
years to be accounted for. If we look at the list of things to be
accomplished before the 490 years were finished, we immediately
see that some prophecy has not yet been fulfilled; the world goes
on in its sin, even as in Daniel's day, and there is no sign of everlasting righteousness.

All becomes clear, however, when we realize that this is a
Jewish prophecy and deals with the history of Israel. God does not
count time while the Jews are not in full possession of the Holy

Land, including Jerusalem and the place of sacrifice. When Christ died 483 years had been accomplished, and God as it were stopped the pendulum of Israel's clock; He has not yet started it going again. Most certainly that seventieth period of seven years will be in earth's future history.

With these factors in mind we can reconstruct the prophecy. Israel was in captivity. A decree was about to be issued for a remnant of the Jews to rebuild Jerusalem, which had been destroyed before the Babylonian captivity. God said to Daniel: Start counting years from the issuance of the decree to rebuild Jerusalem. After 49 years of trouble the street and the wall will be rebuilt. Then continue counting. After 483 years the Messiah shall be cut off, but not for Himself. What a statement! Here is the clear declaration of God that Messiah would die, and that His death would be for others, not for Himself. It was to be a vicarious, substitutionary atonement. He would be cut off for the sins of His people. Thus He would make an end of sins and make reconciliation for iniquity.

THE APPOINTED TIME

The argument I now set forth I take from the great British scholar, Sir Robert Anderson. In his book, *The Coming Prince*, Sir Robert reviews the history of this period and establishes the date of the going forth of the decree to rebuild Jerusalem. Evidence is marshaled to show that this decree was issued in Babylon one springtime. He then demonstrates that the Lord Jesus Christ died on the cross 483 years later—483 years to the very time marked by the promulgation of the decree. This prophecy was fulfilled to the last detail. Like Sir Robert, I believe that the Lord Jesus Christ did die for us "in the fulness of time," "at the appointed time," in accordance with Daniel's prophecy.

Earlier in this chapter I quoted texts from various writers who linked together three ideas: time, the Scriptures, and the death of Christ. It is interesting to note that those quotations were from Paul, Luke, John, Peter, and the author of the epistle to the Hebrews, probably Paul. All these writers understood and took for granted that Christ's life and death fulfilled the Old Testament prophecies. In earlier volumes in this series we set forth the fact that Christ's coming was announced in the Old Testament. Here is the additional fact that His death was also announced; and it occurred just when God said it would.

What conclusions may we draw? The death of Christ having been eternally determined and planned by God and announced in detail in the Old Testament, all His life having been lived and His death consummated on a meticulously accurate time schedule, it follows inexorably that the spiritual results which God announced in connection with the death of Christ have been fully attained. Now we understand our text in relation to the steadfastness of our hope. Since Christ died according to a time schedule, everything promised in connection with the death of Christ is certainly and assuredly ours.

HALLEY'S COMET

In the 17th century the British astronomer, Edmund Halley, using Newton's newly propounded principle of the law of gravity, announced that the brilliant comet of 1682 would return again about the year 1757. He died 15 years before the event, but, at the time set, the comet reappeared in the heavens, and scientists then knew that the principles which had been worked out theoretically in physics and mathematics were sound.

Before the time of Christ, multitudes looked forward to the fulfillment of prophecies about the coming and death of the Savior. Speaking of them in Hebrews 11, the writer says, "Therefore sprang there even of one, [Abraham] and him as good as dead, so many as the stars of the sky in multitude, and as the sand which is by the seashore innumerable. These all died in faith, not having received the promises, but having seen them afar off, and were persuaded of them, and embraced them, and confessed that they were strangers and pilgrims in the earth" (Heb. 11:12, 13). Slowly the years dragged by. Then a star was seen in the sky and wise men came to worship the one who had been born King of the Jews. As years passed the prophecy came closer to its ultimate fulfillment, and finally the springtime, the day of Passover, Calvary, its cross and its death, were followed by the triumphant resurrection. The men of the old covenant were forever vindicated. The groundwork was laid for our confidence and hope. Christ died at the set time, in the fullness of time. And Christ died for the ungodly, for you and for me.

CHAPTER XXIII

God's Love Commended

For when we were yet without strength, in due time Christ died for the ungodly. For scarcely for a righteous man will one die: yet peradventure for a good man some would even dare to die. But God commendeth his love toward us, in that, while we were yet sinners, Christ died for us (Rom. 5:6-8).

GOD is love. That statement implies a dilemma, for love must pour itself out upon its object, but it also wants to be loved in return. For God to love is quite possible, but for God to be loved requires a miracle. We are sinners. A cat may look at a king, but may a sinner look at God? Because He is God, He is unattainable, unapproachable. If a beggar desires a lovely princess, he has a slim chance of some Aladdin-like miracle being performed on his behalf, for he is of the same nature as the princess. But a creature-sinner has everything against him. God stands high above and far away. How can I reach Him?

I early and easily learned that I was ungodly. It is not long before a child becomes aware that he is not like God. Knowledge of our ungodliness is simple to acquire and admit. The knowledge of our helplessness is harder come by, for we are incurably addicted to the evil of wanting to do something spiritually for ourselves. When the man who knows he is ungodly learns that he is weak, helpless, without strength, he no longer will try to approach God but will find that God has approached him. God's way to the heart of the ungodly is through the Lord Jesus Christ and His cross. Here He overcame both our ungodliness and our helplessness.

"For when we were yet helpless, at the appointed, set time, Christ died for the ungodly. It is rare, indeed, that a case will be found where a man will die for a righteous man; someone might be found that would die for a really benevolent man; but God commendeth his love toward us, in that, while we were yet sinners, Christ died for us."

Out of this text we bring three things: human love contrasted with divine love; the oneness of the love of God and Christ, and the implications of that oneness; and the amazing fact that God commends His love toward us.

Human love almost always has a selfish motive. Its highest degree is described by Christ, who said, "Greater love hath no man than this, that a man lay down his life for his friends" (John 15:13). The thoughtless will recall newspaper headlines and assert that there are a great many manifestations of self-sacrificing love.

If we analyze the motives behind the acts, however, we will see that cases of dying for others are extremely rare. First, eliminate all cases where Christians have died for others by going to places of danger or infection. The motivation was the divine love shed abroad in their hearts, and was the outworking of that inflowing love. What we are looking for is the natural reaction of human love.

You then cite acts of heroism of which we read from time to time. Soldiers die for their country; mothers and fathers rush into burning buildings or dive into freezing or rushing waters to save loved ones in peril. There are firemen, policemen, or the passing stranger who die in line of duty for people whom they do not know. I do not count any of these deaths as voluntary. In most cases there is a calculated risk. The stranger or the public servant who loses his life to save another thinks that he will be able to breast the tide of the raging stream, or will be able to get out of the burning building before the walls fall or before he is overcome by smoke and flame. These men of steady nerves have performed similar acts before and have come off successfully. These men are brave, very brave, but they are not voluntarily giving their lives for others.

It is the same of the soldier who dies in battle. He, perhaps, did not want to go into the army in the first place. It was a disagreeable task that had to be performed, so it might as well be performed with stoicism. The orders are to advance against the enemy. The soldier knows that there is a chance of death, but that the mathematical odds of the casualty lists with the total number of men involved give him the chance of survival, and he goes forward, ready to die if necessary. In some cases, as we shall see, he may have calculated the odds and consented in his own mind to give his life for a great cause.

In the case of men and women who have given their lives for

children or other close relatives, there is a psychological involvement. There is no time to decide. The peril for the loved one is there, and the emotions lead the individual into the place of death because there is no time to consider that his own death may result. There have been women who did not know how to swim who have thrown themselves into rushing streams in a futile attempt to rescue children. If there had been time to assess the matter coolly, the act would have been suicide, but now it must be put down to great emotional unbalance which distorted reason and led to disaster.

WILLINGNESS TO DIE

When we have eliminated these types of sacrifice—reckless bravado, calculated risk, emotional unbalance—we have taken care of most instances in which human beings die for others. I would be the last to minimize the bravery or the love involved in such acts, but cold reason will not permit us to set down these deaths in the column of voluntary sacrifice.

We now proceed to examine cases where individuals, in cool possession of their faculties, decide to die for someone else. Thomas Macaulay has given us the key to one category of such deaths in his poem, "Horatius at the Bridge":

> For how can man die better,
> Than in facing fearful odds
> For the ashes of his fathers,
> And the temples of his gods?

I can well understand how many young men of Oxford and Cambridge, at the time of the great blitz in World War II, stepped into their aircraft and went up to fight the enemy, knowing that they were about to see the end of life. They did it with calm calculation and determination, and as Winston Churchill put it, "Never have so many owed so much to so few." They may have had in mind that they were dying for a close handful of special loved ones, but this is doubtful. They were of the number who realized the importance of the great principles of liberty, and were willing to give their lives that the way of life of a whole people might be preserved. Theirs was a love that must be placed in the highest category: "Greater love hath no man than this, that a man lay down his life for his friends."

There are other stories of this same quality such as the tale of a survivor of a mine disaster. He had a wife and three children and was trapped in a mine where gas was escaping. In the falling of debris his gas mask was torn. A young man took off his own mask and forced it on his friend, saying, "You have Mary and the children; they need you. I am alone and can go." When we read of such an act, we feel that we are treading on holy ground.

Another illustration of this same nature gripped my imagination and heart. A little crippled girl, living in the slums, was to undergo an operation that might enable her to walk again. After the operation she needed a blood transfusion, and her fourteen-year-old brother, a tough boy of the streets, volunteered. He was taken to the bedside of his sister, and watched while the vein in his arm was opened so that his blood might flow into the body of the unconscious girl. Time passed and he sat staring in tight-lipped silence. When it was over, the doctor put his hand on his shoulder and told him that he was very brave. After a moment the boy, who did not understand the nature of a transfusion, looked up and said, "Doc, how long before I croak?" As far as his heart and will were concerned, he was dying, drop by drop, slowly and willingly, expecting that her life would mean his own death. There, indeed, is the highest in human love.

In our text the Holy Spirit analyzes the thought of dying for others. Two classes of men are mentioned. "It is rare, indeed, that a man will die for a righteous man; it might be found that someone would die for a good man." We must stop a moment and define the adjectives *righteous* and *good*. The words are used in an accommodated sense, since we have already seen that "there is none righteous, no not one," and "there is none that doeth good." But while in the third chapter the words were used in their strictest sense, in comparison with the righteousness and goodness of God, here they are used in human comparisons. Maclaren explains the difference. "Christ died for us. Would any man do that? No! 'for,' says he, 'it will be a hard thing to find anyone ready to die for a righteous man—a man rigidly just and upright, and because rigidly just, a trifle hard, and therefore not likely to touch a heart to sacrifice; and even for a good man, in whom austere righteousness has been softened and made attractive, and become graciousness and beneficence, well! it is just within the limits of possibility that some-

body might be found even to die for a man that had laid such a
strong hand upon his affections. But God commendeth His love
toward us in that while we were yet sinners Christ died for us.' "

SALVATION BY CHRIST ALONE

Before we leave this question of self-sacrifice in its highest
degree, let me deal with one deplorable doctrine; namely, that
such a high degree of human love was sufficient to purchase entrance
into Heaven. During the first world war, an outstanding Bible
teacher lost a son through enemy action. He preached a sermon in
which he told all who had lost loved ones in the service that such
self-sacrifice would be rewarded by salvation. This shows how
emotion can unbalance even a keen, theological mind. In rebuttal
to this thesis of salvation by dying for one's country, Dr. W. H.
Griffith Thomas answered that, if such were the case, a German
bullet was as efficacious as the blood of Jesus Christ. The proper
procedure would have been to empty the prisons and put all the
depraved and vicious into the front line where shock troops were
sure to be killed, and thus insure their salvation. The Bible presents
the categorical answer that no form of human righteousness can
commend the soul to God's holy love.

A GREAT CONTRAST

We can now contrast the highest form of human love with
divine love. Man must have a motive for his love outside of himself.
God loves because He is love. To die for sinners is divine and
sovereign. The words *lovely* and *lovable* describe attributes in the
object of our love. But when God loved us, we were unlovely and
unlovable. He loved us in spite of what we were. His love engulfed
us when we were helpless, ungodly sinners. He died, the just for
the unjust (1 Pet. 3:18); and we thus judge that if one died for all,
then were all dead (2 Cor. 5:14).

In earlier writings I quoted Augustine's famed prayer, "O God,
Thou hast formed us for Thyself; and our hearts can know no rest
until they rest in Thee." That sounds pretty, but close analysis shows
that our hearts are deceitful above all things and incurably wicked
(Jer. 17:9), and will never find rest, even in God. That is why we
must have new hearts. Evangelists should stop telling unsaved

people to give their hearts to God, and, instead, tell them to receive the grace that God gives because His very being is love.

GOD'S LOVE OUTPOURED

We are brought back, then, to our consideration of the fact that love must flow from God because there is an inner fountain in the heart of God that must flow out to those upon whom He has determined to lavish His love. There was nothing in us to call forth this love; there was everything in us to repel it. In spite of this, the love of God flows. A phenomenon in nature makes me think of the love of God.

In southeastern France, almost due east of Avignon, is the fountain of Vaucluse. The river of the same name flows into the Rhone, but where does it come from? I have followed the stream to its source. The valley grows narrower, and there seems to be no break in the mountain that rises ahead. And indeed, there is none. A cliff rises hundreds upon hundreds of feet to block the valley. As we approach that cliff, there is the chateau where Petrarch lived and where he wrote his poems immortalizing Laura. We pass the chateau and go up the river. The waters are wide, swift, and deep. The arms of the cliff stretch around us, and the river comes toward us in undiminished volume. Suddenly we round the last bend, and there we see the water flowing from the foot of the rock, pouring forth thousands of gallons per minute, probably the greatest spring in the world. Thus flows the love of God.

Our text presses us to the conclusion that Jesus Christ is God. The love of God the Father and the love of Christ are seen to be the same love, and unlike any other love. Things equal to the same thing are equal to each other. The love of Christ is shown by His death on the cross. The cross, then, forms the equation between the love of the Father, and the love of the Son. It is the same love. Therefore the cross is one of the proofs of the Godhead of the Lord Jesus Christ.

The implications of the oneness of God the Father and God the Son are evident. They determined to accomplish our salvation and did so. The Father would give His only begotten Son, and the Son would lay down His life. Salvation becomes a fact, so simple that any child can receive it, yet so profound that no philosopher can fathom it.

"COMMEND"

And the Father will not permit so much love to be poured out in vain. He stoops yet further, to *commend* His love toward us. The word "commend" has some interesting meanings. The Greek word is translated by five different English words in our King James Version: *approve, commend, consist, make, stand.* The root idea was "To place together, to set in the same place, to bring or band together." When two people were brought together, they were "commended" to each other, or "recommended," as we would say in modern usage. In the ancient Greek world the word was used when many things were put together to be exhibited. And at times things were put together to establish facts, to prove something. From this we can understand why the translators have rendered this word by such a variety of English terms. Thus we read that God proves His love towards us; God establishes, confirms, manifests His love; God gives proof of; God demonstrates His love; God commends His love toward us.

Maclaren writes: "When Paul says 'commend', he uses a very significant word which is employed in two ways in the New Testament. It sometimes means to establish, or to prove, or to make certain. But 'prove' is a cold word, and the expression also means to recommend, to set forth in such a way as to appeal to the heart, and God does both in that great act. He establishes the fact, and He, as it were, sweeps it into a man's heart, on the bosom of that full tide of self-sacrifice."

But why should God go about to prove His love toward us? Or why should God set forth a recommendation of His love? And once more the answer comes that perfect love must manifest and demonstrate itself, must set itself forth, since it knows that our good is in receiving the benefits of that love. The verb is in the present tense. We do not read that God "commended" His love. It is a present going forth of that love in proof and recommendation. It is as modern as today and as alive as now. Christ died some thirty years before Paul wrote these words, but Paul feels them as living, pulsing realities. Christ died for him, and for the believers then alive in Rome. And Paul's words have gone on living, in the continuing present tense, and are alive today. "God commends His love toward us . . . Christ died for us."

THE MIRACLE OF LOVE

And the recommendation works, for it brings the miracle of divine love into the barren emptiness of my heart. There was a time when God was not in my life. I knew that I was a sinner, and that knowledge kept God outside. My conscience was the barrier flung up against the holiness of God. When I thought of God, I felt like Peter, who fell before Him crying, "Depart from me, for I am a sinful man, O Lord." My heart was awakened and aroused to its need. Could God love sin? What a horrible thought! and my heart cringed away still farther. But love pursued me and I thought, Could God love a sinner? And then love began to have its way. For though I knew God could never love sin, I learned that God could love a sinner, that He had loved the sinner, that He still loved the sinner, and that His love was ever continuing. I could say, "He loves me!" And I could say it because He recommended the cross to me as proof that He loved me. The historical act was father to the present fact. His death was the source of my life. Love had justified me, and my conscience was stilled forever.

It is a love which, though not repelled by sin, is witnessed by that death to be rigidly righteous. It is no mere flabby laxity of loose-girt affection, no foolish indulgence like that whereby earthly parents spoil their children. God's love is not lazy good nature, as a great many think it to be and so drag it in the mud; it is rigidly righteous, and therefore Christ died. His death bears witness that God's love shrinks from no sacrifices. This Isaac was not "spared." God gave up His Son. Love's very speech is in surrender and God's love speaks as ours does. It is a love which embraces all ages and lands.

> Come ye sinners, poor and needy,
> 　　Weak and wounded in the Fall,
> Jesus ready stands to save you,
> 　　Full of pity, grace, and power.
>
> Let not conscience make you linger,
> 　　Nor of fitness fondly dream;
> All the fitness He requireth
> 　　Is to feel your need of Him.

CHAPTER XXIV

Saved from Wrath

Much more then, being now justified by his blood, we shall be saved from wrath through him (Rom. 5:9).

WE NOW come to a phase of the doctrine of justification that demands special consideration. Read verses one and nine of this chapter together to get further light: "Therefore, having been justified by faith, we have peace with God"; "Much more, therefore, having been justified by his blood, we shall be saved from wrath through him."

In both verses justification is the act of God, performed from Himself and within Himself. But the effects upon us who believe are wonderful and very far-reaching. When we exercise our God-given faith in the work of Christ and believe what God the Father has to say about it, there is immediate peace with God for the believer. The warfare is ended, and God Himself has nothing against one whom He has justified. When my faith lays hold upon that fact, my conscience is stilled forever, my intellect is satisfied with the complete finality of the transaction, my soul has been created anew in Christ. I am henceforth and inseparably in Him.

GOD MUST BE SATISFIED

Now, in this ninth verse we have again presented to us the ground of our justification with another of the results of that justifying work, from the point of view of God Himself; for the importance of the Bible teaching concerning our salvation is not what we think about it, but what God says about it.

It is God who must be satisfied in the matter of our sin. And justification is the expression of the fact that God is satisfied because of what the Lord Jesus Christ has done for us. When we believe it, peace is declared between God and the sinner. To know that God's wrath is forever stilled against us, we must know His word about the ground of our justification—the blood of Jesus Christ.

CHRIST'S ATONING DEATH

There are those who profess to believe in the death of Jesus Christ, yet do not believe in it as set forth in the Word of God. Maclaren exposes the pale thought of these unbelievers. After describing the death of a human martyr for a human cause, Maclaren say: "That is not the depth of the sense in which Paul meant that Jesus Christ died for us. It was not that He was true to His message, and, like many another martyr, died. There is only one way, it seems to me, in which any beneficial relation can be established between the death of Christ and us, and it is that when He died He died for us, because 'He bare our sins in his own body on the tree.' I dare say some of you do not take that view, but I know not how justice can be done to the plain words of Scripture unless this is the point of view from which we look at the cross of Calvary—that there the Lamb of Sacrifice was bearing, and bearing away, the sins of the whole world. I know that Christian men who unite in the belief that Christ's death was a sacrifice and an atonement diverge from one another in their interpretation of the way in which that came to be a fact, and I believe, for my part, that the divergent interpretations are like the divergent beams of light that fall upon men who stand round the same great luminary, and that all of them take their origin in, and are part of the manifestation of, the one transcendent fact, which passes all understanding, and gathers into itself all the diverse conceptions of it which are formed by limited minds. He died for us because in His death, our sins are taken away and we are restored to the divine favor.

"I know that Jesus Christ is said to have made far less of that aspect of His work in the Gospels than His disciples have done in the Epistles, and that we are told that, if we go back to Jesus, we shall not find the doctrine which for some of us is the first form in which the gospel finds its way into the hearts of men. I admit that the fully-developed teaching followed the fact, as was necessarily the case. I do not admit that Jesus Christ 'spake nothing concerning Himself' as the sacrifice for the world's sins. For I hear from His lips—not to dwell upon other sayings which I hear from His lips, 'The Son of Man came not to be ministered unto, but to minister'—that is only half His purpose—'and to give His life a

ransom instead of the many.' You cannot strike the atoning aspect
of His death out of that expression by any fair handling of the words.

"And what does the Lord's Supper mean? Why did Jesus Christ
select that one point of His life as the point to be remembered? Why
did He institute the double memorial, the body parted from the
blood being a sign of a violent death? I know no explanation that
makes the Lord's Supper an intelligible rite except the explanation
which says that He came, to live indeed, and in that life to be a
sacrifice, but to make the sacrifice complete by Himself bearing
the consequences of transgression, and making atonement for the
sins of the world.

"That is the only aspect of Christ's death which makes it of any
consequence to us. Strip it of that, and what does it matter to me
that He died, any more than it matters to me that any philanthropist,
any great teacher, any hero or martyr or saint, should have died?
As it seems to me, nothing. Christ's death is surrounded by tenderly
pathetic and beautiful accompaniments. As a story it moves the
hearts of men, and 'purges them, by pity and by terror.' But the
death of many a hero of tragedy does all that. And if you want to
have the cross of Christ held upright in its place as the throne of
Christ and the attractive power for the whole world, you must not
tamper with that great truth, but say, 'He died for our sins, according to the Scriptures.' "

JUSTIFIED BY HIS BLOOD

This, then, is the meaning of being justified by His blood. I
am well aware that many do not like the word "blood," and seek to
avoid it by all manner of circumlocutions. But while I may be able
to bring to such a word of comfort in one statement I am about to
make, I must bring them to their senses with a sledge-hammer blow
of truth about the blood of the Lord Jesus Christ. First, I confess
that the true meaning of the phrase, "the blood of Christ," has been
obscured by much popular preaching, fundamental preaching, which
contains, all innocently, a great deal of theological error centering
around the term, "the blood of Jesus Christ."

I have heard men criticize a preacher because one entire sermon
did not contain the word "blood." I have preached sermons without
once using this word, but their entire import, value, and life, are
dependent upon the fact that I have peace with God because I have

been justified by faith, and because I know that I am free from wrath to come because I have been justified by His blood.

The error of some faithful preachers lies in thinking that the blood of Christ always symbolizes the death of Christ, whereas it often means the life of Christ. I am not speaking of the life which He lived in Palestine; nor am I speaking of the life which He lived after the resurrection and which He still lives in Heaven. I am speaking of that which animated His body on earth. When He was born, He said, "Sacrifice and offering thou wouldst not, but a body hast thou prepared me" (Heb. 10:5). What made that body alive was the blood flowing in His veins. The blood in that case stands for life, not death. A verse in the book of Leviticus has been called the John 3:16 of the Old Testament: "For the life of the flesh is in the blood; and I have given it for you upon the altar to make atonement for your souls; for it is the blood that makes atonement, by reason of the life" (Lev. 17:11).

SACRIFICIAL DEATH

Instead of saying, "He shed His blood," it would be more accurate to say, "He poured out His life," since that is exactly what He did. And, if you fancy that it suits your aesthetic sense better to say, "He poured out His life," you may certainly do so, provided you do not use the term to contradict the fact that "He shed His blood." In other words, if you say, "He poured out His life," you must put the accent on *poured out*. So you are really back where you started. But in making the journey we have learned a little more about the death of our Savior, and that is well worth while.

There is, perhaps, one other grain of comfort for the aesthete who cringes before the shedding of blood. That may lie in the fact that in one sense the Bible is not speaking of the chemical elements of the blood, the hemoglobin or the white corpuscles, when it tells us what was accomplished on the cross of Calvary. After being reminded that the blood of animals was used in the sacrifices of the Old Testament, and that without shedding of blood there is no remission, we read, "It was therefore necessary that the patterns of things in the heavens [that is, the Tabernacle] should be purified with these [animal sacrifices] but the heavenly things themselves with better sacrifices than these" (Heb. 9:23).

What is this better sacrifice? Read on. "For Christ is not entered into the holy places made with hands, which are the figures of the true; but into heaven itself, now to appear in the presence of God for us. Nor yet that he should offer himself often, as the high priest entereth into the holy place every year with the blood of others. For then must he often have suffered since the foundation of the world; but now once in the end of the age hath he appeared to put away sin by the sacrifice of himself" (Heb. 9:24-26). If you prefer that to "The shedding of His blood," you may use it. But once more we will call you to a sharp halt. You may not use the sacrifice of Himself to deny the shedding of His blood, for the sacrifice of Himself was exactly what it is stated to be; namely, a sacrifice.

THE RESURRECTION BODY

So, perhaps, after all, I have not been of much comfort to the aesthete, for I must come back with the sledge-hammer blow of Scripture: put it as you will, you can never get around the plain Bible teaching that the Lord Jesus Christ lived here on earth with blood in His veins, that He went to the cross where that blood was drained from His body in death by crucifixion, and that He arose from the grave without any blood in His body. That is exactly what is taught in the Scriptures, and is the conclusion we must draw from putting certain Scripture texts together.

Describing the difference between Adam and Christ, the Holy Spirit states, "The first man is of the earth, earthy; the second man is the Lord from heaven. As is the earthy, such are they also that are earthy; and as is the heavenly, such are they also that are heavenly. And as we have borne the image of the earthy [Adam], we shall also bear the image of the heavenly [Christ]" (1 Cor. 15:47-49). Then the Holy Spirit adds this significant line: "Now this I say, brethren, that flesh and blood cannot inherit the kingdom of God." What? No blood in Heaven? That is what it says. And listen carefully to the words of the Savior after He arose from the dead. The disciples in the upper room were frightened because of the Jews; suddenly the Lord Jesus appeared to them in His resurrection body. They were terrified, we read in Luke's account, supposing that they were seeing a ghost. The Lord Jesus said, "Why are you troubled? and why do thoughts arise in your hearts? Behold my hands and my feet, that it is I myself: handle me, and see; for a spirit hath not flesh and bones, as you see me have" (Luke 24:38, 39). He had the same life before and after the cross, but on different principles. His physical life during His ministry was based on the blood flowing in His veins; His physical life after His resurrection (and it was material enough for Him to eat broiled fish) was based on the Spirit, the breath of God. And so will be our resurrection bodies. They are sown as "natural"—literally, soulish—bodies; they are raised as spiritual bodies. A spiritual body is not in contra distinction to the physical, for once more the broiled fish testifies against that idea; a spiritual body is dominated by the Spirit.

In conclusion, all the various phrases in the Bible concerning His death add up to the same thing: "He shed His blood," "He was crucified," "He died," "He gave His life a ransom," and "He put away sin by the sacrifice of Himself." He was "poured out," He was dying Godward. The Father demanded His death in perfect justice, and consented to it in perfect love.

What conclusion is to be drawn from all this? It is that the blood of Christ stilled the wrath of God against all believers. In the second chapter of Romans we saw the basis of the judgment that will come upon the ungodly, the unrepentant. The wrath of God was presented from every angle. When this inevitable consequence of God's holiness was fully revealed, the believer was told to rest in the fact that Christ has died.

MUCH MORE

But need I not fear at all? The Holy Spirit says, You are positively and superlatively safe. Our text says, "Much more, therefore, having been justified by his blood, we shall be saved from wrath through him." Much more! Is there something more than the peace with God which comes from justification through faith? Yes, for having been justified by His blood, there is henceforth absolute certainty about the day of judgment. I am convinced that the Bible teaches that we believers shall not appear before the judgment bar of God at the great white throne.

Frequently the poets who have written our hymns have introduced wrong ideas into our theological thinking. If you were standing by me when I sing hymns you would sometimes hear me change the words and go singing down the page, sometimes without rhyme, but always with reason. When I come to the last verse of "Rock of Ages," for example, I do not sing it as printed.

> While I draw this fleeting breath;
>   When my eyelids close in death;
> When I soar to worlds unknown,
>   See Thee on Thy judgment throne;
> Rock of Ages, cleft for me,
>   Let me hide myself in Thee.

If you were beside me when we came to that verse, you would hear me mumbling along, sometimes making one syllable drag over two notes, sometimes making half a dozen words go for one note. But the idea would be biblical. It would be something like this: "When I soar to worlds now beginning to be quite well-known; Take my place as the bride seated with Christ upon the judgment throne; Because Rock of Ages, Thou were indeed cleft for me, I have long since come to the place of perfect safety and assurance that Thou hast perfectly hid myself in Thee." And while the congregation might go on singing, "Amen," I would be thinking, "And it's done once for all, and forever."

SECURITY

This is the first of four occurrences of the term *much more* in this chapter. We shall refer to it again. The principle is that God never does anything by halves. He did not set out to save us and then leave us to our own devices. Here is the security of the believer, and no honest student of the Scriptures can make anything else out of it. If God moved toward us when we were helpless, ungodly sinners, His enemies, will He be deterred by that helplessness, that ungodliness, that enmity? Let us reiterate that God has never been astonished by anything in us. He did not find anything good in us. He did not love us because we were lovely or lovable, but because His nature is love. This being the case, we know that He will carry the whole plan of redemption through to its logical conclusion.

That conclusion is the final manifestation of His holiness and wrath. He has told us that the day of wrath will surely come. But now He tells us that He has tried the Lord Jesus Christ, found Him guilty in our stead, put Him to death, and so has acquitted and justified us. Having been justified by His blood, we shall be saved from wrath through Him. Much more shall we be saved, because of our position in Christ. I once heard a preacher say that, when the day of God's wrath finally came upon earth, we would stand in

Christ "insulated" against the burning force of God's wrath. The man meant well, but he missed the point of God's declaration. In the day of wrath we shall not be near the place where wrath will strike; we shall be in the place whence wrath originates.

Have you noticed that judgment is announced in the Bible as proceeding from Christ and, in a parallel passage, that same judgment is announced as proceeding from us? It is startling to some who have long been accustomed to the liturgical ideas that the mercy of God is something that must be sought, even after one has become the object of that mercy. In the second Psalm it is written that God the Father will hand over the unbelieving world to Christ for crushing judgment: "Ask of me, and I will give thee the nations for thine inheritance, and the uttermost parts of the earth for thy possession. Thou shalt break them with a rod of iron; thou shalt dash them in pieces like a potter's vessel" (Ps. 2:8, 9). These same words are applied in the New Testament to those who have put their trust in Christ: "To him that overcometh will I grant to sit with me in my throne, even as I also overcame, and am set down with my Father in his throne" (Rev. 3:21). And again, "He that overcometh . . . shall rule them with a rod of iron; as the vessels of a potter shall they be broken to slivers" (Rev. 2:26, 27). This is indeed much more than justification through His blood. This is being saved from wrath through Him, and becoming one with the Judge who visits His wrath upon the unbelieving world.

CHAPTER XXV

His Enemies

For if, when we were enemies, we were reconciled to God by the death of his Son, much more, being reconciled, we shall be saved by his life (Rom. 5:10).

ALL God's work for us was done when we were His enemies. He tells us so, and sets it forth in recommending His love to us. He did not love us when we were lovely or lovable. His love came from His own heart and is ours through the nature of His being. We were helpless, we were ungodly, we were sinners when Christ died for us, and, even more, we were enemies.

THE ENEMY

The enemy! It is a cold, hard word. Its associations bring a chill to our hearts. Every soldier knows what it means. The troops leave their position and march on. After some hours the distant noise of cannon is heard, and yet the column goes on. Then comes the order to spread out, to be on the alert. The sound of artillery is nearer. You climb a short rise and see on a far hill the puff of smoke. Again and again you see it, and then you note the hospital corpsmen carrying stretchers with bleeding soldiers, unconscious upon them. You now crawl from rock to wall, from wall to bush, from bush to haystack, seeking refuge even in a high tuft of grass. A shell whines overhead, changing its sound as it nears and passes you. The ground trembles and there is the dull thud of the explosion, then a cry from a comrade. You now know that right before you are human beings who will kill you if they can. Death is behind those trees. Death is in that village. Death is along that ridge. Your death, if they can possibly effect it. For they are enemies; and what is more, you are their enemy. You will kill them if you can. Their throat is choking with fear even as yours is. It is kill or be killed. That is the enemy. He wants his own way and you want your own way. Either of you will kill to get it. That is the heart of enmity. That is why wanting one's own way is the worst of sins; it is the root of all other sins.

The fields of war are not the only scenes of hatred. There may be lurking enmity in the simple haunts of peace. Something you love is destroyed. Flowers may be pulled up by the roots, or a tree cut around so that it dies. A door may be defaced, a window broken. Or someone may seek to hurt your reputation. The poison pen letter is written; the lie is circulated. Malice shoots the arrow of false rumor. You cannot learn why these things are happening. All you know is that you have an enemy.

CONSCIOUS HOSTILITY

The vocabulary of hatred is a very interesting one. We take, first of all, the simple noun "enemy." It comes from the Latin, *inimicus.* Break that in two and you have *in* and *amicus,* not a friend. *The Oxford English Dictionary* carries a whole section of illustrations of the word "enemy" used in connection with Satan as the archenemy, the great enemy, the enemy of mankind, or simply the enemy. But the primary definition is that of a hostile person who cherishes hatred, who wishes or seeks to do ill to another. The Anglo-Saxon word for "enemy" has given us "foe." The Latin word for "enemy" has given us "hostile." The common German noun for "enemy" has given us the word "fiend."

The Greek word used in the New Testament to describe us as the enemies of God carries all these ideas and implications. Strange that mankind should bear malice toward a kind and beneficent Creator, but that is the heart of the doctrine here set forth. The original word is often used passively for *hated, odious,* or *hateful;* but in its active form, as in our text, it expresses the conscious hostility of one who hates or opposes another.

But is man hostile to God? The eighth chapter of Romans leaves no room for doubt. "For the carnal mind is enmity against God; it is not subject to the law of God, neither indeed can be. So then they that are in the flesh cannot please God" (Rom. 8:7, 8). Does this mean that we are, by nature, hostile to God? That we cherish hatred toward our Creator? That we wish and seek to do Him ill? There may be those who deny such feeling, but Scripture and experience teach that this is true of every member of the human race by nature and by choice.

ADAM'S REBELLION

Let us look at the nature of Adam's original sin. God placed man on earth in a perfect environment and made him lord over all creation except a few square yards of ground which surrounded one tree. Man was to have everything north, south, east, and west of that tree. The forbidden tree was the sign of man's creaturehood and dependence upon God. The New Testament tells us that when Eve sinned she was deceived. She thought she was doing a good thing. The Devil had told her that by eating the fruit she and Adam would be as the gods, knowing good and evil, so she thought that it was a thing to be desired. But when Adam sinned, we are told by the Holy Spirit, he was not deceived (1 Tim. 2:14). He boldly ate the fruit Eve offered him. It was an act of rebellion, the equivalent of a declaration of independence; and from that time the entire human race has wanted to be independent of God.

Only the true believer in Christ has reversed this attitude by coming to God in utter dependence upon Him for salvation and every other good. Adam, in effect, said, "I am tired of having everything north, south, east, and west of this tree. I will be independent. I will run my own affairs." It was not a request that God share the throne of government with man; it was an ultimatum to Him to abdicate and leave full control to man.

Full control of his own affairs—that is what man desires more than anything else, and so man is the enemy of God who, because He is love, exercises restraints upon the human race and presents to His creatures what is best for them. And if someone asks what is best for humanity, the answer is total dependence upon God.

WANTING ONE'S OWN WAY

The worst of all sins is to want one's own way. All other sins are the outgrowth of this one root sin. "All we like sheep have gone astray; we have turned every one to *his own way.*" In simplest terms, man's own way is hostility to God's way. Man is an enemy because he wants his own way instead of God's way.

But with the declaration of independence in the Garden of Eden came the fruits of sin. Into the vacuum caused by the out-rushing of man's dependence upon God, there came the great burden of sin and sense of guilt. Man started to run from God, and he has been running ever since. Were it not for the fact that the pursuing love of God is swifter than man, no one would ever be saved.

BROTHERHOOD

Since he wants his own way and not God's way, man hates God and would do away with Him if he could. But man could not vent his hatred upon God Himself because he could not reach God. But that hatred was poured out against any other man who stood near God. The nearer a man got to God, the greater the hatred manifested toward him. Why did Cain kill Abel? Here was murder at the very outset of the history of the human race. Here was the first exposure of the "brotherhood of man" and its horrible fruits. There always have been two brotherhoods, and there always will be. There is the brotherhood of those who hate God and there is the brotherhood of those who have renounced the choice of Adam and have returned to dependence upon the Lord God. When we receive Christ as Savior, we undo the choice made by Adam. Christ told His disciples in advance what to expect from the world, and forewarned them of its hatred. "If the world hates you, know that it has hated me before it hated you. If you were of the world, the world would love its own; but because you are not of the world, but I chose you out of the world, therefore the world hates you. Remember the word that I said to you, 'A servant is not greater than his master.' If they persecuted me, they will persecute you; if they kept my word, they will keep yours also. But all this they will do to you on my account, because they do not know him who sent me" (John 15:18-21).

MANIFEST HATRED

In some parts of the earth human hatred toward God is publicly manifested. It is impossible, for instance, to belong to the Russian Communist Party without accepting atheism. The *Bezbozhnik,* Society of the Godless, is an important adjunct of Communism. God has been declared nonexistent. Russian dictionaries define all religious words in terms of mythology and relegate God and sin to the limbo of bourgeois thinking.

Elsewhere the hatred of man towards the true God has been manifested by substituting another god for the Lord Jehovah of Hosts, the God and Father of our Lord Jesus Christ. The gods of

Asia are not the God of our Savior and Redeemer. The name of Ram was on the lips of Gandhi as he died, but certainly this was not the name of our God. If anyone claims that it is one and the same, he shows his hatred toward the true God, for we read in the Scriptures, "I am the first, and I am the last; and beside me there is no God" (Isa. 44:6) Ask Elijah if Jehovah and Baal mean the same thing. Elijah lived among men who were intensely religious and who called upon their god with fanatical eagerness. But it was demonstrated that their god Baal was Satan wearing a mask of deity. Thus it is with Allah of the Moslem, and with many who use the name "God" for a being who certainly is not the God and Father of our Lord Jesus Christ.

But, in addition to the atheistic hatred of God in Russia, and the hatred manifested in other lands by the substitution of a counterfeit god, there are hatreds within the borders of Christendom, which are no less real because they are camouflaged. We do not need to spend much time considering the hatred of the criminal world against the true God. The men of lust and blood, the gangsters, murderers, gambling lords, all hate the true God because He stands for righteousness and, consequently, for restraint. And we may include in this number those men who are engaged in businesses which are legitimate, but who know no law in their dealings with the public. Gather from the Psalms a description of these men. "There is no faithfulness in their mouth; their inward part is very wickedness" (Ps. 5:9). "The wicked in his pride doth persecute the poor . . . for the wicked boasteth of his covetousness, and the ravisher outrages and despises Jehovah. The wicked says with arrogance: He does not punish. There is no God; There are all his thoughts. His ways are always successful; Thy judgments are far too high to reach him; as for all his enemies, he puffeth at them. He hath said in his heart, I shall not be moved; for I shall never be in adversity. His mouth is full of cursing and deceit and fraud; under his tongue is malice and iniquity. He sitteth in the lurking places of the villages; in the secret places doth he murder the innocent; his eyes are privily set against the poor. He lieth in wait secretly, as a lion in his den; he lieth in wait to catch the poor, and draweth him into his net. He croucheth, and humbleth himself, that the poor may fall into his claws. He says in his heart, God forgets; he hideth his face; he never looks. Arise, O Jehovah, O God, lift up thine hand; forget not the humble. Wherefore doth the wicked despise God? Why doth he say in his heart, thou wilt not punish?" (Ps. 10:2-13, Heb.).

Yes, man's hatred for God manifests itself in many ways. Not only is there the smoldering hatred against Him on the part of the wicked, but also there is the hatred that relegates Him to the last line of a political speech, and gives Him the polite brushoff of diplomacy. The attempt to organize humanity in the United Nations, for example, is open manifestation of hatred toward the true God. Just as surely as the Tower of Babel rose beside the Euphrates to announce that man hated the true God and did not want Him to reign, so the headquarters building of the United Nations, with its blasphemous room of religion where a shaft of sunlight streams in to illuminate an altar, but where the cross of Christ is not permitted, rises beside the East River in modern Babylon to declare that the carnal mind is enmity against God. But the second Psalm long ago told us, "Why do the nations rage, and the people imagine a vain thing? The kings of the earth set themselves, and the rulers take counsel together against Jehovah, and against his anointed, saying, Let us break their bands asunder; and cast away their cords from us" (Ps. 2:1-3).

One class of people has not yet been described. I can imagine some of them reading this and saying, "He has described the atheists in Russia and the pagans in the heathen world; he has described the criminals, the crooked businessmen, and the politicians, but he has not described me. I do not think that it is necessary to believe in Christ's death. I live a high, moral life, and I hold the most broad and tolerant attitude toward all people, even toward their ideas of God." I maintain that such people are the most subtle enemies of God, and their hatred is the most refined.

They have drawn over themselves the cloak of respectability like the Pharisees of old, and go through the forms of religious purification, prepare to go to a religious service, and turn aside en route to go to the house of Pilate and cry against Christ. Then, having delivered Him to crucifixion death, they go about their religious service. The man who does not believe God's Word makes Him a liar and so is among His enemies. The man who does not accept the death of the Lord Jesus Christ as the substitutionary atonement for sins continues to manifest his innate enmity against God.

We must understand that man's attitude toward Christ did not begin at the cross but is a continuing manifestation of the natural heart of unbelief. Cain's hatred of the atonement and a twentieth-century manifestation of such hatred are, of course, identical. In the epistle to the Hebrews we read of the judgment to come upon those who continue such enmity. We read, "He that despised Moses' law died without mercy under two or three witnesses. Of how much sorer punishment, suppose ye, shall he be thought worthy, who hath trodden under foot the Son of God, and hath counted the blood of the covenant, wherewith he was sanctified, [as] an unholy thing, and hath despised the Spirit of grace?" (Heb. 10:28, 29).

ENEMIES OF THE TRINITY

It should be noted that man's enmity against God is manifest toward each of the three members of the Godhead. First, he despises Christ, not as the Son, but as the emissary of God the Father. The Lord Jesus came from the Father and must be considered, first of all, as representing the divine majesty. He who rejects the Lord Jesus Christ is rejecting God the Father. Christ set this forth in the parable of the householder who sent servants to collect his share of the fruits from the husbandmen who tilled his vineyard. They beat one, killed another, and stoned a third. "Again, he sent other servants more than the first; and they did to them likewise. But last of all he sent to them his son, saying, They will reverence my son. But when the husbandmen saw the son, they said among themselves, This is the heir; come, let us kill him, and let us seize on his inheritance. And they caught him, and cast him out of the vineyard, and killed him" (Mt. 21:33-39). Here the Son is the representative of the Father, and out of hatred for the Father they mistreated the prophets and slew the eternal Son.

Second, the hatred against the Lord Jesus Christ Himself is so well known that we need not enlarge upon it. He was crucified, and it was by the likes of you and me. Mankind despised His blood in life, and even in death while He was shedding that blood upon the cross.

Third, hatred for the Holy Spirit is a continuing one. The Holy

Spirit pleads with men and they reject His plea. He points to God the Father in nature and seeks to teach men that the goodness of God in supplying mankind with so many blessings should lead them to repentance. But men take the gifts and reject the giver. The Holy Spirit points to God the Son in redemption, and tells men that love that bleeds for them is love that means all good, and calls them to love in return. But man crucifies Christ afresh and puts Him to an open shame. There is nothing left for the Holy Spirit to do, for He will not talk about Himself: He was sent to talk about Christ. And the world cannot receive Him because it seeth Him not (John 14:17). So the circle of hatred is complete. The Holy Spirit is grieved; and men, having sinned against Him, can do no more, for God is but three persons.

GOD'S LOVE

The Lord now brings us to the climax of this teaching concerning His love. He points out that, while we were in that state of enmity, He moved toward us. He did not wait for us to become friends, for He would have waited in vain. He moved toward us although He knew that He was moving to His death. So inevitably does hatred follow sin, and strike out against the love of God that God could speak of Christ as the Lamb slain from the foundation of the world (Rev. 13:8). And that love ultimately triumphed. An innumerable company of believers was made alive in Christ. In an instant ungodly men were declared righteous while still unchanged, and enemies became sons. Men were transferred from darkness to light; from the kingdom of Satan to the kingdom of God's dear Son.

As Christians we can never forget the hole of the pit from which we were digged. What we are in Christ shines against the background of what we were. We were enemies, but Christ died for us. That is the motivating power which takes us onward and upward in Himself. He died for us when we were enemies. There never was such love.

CHAPTER XXVI

Reconciliation

Much more then, being now justified by his blood, we shall be saved from wrath through him. For if, when we were enemies, we were reconciled to God by the death of his Son, much more, being reconciled, we shall be saved by his life (Rom. 5:9, 10).

MUCH more—much more—that is the theme of the central portion of the fifth chapter of Romans. The argument of the book moves to a new phase. Having been justified, the believer has access into the grace wherein we stand, and the indwelling Holy Spirit, by whom the love of God is poured out in a gushing stream, brings all other blessings. All this was done without regard to what we were, yea, even in spite of it, for we were helpless, ungodly sinners, and were enemies, when God moved to save us. Much more, then, shall we be sure of being saved from wrath through Him. And again, having been reconciled to God by the death of His Son, even when we were enemies, much more shall we be saved by His life.

"RECONCILE"

The word "reconcile" comes from the Latin and means to "bring a person again into friendly relations to or with oneself or another after an estrangement." That there has been estrangement between the soul and God has been made abundantly evident in the early chapters of Romans. Man sinned and fled from God and became His enemy. It would normally appear that the offended God would have to be reconciled to man, but this is not the way the Bible puts it. Tennyson in "The Lotus Eaters" says, "The gods are hard to reconcile," meaning that those who have been offended will not easily smile again. But God, who is Light, holds nothing against the sons of darkness and is willing to bring them into the Light, if they will only come.

AN EVEN EXCHANGE

The Greek word translated "reconciled" comes from the world of the moneychanger. If you give two dimes and a nickel in exchange for a quarter, or *vice versa,* you have made an equal exchange.

This was the original meaning of the word as used by Aristotle and others. Later the word was used for the adjustment of a difference in business dealings, and finally for a difference between two personalities who had become estranged. The transition from the material to the emotional and psychological was made, and the word was used as in Shakespeare's *Richard III:* "I desire to reconcile me to his friendly peace."

Perhaps I have spent more time on this Greek word and its meaning than on almost any other, for I find myself differing with some of the commentators on its significance. Thayer thinks that the word means "the restoration of the favor of God to sinners that repent and put their trust in the expiatory death of Christ." I wish to show that the New Testament meaning of the word is quite different. Again, Thayer adduces two arguments to prove that God has reconciled us: "First, that He does not impute to men their trespasses; second, that He has deposited the doctrine of reconciliation in the souls of the preachers of the gospel."

THE LOVE OF GOD

But I am sure that there is something much greater than this. It should be noted that the word "reconcile" is never used of God. It is used only of men. This, at the outset, is extraordinary and quite contrary to human practice. But we are not to be astonished at this, for God's ways are not our ways. The whole argument of our paragraph in Romans is that God took the initiative. God did not have to be reconciled to man because God is love. Man had to be reconciled to God because man was a helpless, ungodly enemy.

Man by the fall was estranged from God; he would not come back to God of his own will, and he could not come back to God because he had been rendered incapable of so doing. He was nonetheless responsible, and God was going to do something about it. He was going to save those on whom He had eternally set His love. God never had to be reconciled, for He is love. Those who refuse His love and continue in their own selfish way must incur His wrath.

All this is specifically set forth in 2 Corinthians 5:17-19: "For if any man be in Christ, he is a new creation; old things are passed away; behold, all things are become new. And all things are of God, who hath reconciled us to himself [note that it does not say that He reconciled Himself to us] by Jesus Christ, and hath given to us the ministry of reconciliation; that is to say, that God was in Christ, reconciling the world unto himself, not imputing their trespasses unto them; and hath committed unto us the word of reconciliation."

Go back to the root meanings of "reconcile": to exchange coins of equal value, and to adjust a difference. The context of our verse in Romans shows us that we were helpless, ungodly sinners, and not only so, but also that we were enemies. God came in Christ and died for us. That satisfied every demand of His nature for righteousness and true holiness, and now His love may pour itself out to us. God sets Himself up as a banker in the market place and calls out to sinners, "Change your money here! Change your money here! I will give my power for your helplessness! I will give my godliness for your sinfulness! I will give my love for your enmity!"

PREACHING RECONCILIATION

This is the message of reconciliation which we are supposed to preach. It has almost disappeared from the Christian pulpits. Multitudes of liberals preach a gentle and ineffective reminder to sinners that Christ was a very fine example of martyrdom and willingness to die for a cause, and that mankind should show its good will by joining in all good causes, and therefore in this cause. It is all very vague and fruitless. On the other hand, even fundamental evangelists are not really exercising the ministry of reconciliation. "Now then we are ambassadors for Christ, as God did beseech you by us; we pray you in Christ's stead, be ye reconciled to God. For God hath made him [Christ] to be sin for us, who knew no sin; that we might be made the righteousness of God in him" (2 Cor. 5:20-21).

Let us examine some of the phrases used by evangelists which have been passed around so often that they carry the sanctity of divine utterance in some quarters, even though they are quite false and should never be used by gospel preachers. Take, first of all, the common invitation for the sinner to give his heart to God. As James McKendrick, the Scotch evangelist, said, "What would God do with the dirty thing anyway?" Never in the Bible is an unsaved man asked to give his heart to God. God first takes away the heart of stone and gives the believer the heart of flesh. Then He says, "My son, give me thine heart" (Prov. 23:26). But this is not a request for the old, foul heart, which God says is deceitful above all things and incurable (Jer. 17:9).

Again, evangelists frequently say, "If you do not receive Christ as your Savior, you will be lost." At first glance this appears to be good coin, but it is counterfeit when subjected to the acid test of Scripture. Such an invitation exalts the sinner to the throne where God and the Devil bow before him. The sinner has the heady intoxication of thinking himself in a position to confer an enormous favor upon one or the other of the suppliants. But the Bible presents us no such elevation of the sinner above God. The true proposition is, "If you do not receive the Lord Jesus as your Savior, you will remain lost. You always were lost. You were born lost. You are lost, and now we invite you to be reconciled to the true God who is all love toward you."

THE WILL OF GOD

Most common of the honest errors made by evangelists is the appeal to the human will, especially through the emotions. There is no authority for such an appeal in Scripture, and there are flat statements to the contrary. "Being born again, not of blood, nor of the will of the flesh, nor of the will of man, but of God" (John 1:13); and, "So then it is not of him that willeth, nor of him that runneth, but of God that sheweth mercy" (Rom. 9:16). Therefore, any preaching addressed to the will of the listener is in contradiction to the plain statements of the Word of God. Such preaching may be sincere, but it is not the ministry of reconciliation which has been committed to us as the ambassadors of Christ.

Still another error of many evangelists is the false presentation of the doctrine of repentance. We must not be misunderstood at this point. There is a biblical repentance, but there is also a non-biblical repentance. The false doctrine is the penitential idea of repentance. To tell an unsaved man to be sorry for his sins is like asking a corpse to give itself a blood transfusion. The repentance which in the Bible is called godly sorrow can be experienced only by a godly person (2 Cor. 7:10). How can an ungodly man experience godly sorrow?

ABOUT FACE!

The basic meaning of the original word, repentance, is "to change one's mind," and, since the idea of mental direction is involved, it is the equivalent to the military command "About face!"

Change of direction is involved in the process of becoming a Christian, but this must not be allowed to degenerate into the false idea of weeping for sin before salvation can be secured. (Soon after that, one would think that there must be further suffering for sins after death, and thus we would deny the finished work of Christ.) Biblical repentance may be described thus: the sinner has been trusting in himself for salvation, his back turned upon Christ, who is despised and rejected. Repent! About face! The sinner now despises and rejects himself, and places all confidence and trust in Christ. Sorrow for sin comes later, as the Christian grows in appreciation of the holiness of God and the sinfulness of sin.

As we comprehend the love that stooped to save us, that love will constrain us. Paul had written several epistles before he wrote, "I know that in me, that is, in my flesh, dwelleth no good thing" (Rom. 7:18). In one of his earliest writings he rated himself as number twelve or thirteen, saying, "I am the least of the apostles" (1 Cor. 15:9). Later in his ministry he classified himself as number 500,000 or thereabouts, writing, I "am less than the least of all saints" (Eph. 3:8). But as an old man in prison and about to die, he wrote to young Timothy, "Jesus Christ came into the world to save sinners; of whom I am chief" (1 Tim. 1:15).

Experimentally, I knew nothing of true godly sorrow for my sin for years after I was saved, and, indeed, I ask God even now to increase that sorrow that I may have an ever-growing horror of sin and an increasing sensitiveness to sin in its every subtle variation. Such godly sorrow leads to repentance not to be repented of (2 Cor. 7:10).

God has not committed to us the ministry of calling incurable hearts to be offered to Him; He has committed to us the ministry, the word, of reconciliation. God has not committed to us the ministry of high-pressuring unstable souls; He has committed to us the ministry of reconciliation. God has not called us to stir up the emotions of the psychologically impressionable; He has called us to the ministry of reconciliation.

"BY THEIR FRUITS"

What is this ministry of reconciliation committed to us? Let me exercise it rather than describe it. First, my credentials: "Now then we are ambassadors for Christ, as though God did beseech

you by us: we pray you in Christ's stead, be ye reconciled to God"
(2 Cor. 5:20). Others make the same claims, but do they have the
authentication of the Word of God and of the Holy Spirit? I do
not present my claim upon the basis of the fancied validity of
ordination through a church. Ambassadors are not chosen by apostolic succession but by clear appointment. The reality of the appointment is to be judged by the faithfulness of the ambassador to the
Word of God, which is in the hands of all men. If you do not check
all preaching by the Bible and the Bible alone, you will be held
responsible by God. But what about all who claim to minister according to the Bible? The answer is, look at their converts. "By their
fruits ye shall know them" (Mt. 7:20). Not by their proselytes to a
set of ideas, but by the lives that are transformed under their
ministry. Appraise them not by the statistics of people who come
forward in an after meeting, but by the number of young men who
enter the same faithful ministry of reconciliation.

But now to the ministry of reconciliation itself. Consider that
I am speaking to a group that includes a Moslem, a Devil-worship-
per from Africa, an atheist from Russia, an agnostic from the faculty
of one of our great universities, a follower of a cult that talks about
the love of God but denies the salvation provided by the blood of
the cross. Finally, in the group with the Moslem, the pagan, the
atheist, the agnostic, and the cultist, there is you. To you all I speak,
as though God did beseech you by us. Even as the Lord said to
Moses, "Behold, I have made thee God [thus the Hebrew] to
Pharaoh, and Aaron thy brother shall be thy prophet" (Ex. 7:1). Thus
I speak to you:

You are a sinner, estranged from God. You have been running
away ever since the garden of Eden. God declares that you are now
in a condition of total helplessness, ungodliness, and sinfulness, and
that you are His enemies. He commands me to tell you that He has
fully dealt with your sin by sending Christ to die for you. Christ's
blood cried out, silencing God's wrath against you, so that He is
now propitiated. God is thoroughly satisfied with the death of Christ
instead of your death. I declare to you on the authority of God
that He is not imputing your trespasses to you. Every sin which you
ever committed or ever will commit has already been charged to
the account of Christ, and God holds nothing against you. He knows
that you are still afraid and are acting as an enemy, but He loves

you. He authorizes me to say that all has been forgiven and that you must simply turn around and come home.

JUST AS YOU ARE

You are to come just as you are. You are not to wash your face or brush your clothes. He will cleanse you and give you new garments, but He will not do so until you step inside the door with all your filth and ungodliness. After He has bathed you, you can keep yourself washed. After He gives you new garments, you may keep them brushed. Leave all your baggage outside and come with empty hands. He will give you new luggage, and you will pack it from His bounteous store. But He will not tolerate your bringing anything with you.

BRING NOTHING, DO NOTHING

O be ye reconciled to God. He loves you. He has nothing against you. He must take you as you are. Moslem, leave your Koran and come as a naked sinner. Pagan, leave your fetishes and come as you are. Atheist and agnostic, leave your doubts and fears and intellectual pride and come as bankrupts. Member of a false cult, leave your horrible caricature of God and come knowing that the blood of Christ has been shed by God Himself to pay your fine. Whoever you are, drop all confidence in baptism or church membership, and come to God; be reconciled to Him, for He has forgotten your sins, has put them behind His back, will remember them against you no more forever. Bring nothing, do nothing, say nothing. Come as you are.

That is the ministry of reconciliation. That is the gospel. God commands you to repent, to turn away from all that you are or have, and to come to Him through the Lord Jesus Christ.

CHAPTER XXVII

The Power of Resurrection Life

For if, when we were enemies, we were reconciled to God by the death of his Son, much more, being reconciled, we shall be saved by his life (Rom. 5:10).

WITH this text the epistle turns from the past toward the present and future. Up to now the apostle has been considering our past imperfect in sin, as well as the past perfect of the redemptive work of the Lord Jesus Christ. Here Paul stands on the crest of the divide and looks into our present active and future perfect with Christ in glory.

PRESENT POWER

We now occupy ourselves with the announcement of the divine reality of present power and position through the resurrection life of Christ. Our text says that we shall be saved through His life, and that this is "much more" than our reconciliation with God. It is important, therefore, to note that we are to experience in daily life the power of Christ's resurrection. The life of Christ is made known to us in different phases which we must carefully differentiate. Christ eternally existed in the Father and represented us in the eternal counsels of the Godhead. Then, in the fullness of time, God sent forth His Son, made of a woman, made under the law (Gal. 4:4). For some thirty years He lived the second phase of life here on earth. Third, He went to the cross and during six hours of light and darkness poured His life out for us, thus satisfying God, laying the groundwork for our reconciliation, and establishing the basis for righteous condemnation of the world. The fourth phase of Christ's life followed His resurrection and for six weeks He manifested upon earth, establishing the material proofs of His resurrection: He invited Thomas to touch His hands and side; He appeared in the upper room and ate broiled fish with the disciples to demonstrate that the body which He now possessed was not a ghostly apparition but a body of flesh and bones (Luke 24:39). In the fifth phase He ascended into Heaven, and the cloud of shekinah glory received Him (Acts 1:9). He took His place on the throne of Heaven at the right hand of God the Father, and is there today, occupied as our mediator and intercessor. In the sixth phase, He will come forth as judge to put down all sin and unrighteousness. And, seventh and last, He will finish His work of judgment, turn the kingdom over to the Father, and enter into the eternal phase of His life with us as His bride.

THE SHED BLOOD

I have set forth these seven phases of the life of Christ because some Bible students have used this and similar texts to teach that it was not necessary for Christ to shed His blood. This is not a matter of opposing interpretations. It is ignorant unbelief versus knowledge of the revelation of God. If any one asks by what right we speak so dogmatically, we reply that it rests on the Lord Jesus who told the woman at the well, "Ye worship ye know not what: we know what we worship: for salvation is of the Jews" (John 4:22). He was pointing out that the whole scheme of redemption by blood (and that shed only in Jerusalem) was God's method of salvation. He never taught salvation from sin by following His example. The idea that adherence to a system of ethics could save a soul was everywhere denied by the Lord Jesus. He came not to be ministered unto, but to minister, and to give His life a ransom for many (Mt. 20:28). He came to seek and to save that which was lost (Luke 19:10).

THE PASSOVER LAMB

This truth is illustrated in the Passover as observed in Egypt. Each family of Israel was to secure a lamb, a firstling of the flock, without spot or blemish, take it into the household on the tenth day of the month, keep it there for three days, and kill it on the fourth day. Its blood was then to be sprinkled on the two side posts and the upper door post of the house (Ex. 12:7). Can you imagine the scene when a lamb was brought into the house? We may be sure that the children cuddled and petted the lamb; perhaps they tied ribbons around its neck, and, in general, behaved as children do when confronted with the wonder of warm life throbbing beneath their touch in the woolly beast. But the day came when it was necessary to kill that little lamb. If this had not been done, the eldest son in the house would have died under the stroke of the angel of death passing over the land. The death angel would be unmoved by the warmth and beauty of the lamb; although shedding its blood was an ugly thing. Death is always ugly. It is almost as ugly as the sin that caused it. No argument could avail: the lamb must die.

THE LAMB OF GOD

And thus the Lord Jesus Christ was taken into the house of Israel for three years. John the Baptist—John the Identifier—looked over all the men of Israel and saw not one without spot or blemish. When the Holy Spirit led John to look at Jesus Christ, he cried out, "Behold the Lamb of God, which taketh away the sin of the world!" (John 1:29). John's identification of Christ could pass so far as His outward appearance was concerned, but God Himself declared from Heaven, "This is my beloved Son, in whom I am well pleased" (Mt. 3:17). For three years after Christ's baptism, He went about doing good, healing the brokenhearted, causing the blind to see, the deaf to hear, and the lame to walk. He cleansed the leper and raised the dead. He spoke as never man spoke. Is this enough? Can this matchless life save any man? No! The Lamb must go to the cross and die. He must shed His blood to satisfy the justice of God. So the Lamb was put to death. There is no merit in the life; there is life and health and peace in His death. All blessings flow from the Christ of Calvary.

Much more, then, having been reconciled by the pouring out of His life in death, we shall be saved through the welling up of His life in resurrection. When we were dead, He died for us; much more, now that He is alive, He lives for us; much more, being reconciled, we are kept saved through His being alive. On earth He said, "It is advantageous for you that I go away" (John 16:7-Gk.). We are the gainers by His absence, for it makes possible His resurrection life in us.

One day since the day of Pentecost overbalances many days before Pentecost. In our age, there is depth of salvation available for the believer which not even Abraham, Moses, or David knew, and which Peter, James, and John did not know before Pentecost.

THE DEATH OF THE TESTATOR

These advantages were bought and paid for by the death of Christ. We all know that there is no advantage in being a beneficiary unless the testator has wealth to meet its provisions, and dies while the will is in force. We read, "For where a testament is, there must also of necessity be the death of the testator. For a testament is of force after men are dead; otherwise it is of no strength at all while the testator liveth" (Heb. 9:16, 17). God made a multitude of promises but those promises were of no value until the death of the Lord Jesus Christ put them into effect. Now the assets of God's estate are credited to our account.

OUR RISEN EXECUTOR

Furthermore, the advantages that are now available to us are secure and certain because He, "much more" in His resurrection life, is living in order to take care of our interests.

When the Lord Jesus Christ died, He left us a vast estate. But how would it be managed? Would it be possible for our assets to be dissipated or lost? Not with such a God as our God and such a Savior as our Savior. On the third day the Lord Jesus Christ rose from the dead and became executor of His own estate. He lives in order to take care of us for whom He died. The argument of our text is: Since He died in order to make available to us all the riches of God, much more can we be sure of our possessions because He arose from the dead in order to manage our affairs. And that is exactly what He is doing today. He will never defraud us because He is the bridegroom and we are the bride, and His banner over us is love. If we believe not, yet He abideth faithful; He cannot deny Himself (2 Tim. 2:13).

PRESENT TRIUMPH

Much more, then, having become reconciled, we shall be kept saved and safe by His resurrection life. The fruit of His resurrection is His present life for us and in us, buttressing our hearts with strong confidence and sustaining our hope of present triumph and future union with Him forever.

Let us consider the fact that we have been joined to Christ in His resurrection. During His earthly life he said, "Because I live, ye shall live also" (John 14:19). As time went on, this preliminary announcement was expanded and explained until we have before us a prospect of life in Christ that is beyond imagination. But the tragedy is, so few professing Christians appropriate that life. For the Lord was not talking about life in Heaven, but about the life of triumph here after we are saved.

On the day of Pentecost Peter set forth the facts concerning the death and resurrection of the Lord Jesus Christ and then went on to link the resurrection of Christ with His present position and power in our behalf: "This Jesus hath God raised up, whereof we all are witnesses. Therefore being by the right hand of God exalted, and having received of the Father the promise of the Holy Spirit, he hath shed forth this which ye now see and hear" (Acts 2:32, 33). In the eighth chapter of Romans this is carried one step further: "Who is he that condemneth? Christ has died, yea rather, he is risen again, who is even at the right hand of God, who also maketh intercession for us" (Rom. 8:34).

> The Father hears Him pray,
>   His dear anointed One;
> He cannot turn away
>   The presence of His Son:
> His Spirit answers to the blood,
>   And tells me I am born of God.

GOD'S PURPOSE FOR US

Christ intercedes not merely to remind the Father that we have been justified and that our sins have been dealt with forever. If we will surrender to His power and recognize our oneness with Christ, we shall know the heights of God's purpose for us. "Wherefore he is able also to save them to the uttermost that come unto God by him, seeing he ever liveth to make intercession for them" (Heb. 7:25). To be saved to the uttermost is the design which God has formed on our behalf.

As a boy I first memorized this verse as though it read that He is able to save us from the uttermost. I thought of the drunkards I saw around town and imagined that this was a promise that God was able to stoop very low—lower than anything I knew by experience. A few years passed, and I learned the truth of the verse in the following manner. Mel Trotter, the famous mission worker, was telling how God saved him from the lowest ranks of sinfulness. Then he climaxed his story thus: "God saved me from the guttermost to the uttermost." I rapidly checked with my Bible and discovered that the text did indeed teach that God was able to save to the uttermost. It is true that God can and does stoop to save men from the depths of iniquity. But—"much more"—salvation in highest triumph is a superlative possibility for our present existence and, alas, one which few Christians ever know. However, if you can catch a vision of the meaning of our text—much more shall we be saved by His life— you may enter now into that *much more* salvation which He has so bountifully made available.

THE SOURCE OF POWER

When the Lord Jesus Christ was here on earth, He added the links to the chain which brings power from Heaven direct to us for daily appropriation and use. In the Psalms our God is shown as the source of all power. "Once God has spoken; twice have I heard this, that power belongs to God" (Ps. 62:11). That is wonderful to contemplate. To know that the source of all power is in God makes us rest quietly in a world where wickedness seems to be victorious. Paul, later in the epistle, says, "There is no power but of God; the powers that be are ordained of God" (Rom. 13:1). But the Lord Jesus, after His resurrection, flatly stated, "All power is given unto me in heaven and in earth" (Mt. 28:18). Today, God the Father is doing nothing apart from God the Son. The Lord Jesus is the repository of all the power of the universe. There is no power other than the power that is in Him.

But what does Christ choose to do with all that power that is now lodged in Him? His very last words here on earth were these: "But ye shall receive power, after that the Holy Spirit is come upon you; and ye shall be witnesses unto me" (Acts 1:8); beginning with where you are, extending to the territory around about you, and the territory a little farther off, and even to the uttermost parts of the earth. The power which resides in God was transmitted to Christ in His resurrection and made available by Him to us before His ascension. This is why Paul cries out, "That I may know him and the power of his resurrection" (Phil. 3:10). And having learned some of the lesson, Paul is able to say to the Philippians in the next chapter, "I can do all things through Christ who strengthens me" (Phil. 4:13).

The channel of power has been fully prepared. It runs from the heart of God through the Lord Jesus Christ; flows down upon us from the cross and floods the open tomb; it carries us along on its flow, even to the throne of God, where we have been raised to sit together in the heavenly places in Christ (Eph. 2:6). O mighty flow of love! O blessed flood of grace! May we ever be crested on its wave and carried beyond all the rocky trials of this life, to find forever our full rest in the heart of God through our Lord Jesus Christ. Much more! Much more! We shall ever be kept safe in His life.

CHAPTER XXVIII

None Like unto Our God

And not only so, but we also rejoice in God through our Lord Jesus Christ, by whom we have now received our reconciliation (Rom. 5:11).

WITH the eleventh verse of the fifth chapter of Romans the revelation sweeps to a climax. Christ has died, and in His death we have been justified. Having been justified, we have peace with God through our Lord Jesus Christ, and by Him we have also received access into the grace wherein we stand. All the experiences of life contribute to our growth in Christ as the love of God is shed abroad in our hearts. For when we were helpless, ungodly sinners God reached down, down, down to lift us. Yes, when we were enemies, Christ died for us, and in His death furnished the basis for our reconciliation, so that having been justified we were sheltered from the wrath to come. Even more, much more, now that He is alive, He lives for us. Oh joy! Oh joy! Oh joy!

THE SUMMIT OF GOD'S LOVE

And not only so, but we also rejoice through our Lord Jesus Christ, by whom we have now received the reconciliation. That joy is the climax of all that we have seen. We have been brought to the very summit of the mountain of God's love, and there survey our glorious position in God.

The cross of Jesus Christ is a two-way street. We have been brought to God, and God has been brought to us. Once more Paul speaks of the reconciliation as having come to us through the Lord Jesus Christ. The Holy Spirit continually reminds us of the cross of Jesus Christ as though to keep before us the thought that no blessing can come to us in any way other than by this great act of God in satisfying justice with the payment of the fine and in satisfying love through the release of the guilty one. Apart from this we are afar off, dead in trespasses and sins. Through the cross we who were once alienated from the life of God are brought back into fellowship with Him, and our sins have been fully dealt with forever.

THE ATONEMENT

It is rather unfortunate that the King James translation has used the word "atonement," for this has given rise to a false doctrine. There have been those who have tried to break the word apart and use its syllables to make the word "at-one-ment." In false cults such as Christian Science, New Thought, and Unity, the word has been used to eliminate the blood of the Savior. Mrs. Eddy says, "Atonement is the exemplification of man's unity with God, whereby man reflects divine Truth, Life, and Love. Jesus of Nazareth taught and demonstrated man's oneness with the Father, and for this we owe Him countless homage." This same writer says, "Jesus bore our infirmities; He knew the error of mortal belief, and 'with his stripes [the rejection of error] we are healed.'" And again, "He to whom 'the arm of the Lord is revealed' will believe our report, and rise into newness of life with regeneration. This is having part in the atonement; this is the understanding in which Jesus suffered and triumphed. The time is not distant when the ordinary theological views of atonement will undergo a great change—a change as radical as that which has come over popular opinions in regard to predestination and future punishment." In other words, Christian Science says that the masses no longer believe the Bible teaching about the doctrine of the sovereignty of God or eternal punishment, and that they will soon throw away the doctrine of Christ's substitutionary death for sinners. Mrs. Eddy continues, "Does erudite theology regard the crucifixion of Jesus chiefly as providing a ready pardon for all sinners who ask for it and are willing to be forgiven? Does spiritualism find Jesus' death necessary for the presentation, after death, of the material Jesus, as proof that spirits can return to earth? Then we must differ from them both." I would underline that last sentence, "We [i.e., Christian Science] must differ from them both." In other words, Christian Science, on its own admission —indeed, on its boast—denies salvation by the death of the Lord Jesus Christ and denies His bodily resurrection. This is open rejection of the substitutionary propitiation for the sins of men through the shedding of Christ's blood. And since death is looked upon as unreality, it follows naturally that resurrection is absurdity.

REJOICING IN GOD

In our text, the Greek word is the same as that translated "reconciliation" in several previous verses; thus it should be here, and the modern revisions so translate it. The atonement which the Lord Jesus Christ has brought to us is reconciliation. It is the Lord Jesus Christ becoming man in order that He might have a human body to be put to death on the cross for the payment of our fine to the justice of God. It is because of all that He has done for us there that we may now make our boast in God.

This amazing thought takes us to the highest point of Christian truth. The King James Version says, "We joy in God." But the meaning of the word suggests such rapture that we can scarcely contain ourselves. Other translations make the meaning more evident. "We rejoice in God," says the Revised Standard Version. The Confraternity edition renders it, "We exult in God." The French translation of Segond renders it by the word we use in the hymn, "In the Cross of Christ I Glory." Goodspeed says, "More than that we actually glory in God." The Phillips paraphrase reads, "Nor, I am sure, is this a matter of bare salvation—we may hold our heads high in the light of God's love because of the reconciliation which Christ has made." Williams says, "We shall continue exulting in God." The only translation I have found which renders the Greek with absolute literalness is the German translation, which uses the expression *sich ruhmen,* "We boast in God."

For *kauchaomai,* used here, is the common Greek verb for "boast." It was so twice in chapter two, "Thou makest thy boast in God" (2:17), and "Thou that makest thy boast in the law" (2:23). The same word appears earlier in this fifth chapter: "We rejoice in hope of the glory of God" (v. 2); and "we glory in tribulations" (v. 3). It is used 21 times in the Corinthian epistles for boast and glory. It is found in two well-known texts, "God forbid that I should glory, save in the cross of our Lord Jesus Christ" (Gal. 6:14); and "Not of works, lest any man should boast" (Eph. 2:9).

OUR BOAST IN HIM

How does this word describe our feelings toward our God? How can we glory in Him? How do we make our boast in Him? The answer can be found by comparing some of the ways in which men boast about other men.

We smile tolerantly when a young man makes the great discovery of love. He begins to boast about his love for the girl as though he were the inventor of love and as though it had been unknown before him. He talks about her hair, her eyes, her cheeks, and enthusiastically declares, "There is absolutely no one like her!" And since we hear such declarations made about people of all types and kinds, we come to the conclusion that there is no one so ill-favored that she may not excite the admiration and devotion of some swain. We see that almost any pair of eyes becomes the only pair of eyes for someone.

But when we turn to the Word of God, we find this expressed quite differently, about God. In the Psalms David, inspired by the Holy Spirit, makes his boast in God. Time and again he declares, "There is none like unto thee, O God." When we cry out that this is our God, we are fulfilling our text in Romans. We joy in God. We exult in God. We glory in God. We boast in God. There is none like unto our God.

HIS NAMES

If I were to name the names of my God, you would see that there is none like Him. How shall we call Him who has revealed Himself in so many ways? For He is the Creator; He is Jehovah; He is the Father; He is the Son; He is the Holy Spirit. His names reveal His power, wisdom, holiness, justice, truth, lovingkindness, and ineffable, measureless wonder. His name is wonderful, counselor, the Mighty God, the everlasting Father, the Prince of Peace. He is the rose of Sharon, the lily of the valley, the bright and morning star. He is the fairest of ten thousand; the Alpha and the Omega; the beginning and the ending; the first and the last. He is the Most High God, possessor of Heaven and earth. He is the Eternal, Almighty God. He is the God and Father of our Lord Jesus Christ. His name is Jesus, Savior, Redeemer, and Lord. He is the shadow of a rock in the weary land. He is our light and our salvation; our fortress and our high tower.

O let me boast in my God! There is none like unto Him! He is the Ancient of Days, seated upon the throne of Heaven. He is the Man of Sorrows, walking upon the earth. He is *El Olam,* Father of Eternity, and He is the Babe of Bethlehem. He is the way, the truth, and the life; He is the light of the world; the bread of life;

the good shepherd that giveth His life for the sheep. O let me boast in my God! There is none like unto Him! He is the water of life, the living vine, the living bread from Heaven. He is the door by which we enter Heaven; He is the resurrection and will bring us out of our earth and into life eternal. O let me boast in my God, for there is none like unto Him!

HIS MATCHLESS WORTH

He is divine Providence, the author and finisher of our faith. He is the Provider for all our need. He is our shield and exceeding great reward. He is the Lord God of Hosts. He is the God of Abraham, of Isaac, and of Jacob. And He is not ashamed to be called their God, and mine. O let me boast in the Lord, my God! There is none like unto Him! He is the God of Heaven and the man of Galilee. He is the God of gods, the Lord of lords, the King of kings.

> O could I speak the matchless worth,
>   O could I sound the glories forth
> Which in my Saviour shine!
>   I'd soar and touch the heavenly strings
> And vie with Gabriel while he sings
>   In notes almost divine.
>
> I'd sing the characters He bears,
>   And all the forms of love He wears,
> Exalted on His throne:
>   In glorious songs of sweetest praise,
> I would to everlasting days
>   Make all His glories known.

Listen to David in the 135th Psalm joying and rejoicing in God. "Praise ye the Lord, Praise ye the name of the Lord; praise him, O ye servants of the Lord. . . . Praise the Lord; for the Lord is good: sing praises unto his name; for it is pleasant. . . . For I know that the Lord is great, and that our Lord is above all gods. . . . Thy name, O Lord endureth for ever; and thy memorial, O Lord, throughout all generations. . . ."

THE ONLY GOD

We could go beyond the limits of time and space, singing with David the Psalms of praise which came from his harp and lips under the inspiration of the Holy Spirit. But we will confine ourselves to three expressions which speak of the uniqueness of our God, of His solitude in the universe as the one and only God. David had trusted the revelation of the heart of God and found in Him a refuge for his old age. Far better than any system of social security and old-age benefits is that of which David sang: "O God, thou hast taught me from my youth; and hitherto have I declared thy wondrous works. Now also when I am old and greyheaded, O God, forsake me not; until I have showed thy strength to this generation, and thy power to every one that is to come. Thy righteousness also, O God, is very high, who hast done great things: O God, who is like unto thee!" (Ps. 71:17-19).

Not only for his old age, but also for the day of trouble, David found that there was none like unto our God. He sings: "Give ear, O Lord, unto my prayer; and attend to the voice of my supplications. In the day of my trouble I will call upon thee: for thou wilt answer me. Among the gods there is none like unto thee, O Lord; neither are there any works like unto thy works" (Ps. 86:6-8).

And as it was for a day of trouble, so it was for the confirmation of a promise. God swore to David that He would be his God, and that He would make His covenant with David, building his throne and establishing it to all generations. And then David sings: "And the heavens shall praise thy wonders, O Lord; thy faithfulness also in the congregation of the saints. For who in the heaven can be compared unto the Lord? who among the sons of the mighty can be likened unto the Lord?" (Ps. 89:5, 6).

Listen to Moses sing after the children of Israel had been brought through the Red Sea: "Who is like unto thee, O Lord, among the gods? who is like thee, glorious in holiness, fearful in praises, doing wonders?" (Ex. 15:11). Listen to Hannah when the Lord promised her that Samuel should be born unto her: "My heart rejoiceth in the Lord, mine horn is exalted in the Lord: my mouth is enlarged over mine enemies; because I rejoice in thy salvation. There is none holy as the Lord: for there is none beside thee: neither is there any rock like our God" (1 Sam. 2:1, 2). Moses was rejoicing in the God of power. Hannah was rejoicing in the God of lowly tenderness. This is why we can rejoice in our God. Our great matters are little to His infinite power, and our little matters are very great to His Father-love.

ISAIAH'S TESTIMONY

And, finally, let us turn to Isaiah. For three chapters he sets forth the folly of any imitation of God, of any attempt to serve a god that is not our God. "Thus saith the Lord that made thee, and formed thee from the womb, which will help thee; Fear not . . . for I will pour water on him that is thirsty, and floods upon the dry ground: I will pour my spirit upon they seed, and my blessing upon thine offspring. . . . Thus saith the Lord the King of Israel, and his redeemer the Lord of hosts; I am the first, and I am the last; and beside me there is no God. . . . Fear ye not, neither be afraid: have not I told thee from that time, and have declared it? ye are even my witnesses. Is there a God beside me? yea, there is no God; I know not any" (Isa. 44:2-8).

And in the next chapter: "I will go before thee, and make the crooked places straight: I will break in pieces the gates of brass, and cut in sunder the bars of iron: and I will give thee the treasures of darkness, and hidden riches of secret places, that thou mayest know that I, the Lord, which call thee by thy name, am the God of Israel. . . . I am the Lord, and there is none else, there is no God beside me: I girded thee, though thou hast not known me: That they may know, from the rising of the sun, and from the west, that there is none beside me. I am the Lord, and there is none else. . . . Tell ye, and bring them near; yea, let them take counsel together: who hath declared this from ancient times? who hath told it from that time? have not I the Lord? and there is no God else beside me; a just God and a Savior; there is none beside me. Look unto me, and be ye saved, all the ends of the earth: for I am God, and there is none else. I have sworn by myself, the word is gone out of my mouth in righteousness, and shall not return, That unto me every knee shall bow, and every tongue shall swear" (Isa. 45: 2, 3, 5, 6, 21-23).

And He completes it, saying "And even to your old age I am he; and even to hoar hairs will I carry you: I have made, and I will bear; even I will carry, and will deliver you. To whom will ye liken me, and make me equal, and compare me, that we may be like? . . . Remember the former things of old; for I am God, and there is none else; I am God, and there is none like me" (Isa. 46:4, 5, 9).

Before we pass on to the subjects that follow in the next

volume, let us note the astounding distance we have traveled since the third chapter of this epistle. There we were silent. Sin had closed the mouth of each member of the human race. All stood condemned. The giving of the law effectively stopped boasting on the part of man. The law was given that every mouth might be stopped and all the world be brought guilty before God. Now we discover that grace has opened the mouth of each believer. And from the opened mouth comes a shout of praise. The believer is not born mute. There cannot be any dumb children in the family of God. We joy and rejoice in God. Our praise goes forth to Him who opened our mouth. David puts the whole progression in one sequence of a Psalm: "He brought me up also out of an horrible pit, out of the miry clay, and set my feet upon a rock, and established my goings. And he hath put a new song in my mouth, even praise unto our God: many shall see it, and fear, and shall trust in the Lord" (Ps. 40:2, 3). We were in the pit; we are on the rock. We were struck dumb with sin; we have a new song in our mouths.

Is it any wonder that the Wesleyans in England put Charles Wesley's greatest hymn of praise as the number one hymn of their great collection?

> O for a thousand tongues to sing
> 　My great Redeemer's praise,
> The glories of my God and King,
> 　The triumphs of His grace!
>
> My gracious Master and my God,
> 　Assist me to proclaim,
> To spread through all the earth abroad
> 　The honors of Thy name.
>
> Jesus! the name that charms our fears,
> 　That bids our sorrows cease;
> 'Tis music in the sinner's ears,
> 　'Tis life, and health, and peace.
>
> He speaks, and listening to His voice,
> 　New life the dead receive,
> The mournful, broken hearts rejoice,
> 　The humble poor believe.
>
> He breaks the power of canceled sin,
> 　He sets the prisoner free;
> His blood can make the foulest clean,
> 　His blood availed for me.

> See all your sins on Jesus laid:
>   The Lamb of God was slain,
> His soul was once an offering made
>   For every soul of man.

And, above all, this verse

> Hear Him, ye deaf; His praise, ye dumb,
>   Your loosened tongues employ;
> Ye blind, behold your Saviour come;
>   And leap, ye lame, for joy.

Yes! Let us make our boast in God. Let us joy in God and rejoice in Him. And let us praise our God that He has told us, even in the garden of Gethsemane in the midst of His last prayer for His people while here on earth, "This is life eternal, that they might know thee the only true God, and Jesus Christ, whom thou hast sent" (John 17:3). Truly, we joy in God. We rejoice in God. We vaunt ourselves in Him. We boast in our God. In Him we glory.

ΩΙ Η ΔΟΞΑ ΕΙΣ ΤΟΥΣ
ΑΙΩΝΑΕ ΤΩΝ ΑΙΩΝΩΝ
ΑΜΗΝ

INDEX

Aaron, 36, 37

Abel, 34, 35

Abraham, justified by works, 14; sacrifice of faith, 35, 170

Access, through Christ, 24-31; under the Law, 35

Adam, contrasted with Christ, 186; original sin, 192

Ambassadors, for Christ, 202; not by apostolic succession, 203; Russian, 20

Anderson, Sir Robert, quoted, 172

Angels, Christians will not be, 51; death, 207; domestics of Heaven, 52

Aristotle, 199

Atheists, 203-4

Atonement, 213

Augustine, St., quoted, 178

Baptism, a second work, 124, 127; change of identity, 125, 130; does not save, 204; of Holy Spirit, 118, 124; meaning of, 124; water, 124, 125

Beveridge, Bishop, quoted, 165

Bible, Devil hates, 87; how to interpret, 168; supreme authority, 33; symbols in, 51

Bonaparte, Napoleon, quoted, 17

Booth, William, 66

Burns, Robert, quoted, 17

Bunyan, John, quoted, 53, 152

Cain, hated atonement, 196, why he killed Abel, 193

Calvin, John, quoted, 38, 39, 92

Carrel, Alexis, 126

Cellini, Benevenuto, 82

Chastening, through suffering, 79

Chiang Kai-Shek, Mme., 65

Christian, ashamed of moderation, 30-1; blessedness of, 105; citizens of Heaven, 68; entrance to Heaven, 58; expendable, 90; following Christ, 43; freedom from sin, 53;

future planned, 78; glory in tribulation, 72-3, 76; God surrounds, 88; good works, 42; growth, 42-3; hope of, 48-9; hypochondriac, 106; judge the world, 189; live as paupers, 45; no fear of death, 56, 58-9; not angels, 51-2; objects of fulness of Holy Spirit, 128; otherworldly, 71; out of God's will, 80; pilgrims on earth, 68; present triumph, 208; sealed, 140; secure, 141; suffering 77-91; Temple of Holy Spirit, 129-30; 132, 133, 137; three things to know, 48; unequally yoked, 132-3; what is a, 41

Christianity, responsible for social betterment, 67-8; impartation of new life, 145

Church, body and bride of Christ, 122; infant, 128; not an authority, 135; pulpit replaces altar, 39, 50; schisms and divisions, 117, 135-6; tares and wheat in, 136

Church of England, 118

Churchill, Sir Winston, quoted, 176

Clark, Glenn, 43

Communism, 193, See Russian

Confraternity Version of New Testament, quoted, 10, 14, 60, 92, 95, 152, 161, 166, 167, 214

Crosby, Fanny, 52

David, 138, 216-7

Denominations, schism over Holy Spirit, 117-8

Dryden, John, quoted, 153

Eddy, Mrs. Mary B., 213

Elijah, 194

Enemies, 190-7

Engels, Friedrich, 66

Evangelism, 145, 178

Faith, access to God by, 24; gift of God, 121; justification by, 121

Flatland, 112

221